REAL-TIME STRATEGY

IMPROVISING TEAM-BASED PLANNING FOR A FAST-CHANGING WORLD

REAL-TIME STRATEGY

IMPROVISING TEAM-BASED PLANNING FOR A FAST-CHANGING WORLD

Lee Tom Perry

Randall G. Stott

W. Norman Smallwood

John Wiley & Sons, Inc.

New York • Chichester • Brisbane • Toronto • Singapore

TRADEMARKS

Gore-Tex
Teflon
WINDOWS
WORD

Copyright © 1993 by Lee Tom Perry
Published by John Wiley & Sons, Inc.

Library of Congress Cataloging-in-Publication Data

Perry, Lee Tom.
    Real-time strategy : improvising team-based planning for a fast-changing world / Lee Tom Perry, Randall G. Stott, W. Norman Smallwood.
        p.   cm.
    Includes index.
    ISBN 0-471-58564-5
    1. Strategic planning.   2. Management—Employee participation. 3. Work groups.   I. Stott, Randall G.   II. Smallwood, W. Norman. III. Title.
    HD30.28.P357   1993
    658.4'012—dc20   92-34982

Printed in the United States of America

10 9 8 7 6 5 4 3 2 1

For our fathers—
L. Tom Perry, George H. Stott,
and Kenneth L. M. Smallwood

Contents

Preface

In the new world economic order, strategic planning has lost its edge. When U.S. companies dictated the ebb and flow of world commerce, strategic planning worked effectively, but today's global economy is too complex, too dynamic, and too unpredictable for companies to place their faith in the centralized, plan-and-control model of management.

This book introduces an alternative to strategic planning. We call it *strategic improvising.*

Strategic improvising is designed to meet the challenges of today's global economy:

- It assumes that strategic responsibility needs to be widely distributed throughout organizations;
- It emphasizes putting strategic tools in the hands of self-directed team members;
- It promotes team-based actions and learning that will support strategic objectives.

Our thinking about strategic improvising has been influenced by both the music and the culture of jazz. We are not jazz musicians, but we greatly admire the music that skilled jazz musicians can create by exercising freedom within a limited form. Ray Smith, Bob Taylor, Steve Call, Lars Yorgason, and Ron Brough, all wonderfully talented jazz musicians, have been our teachers. They have a rare capacity for both playing and talking about their music. They are also our good friends, and we thank them for sharing their knowledge with us and for deepening our understanding of this uniquely American form of music.

As we learned about jazz improvisation, we began to develop a new way of thinking about strategy. We gained wonderful insights about the differences between strategic planning and strategic improvising when we compared the protocols of symphony orchestras with those of jazz groups. Through these metaphor-based insights, our ideas about strategic improvising became animated and viable.

Writing *Real-Time Strategy* has been a splendid education in team-based learning. While we were developing our ideas about team-based strategies, we experienced the highs and lows of teamwork. On some days, everything clicked. We were creatively in step, engaged, productive, and having the time of our lives. On other days, we did not want any part of being a team: the experience was too painful. Our stubbornness was probably our ultimate bonding agent. We refused to surrender to the forces dividing us because we wanted to write about teams as they really are, in a book that was truly a team product.

Our ideas were never blended automatically. We are three individuals who have strong opinions and different sets of experiences to support them. We worked very hard, and not silently, at understanding each other's views and then defining the common ground. In the process, we learned to respect each other's ideas as much as our own. Moreover, we came to appreciate the benefits of exploring and linking multiple perspectives.

Along the way, each of us had a private moment of truth about our attitude: individual accomplishments had to yield to team accomplishments. Our focus had to be on whether the team was accomplishing what it set out to do, not on who was getting what credit. The longer we worked together, the more our individual contributions became interrelated. Were there times when each of us wanted to claim individual ownership of ideas? Absolutely; but we eventually realized that none of us wanted a book with our own proprietary credit lines. We needed to trust each other enough to share the ownership of our ideas. The result is a far better book than any one of us could have written alone.

Writing *Real-Time Strategy* also involved real-life experience with improvising. In the beginning, we knew only the general direction we wanted to take. The specific ideas needed to be improvised. If our ideas had been fully developed, we could never have worked collectively. Because our ideas were still in a formative stage, we were able to grow and develop them together.

Real-Time Strategy makes several unique contributions to the study of strategic management. The book delivers a wide assortment of empowering, strategic tools that combine to form an alternative, team-based planning technology. Readers will find here both an inside-out and an outside-in approach to strategic thinking; coincident and equal attention is given to organizational capabilities and to opportunities in the business environment. *Real-Time Strategy* updates strategic thinking by incorporating new, real-time information technologies into the logic of strategy. Our method is faster and more responsive than others because it empowers people in two ways: first, by providing strategic tools that work (they have been site-tested in more than 50 businesses), and second, by showing members of self-directed teams how to use the tools together, as a means of improvising operational strategies.

Many organizations and people contributed to the development of this book. Our clients have been an accessible well from which we have drawn insight and understanding. Although we are tempted to acknowledge each of them separately, we prefer to recognize their collective contribution. All of our clients have been part of this team effort, and the key players know who they are.

We are indebted to Jon Younger, our partner and colleague at Novations Group, Inc., for his contributions to this project. Jon is the co-creator of the resourcing model described in Chapter 4. Many other ideas in the book can be traced to informal discussions with Jon. His demanding style and uncompromising standards of excellence have leavened our work.

Gene Dalton, also a partner at our firm, has provided both encouragement and constructive feedback. He was the first to warn us about the pitfalls of coauthoring a book. Fortunately for us, he was an advocate for persistence when the going got tough.

Other colleagues at Novations deserve special recognition. Even when we were not crystal clear about what we were trying to accomplish, Sarah Sandberg had an uncanny knack for implementing our ideas. Sarah's ability to persuade clients to try the untried has aided our work immensely. Kurt Sandholtz, an accomplished jazz pianist, first introduced us to the power of the jazz metaphor for understanding organizations. During our discussions with Kurt, the first seeds of strategic improvising were planted. Joe Hanson made us keenly aware of the financial implications associated with strategic improvising. His current work about the relationship between shareholder value and real-time strategies holds great promise for the future. Paul McKinnon's ongoing study of executive leadership has revealed to us some ways to ease senior executives' discomfort about their loss of top-down control, which they may see as an exclusive trait of strategic improvising. Joe Folkman's skill at measuring the impact of change was an enormous help. He has pushed forward the technology for gathering real-time information about customers, employees, product quality, organizational arrangements, and stakeholders. Nigel Bristow, Vern Della-Piana, Murray Low, Troy Scotter, and Kendall Lyman contributed important ideas and concrete experiences. The Novations marketing staff—Ron Olthuis, Courtney Rogers, and Carolyn Low—provided us with direct feedback from clients about ways to make our ideas more useful. To Judy Seegmiller, Linda Christensen, Stacey Hill, Stacy Keith, and Krista Lewis we owe special thanks for their support in preparing the manuscript.

There are many colleagues and friends at Brigham Young University whom we want to recognize for their support. Fred Skousen, Dean of the Marriott School of Management, has been a steady ally of this effort. Alan Wilkins, Gibb Dyer, Bonner Ritchie, Heikki Rinne, Gary Cornia, and Pete Clarke have all had a profound influence on our thinking. The students in Lee Perry's Winter 1992 graduate strategy seminar read and reacted to the first draft of the manuscript and provided useful suggestions that were incorporated into subsequent drafts. Several of Lee Perry's former students, especially Greg Pesci, Mark Nyman, Paul Carlile, and Eric Rebentisch were also helpful during *Real-Time Strategy*'s earliest stages.

We are fortunate to have had a wonderful group of publishing professionals running with us in the anchor lap. Our literary agent, Michael Snell, helped connect us with the right people at John Wiley & Sons. John Mahaney, our editor, who played a significant role in fine-tuning the manuscript, has been a good friend and an understanding adviser. We have also appreciated the administrative support provided by Gloria Fuzia and the production management provided by Nana Prior. The skilled copyediting of Maryan Malone of Publications Development Company significantly improved the book.

Most of all, we are grateful to our wives—Carolyn, Jolene, and Diana—and our children. They have sacrificed for us, provided us with unwavering support, and lifted and loved us as we have worked on the book. We can never repay our debt to them, but we intend to keep trying.

LEE TOM PERRY
RANDY STOTT
NORMAN SMALLWOOD

Provo, Utah
January 1993

REAL-TIME STRATEGY

IMPROVISING TEAM-BASED PLANNING FOR A FAST-CHANGING WORLD

PICKUP: AN INTRODUCTION TO STRATEGIC IMPROVISING

1

Pickup An introductory phrase, usually one or two bars, leading into a new selection or a chorus. Used for synchronization, to help a jazz group come in together and play as a unit from the first regular bar of the piece.

Taco Bell, a subsidiary of PepsiCo, made McDonald's blink. Taco Bell concentrates on one group of customers—frequent fast-food eaters—and offers them low-cost, good-tasting food. With 20 menu items under a dollar, 39-cent fiesta tacos, burritos, and tostadas, and 20 percent annual profit margins, Taco Bell was driving the fast-food giant crazy. McDonald's responded by offering a 59-cent hamburger, creating a healthier menu that featured salads and the McLean Deluxe hamburger, and using biodegradable packaging. The most telling move by McDonald's was the one it should not have made: it added chicken fajitas and breakfast burritos to its menu. Taco Bell had stared into the giant's face and the giant blinked.

Taco Bell would have made a comparable mistake if it had added hamburgers like McDonald's to its menu. Instead, it gained an advantage by keeping its menu simple and consistent. The company, however, decided to develop a new business that could compete directly against McDonald's without imitating it.

After considering several hamburger concepts, Taco Bell acquired Hot 'n Now, a small chain of hamburger shops based in Michigan. The Hot 'n Now concept was intriguing to Taco Bell's management because it offered value to customers in two ways: it saved them time (the hamburgers were served in 30 seconds or less) and it gave them a unique product at an attractive price (39 cents).

Hot 'n Now's concept had, however, started to break down. Its prices remained low, but its service had become progressively slower. Hot 'n Now was still the fastest in the fast-food business, but its speed did not always meet customer expectations for hot food *and* immediate service.

Taco Bell owned the management expertise and discipline to get Hot 'n Now back on track—and the resources to grow it fast. Taco Bell managers joined Hot 'n Now managers to form a *new* Hot 'n Now management team. Its first agenda item was a discussion of the principles of the business. Every decision that was made was first run through the strategy filter. This ensured that members of the management team would maintain a constant focus on saving the time and the money of frequent fast-food eaters.

One of the fundamental principles underlying Hot 'n Now's present strategy is the "self-management" of stores: teams of employees are responsible for making work assignments, handling people issues, and coordinating performance. The only assistance received by unit teams is from a multiunit manager, who is charged with providing guidance to three or four unit teams.

Supporting the principle of self-management is another principle restricting the proliferation of cumbersome policies and procedures. The management team wanted to provide a framework for unit teams, but it did not want to stifle creative problem solving. In the middle of every Hot 'n Now store, there is a standing area equipped with a whiteboard. Unit teams are expected to huddle there to make key operational decisions. When, for example, a bus with 50 people aboard pulls up to a Hot 'n Now store, the team huddles and develops a strategy for dealing with the flood of customers.

Once the principles of the business were in place, Hot 'n Now's management team acted quickly. They tried different *incomplete* solutions in a few test stores, to see what worked or did not work. They continuously experimented with new ideas that did not violate the dual strategic concepts of low cost and high speed. They also encouraged every unit team to experiment with new ideas and share the results with management.

Hot 'n Now's management team acknowledged that, initially, operations would not run smoothly, but they saw in each failure an opportunity to learn how to make the business better. For example, they tried a bonus system to improve unit team performance. When the bonus system failed to achieve its desired results, they found out why and made the needed adjustments. The management team consistently returned to Hot 'n Now's underlying strategy and principles for guidance in making these adjustments.

Hot 'n Now is among the businesses that operate in the more dynamic sectors of today's global economy. In these businesses, individuals and teams, working together, formulate and implement competitive strategies in real time. This is the core of *strategic improvising,* an approach to strategic thinking designed for businesses like Hot 'n Now, in which rapid-fire change is a way of life.

The Hot 'n Now example reveals three important differences between strategic improvising and traditional strategic planning.[1] Perhaps the most obvious difference is that, with strategic improvising, strategic decisions are made at all organizational levels, not exclusively at the top. Strategic improvising is a *team-based,* not a top-down, approach. Strategic responsibilities are assigned to the team nearest the action.

Second, strategic improvising involves a high-frequency (and, typically, low-impact) approach; strategic planning is clearly a low-frequency (typically, high-impact) approach. Strategic improvisers launch a lot of strategic thrusts, hoping to hit for a high average; strategic planners agonize over each strategic thrust they launch, intent on hitting a few home runs.

A more important difference is that strategic plans are front-loaded: top managers plan before they act. Strategic improvising occurs in real time. Strategic improvisers act before they plan, because they believe action informs strategic thinking.

TEAM-BASED STRATEGIC THINKING

Strategic improvising works only when self-managing teams are given strategic responsibilities *and* strategic tools are placed in the hands of team members. In the Hot 'n Now example, two types of teams were discussed: the management team and the unit teams. The management team had the responsibility for blending Taco Bell's strategy with the Hot 'n Now concept, and then defining a clear and focused business strategy. The strategic tools the management team used were the higher-order tools used to set strategic direction. However, the strategic direction established by the management team was not overspecified. In fact, the management team consciously resisted developing detailed policies and procedures because they wanted the unit teams to assume the responsibility for improvising operational strategies.

People might mistakenly assume that the improvisation of Hot 'n Now's unit teams is tactical, not strategic. However, thinking is not defined according to the organizational level at which it occurs. Tactical thinking by a CEO is not strategic thinking, and strategic thinking by Hot 'n Now's unit teams is not tactical thinking. Moreover, what appears to be a "tactic" to Hot 'n Now's management team may be a "strategy" to members of its unit teams if it determines the ultimate success and viability of their store. According to James Brian Quinn, professor emeritus at Dartmouth's Tuck School of Business Administration:

> [Tactics] are the short-duration, adaptive, action–interaction realignments that opposing forces use to accomplish limited goals after their initial contact. Strategy defines a continuing basis for ordering these adaptations toward more broadly conceived purposes.[2]

Organizational designers, particularly those steeped in sociotechnical systems models, are redesigning organizations around self-managing teams. In most of these redesign efforts, teams are charged with implementing, but not formulating, competitive strategies. This is a serious oversight because, without the license to formulate and implement strategies together, teams are severely limited in their scope of work.

When strategic responsibilities are withheld from self-managing teams, their efforts often miss the mark. One of our colleagues recently attended a session at a major national conference in which he heard an organizational design consultant discuss a new intervention. The consultant's presentation recounted impressive changes in the sociotechnical system of a company using self-managing work teams and other organizational redesign tools. Everyone seemed persuaded by the presentation until someone innocently asked about the progress at the company where the redesign had occurred. The consultant admitted that, before the company's organizational design had passed through the final round of fine-tuning, the company had gone out of business because of problems with its strategy.

According to the consultant, the organizational redesign was an unmitigated success in spite of the company's demise. Our view is that the redesign was an unmitigated failure. Because self-managing teams were never given strategic responsibilities, their work was not guided by strategic considerations. The company drifted toward ultimate dissolution because teams lacked strategic direction.

It is not enough to equip self-managing teams with strategic tools. Before team members can accept responsibility for strategic improvising, they need to be coached in the *use* of strategic tools. At Hot 'n Now, the principal responsibility of multiunit managers is to coach people, not manage them. Instead of exercising authority over people, multiunit managers are expected to train unit teams in the use of strategic improvising tools and shepherd them toward becoming self-managing.

Alfred Chandler, professor emeritus of history at Harvard Business School and widely recognized as the leading authority on American business history, once proposed that the art or science of strategy was so crucial and complex that it required specialized guidance by senior executives. He called these executives "the key few men in any enterprise."[3] Chandler's observations were used to define strategic planning as a top-management function, and they support the model of management depicted in Figure 1–1(a). Detailed corporate strategic plans provide a context for detailed business strategic plans; together, they nearly eliminate discretion at the operating level.

In contrast, the Hot 'n Now example demonstrates that another model of management is possible (see Figure 1–1(b)). A few key

(a) Strategic Planning	**(b) Strategic Improvising**
Corporate Strategies Business Strategies Operational Strategies	Corporate Strategies Business Strategies Operational Strategies

FIGURE 1–1. **Strategic planning versus strategic improvising: the relationship among corporate strategies, business strategies, and operational strategies.**

individuals may be necessary to clarify strategic direction at the corporate and business levels, but lower-level teams of individuals can assume critical strategic responsibilities if they are given strategic improvising tools and coached in how to use them. Strategic improvising invites members of self-managing teams to exercise significant freedom in formulating and implementing operational strategies within the limited form provided by corporate and business strategies.

HIGH-FREQUENCY STRATEGIES

Strategic improvising involves the continuous, rapid firing of strategic thrusts within an established strategic direction. Given that almost every business is constrained in its use of resources, the rapidity of strategic thrusts affects their intensity, which will inevitably vary. Strategic improvisers practice the *theory of the small win*. Their goal is to accumulate maximum understanding about a rapidly changing business environment as quickly as possible, by making low-cost, fast-paced, successive approximations.

In contrast, strategic planning is typically a low-frequency, higher-impact approach to strategic thinking. It involves a surfeit of policies—thorough market research, competitor benchmarking, and industry structure analysis, for example—to raise the odds of success and get the *biggest bang* from each strategic thrust.

At Hot 'n Now, overall success equals the pooled contributions of hundreds of individual strategic thrusts. Because it is acceptable to try out incomplete solutions in the culture created at Hot 'n Now, teams keep the strategic thrusts coming. Teams at all levels of the business are involved in the process. Because there are many more teams at the unit level than at the multiunit and business levels, most of the strategic thrusts are launched by unit teams.

The sheer volume of strategic thrusts, not their variety, characterizes strategic improvising. Strategic improvisers at Hot 'n Now shoot a tight pattern of strategic thrusts because they aim in a single strategic direction. Although strategic improvising has a clear bias for action, it is not necessarily a *ready, fire, aim* approach to strategic thinking. The reasons for this should be obvious. One of the keys to strategic improvising's success is everyone's involvement, but everyone would end up going everywhere pointlessly, without some guidance and discipline. Teams of strategic improvisers do not aim carefully before they fire the first shot, but they make sure they are turned in the same direction as everyone else in the business.

High-frequency strategies create a lot of advantages for businesses. When multiple teams, on multiple levels, fire in the same direction, they generate many ways to learn about many things. Multiple strategic thrusts can also overwhelm and confuse competitors. Because competitors see strategic thrusts individually, it takes them time to recognize the underlying strategic direction. This point was made 3,000 years ago by Sun-tzu, a Chinese military strategist, when he observed, "All men can see the tactics whereby I conquer, but what none can see is the strategy out of which great victory is evolved." High-frequency strategies in which all of a business's teams are turned in the same direction have another definite advantage: it is easier for teams to learn from each other.

Hot 'n Now supports high-frequency strategic thrusts by literally redefining the meaning of failure. The purpose of strategic improvising, like the purpose of all strategic approaches, is to promote success, not failure. When failure inevitably occurs, strategic improvisers are ready and willing to learn lessons from it. At Hot 'n Now, people joke about failing at more new concepts than their competitors launch. The joke would not be the least bit funny except for two differences between Hot 'n Now and its competitors: teams never let the store ride on a single strategic thrust, *and* they never feel locked in to an initially good-sounding idea when it begins to go bad.

REAL-TIME STRATEGIES

"People formulate strategy with their fingertips," says Andrew Grove, Intel's CEO.[4] By proposing that fingertips are the principal tool, Grove is not suggesting that strategy formulation is a mindless activity. He is suggesting that strategy is reflected in what people *do* in organizations. As employees design, manufacture, sell, and support a company's products, they also form and refine competitive strategies in real time.

Some strategists discuss time as a new source of competitive advantage, noting that, if the design cycle in the automobile industry could be cut by two years, new car models could incorporate technology that is two years newer.[5] The same logic applies to strategies and information. The more the strategists reduce the time between strategy formulation and strategy implementation, the more current is the information they factor into their strategies. When strategies are formulated and implemented together in real time, strategists can use real-time information. Because the business environment is a constantly moving target, real-time strategies offer significant advantages over outdated strategic plans.

Before they can engage in real-time strategizing, however, teams need ways to access real-time information. As noted earlier, Hot 'n Now created an area in each store where unit teams were to convene to do real-time strategizing. The teams soon discovered, however, that members needed to be better informed if they were to participate actively in the process. The most informed persons on the unit teams—the order takers—both called and dominated most of the huddles; they were the only personnel with access to real-time information. Unit teams quickly recognized the problems, described to their multiunit manager what they were experiencing, and then proposed some obvious design solutions. Their proposal led to two important modifications in the design of stores. Loudspeakers were installed so that every unit team member could hear an order as it was being received, and monitors were placed at key locations throughout the stores so that everyone could see the drive-through vehicles lined up to place orders.

Hot 'n Now's unit teams were still not home: they discovered that they needed an ongoing way of thinking about strategy. As consultants to Hot 'n Now, one of our important contributions was teaching teams about strategic alignment and the tools that will achieve it.

Business organizations can be viewed as systems that are constantly falling out of alignment. At Hot 'n Now's unit-team level, the most common misalignment was between the way team members were organized to work and the flow of customers. Team members' positioning and the rate at which they worked during the slow periods were insufficient when a busload of people suddenly pulled in. The system had fallen out of alignment, and team members had to huddle to figure out a solution. To correct this horizontal misalignment, a meeting for a strategic purpose was used as a tool.

The bonus system designed by Hot 'n Now's management team, and initially proposed at Hot 'n Now, had created a vertical misalignment. It was not having the desired effect at the unit-team level. Hot 'n Now's management team used another strategic alignment tool, up-close-and-personal contact, to help realign the system. Members of the management team met directly with several unit teams to ask questions about what was wrong with the current bonus system and to receive suggestions for designing a new and improved bonus system.

Helmuth von Moltke, a 19th-century Prussian military strategist, believed that, although the central idea that guides a strategy is front-loaded, it evolves in real time through continually changing circumstances. Front-loaded strategic plans work like a detailed map on which specific routes and destinations are already prescribed; real-time strategic improvising operates more like a compass. Strategic improvising is not based on knowing enough about the future to make a detailed map, plot a course, and decide on the optimal destination. Instead, individuals and teams select a two- or three-degree arc from a 360-degree circle of possibility and focus their business efforts on that small segment. From then on, strategic improvising, like a compass, channels adjustments in real time to ensure that high-frequency strategic thrusts all go in the same strategic direction.

JAZZ GROUPS AND SYMPHONY ORCHESTRAS

Many of our more significant insights about strategic improvising have been born of comparisons between jazz groups and symphony orchestras. Strategic improvising and jazz improvisation share many similarities. Because jazz groups invent team-based, high-frequency, real-time music, we have learned volumes about strategic improvising from observing them. Symphony orchestras seem to operationalize all the characteristics of strategic planning. Control is centralized (top-down), the music is preset (front-loaded), and preparing an orchestra to perform a single symphony requires a huge investment of resources and time (low-frequency, high-impact).

This use of metaphor enables us to see strategic planning and strategic improvising as integrated packages, rather than as a collection of characteristics. This perspective is useful in answering three important questions about strategic improvising:

1. *How does strategic improvising provide direction to business?* A strategic plan is like a conductor's score. For example, a page from the conductor's score of Hector Berlioz's "Fantastic Symphony," shown in Figure 1–2, provides detailed musical instructions to every musician in an orchestra. The score simplifies the role of individual musicians: they are required to play only their line of music. Because the composer and the

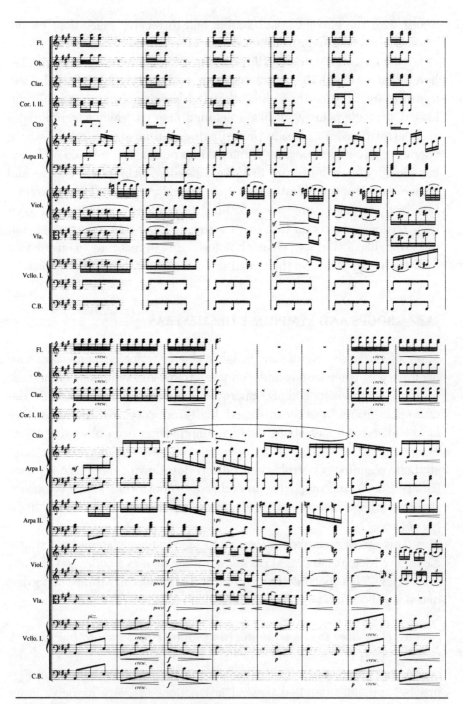

FIGURE 1–2.   An orchestra conductor's score sheet.

conductor must deal with the entire score, however, their roles are incredibly complex. One look at a conductor's score leaves little doubt about why there have been relatively few world-class composers and conductors in the history of the world. Their roles require incredible individual genius.

During the 18th century, when orchestras were smaller, composers wrote less detail into their music than they do today. Composers—Handel, for example—expected musicians to improvise. Johann Sebastian Bach, a contemporary of Handel, was a talented improviser. Frederick the Great, the King of Prussia at the time, asked Bach to develop some variations for one of his favorite melodies. Bach improvised several variations on-the-spot; when he returned to his home, he wrote several others. In all, Bach wrote 32 variations of the same melody and sent them to Frederick the Great for his birthday.

Bach's music is markedly different from Handel's. Most of the printed page of a composition by Handel is white space; a page from a Bach composition is filled with cascades of notes. Bach, the talented improviser, wrote every possible detail into his compositions *to discourage improvising*. Like strategic planners, Bach did not trust others to take liberties with the work of his genius. He wanted to ensure that everything went according to *his* plan.

Businesses clarify a strategic direction to guide strategic improvising. A strategic direction is like the lead sheet of a standard jazz composition. The lead sheet provides the minimum critical specifications—melody line, key, and basic form—necessary for a small group of jazz musicians to improvise together. The lead sheet for a well-known jazz tune, "Satin Doll" (see Figure 1–3), has much more white space on the page (or room for improvising) than the conductor's score in Figure 1–2. Strategic direction offers a similar invitation to improvise because it shows businesses only where to go, not how to get there.

Igor Stravinsky, a famous Russian composer, once said that it was extremely difficult for him to compose with absolute freedom, but his creative juices began to flow once a *simple idea* was introduced to guide his efforts. Stravinsky's statement helped us to clarify our view of the role of strategic direction. We are not comparing strategic improvising to avant-garde jazz, in which nothing—not even a melody—is preset. Strategic improvisers need strategic direction to complete an incomplete strategy in their own highly personalized way.

Satin Doll

**WORDS & MUSIC BY
BILLY STRAYHORN, DUKE ELLINGTON & JOHNNY MERCER**

FIGURE 1–3.   A jazz lead sheet.

2. *How are organizations that practice strategic improvising differ-ent from organizations that practice strategic planning?* Comparisons be-tween symphony orchestras and jazz groups suggest several organizational differences between strategic planners and strategic improvisers. Gener-ally, strategic improvisers are more participative and more responsive, and they engage in more lateral communications than strategic planners do.

- *Participation.* Many organizational scientists have used symphony or-chestras as models of ideal organizations. One of the most impressive characteristics of symphony orchestras is their high level of coordi-nated effort. Nevertheless, a significant cost is associated with the centralized way in which they achieve coordination. They are not highly participative organizations because they do not access the full range of human potential. Conductors vary in terms of the amount of participation they allow in the practice room, but they are clearly in charge during performances, and musicians are expected to perform only as directed. Although this is a satisfying arrangement for some musicians, many others feel underutilized.

    A defining characteristic of jazz is its reliance on the collective genius of the group. Leaders of jazz groups are the persons who get the "gig" (the booking). The leader is always a member of the group, but the role of leader is often rotated among group members. This gives members of jazz groups experience at both listening and being listened to. When they are in the role of leader, they are inclined to listen to the suggestions of other group members because, on another night, their roles might be reversed.

    A story told at W.L. Gore & Associates, about a four-day meet-ing that was attended by most of the business leaders of the company, is relevant here. On the last day, as the meeting was winding down, someone asked Bob Gore, the company president, "What are we sup-posed to do as a result of this meeting?" Bob answered, "I don't think we're *all* supposed to do any one thing. I've come away from this meeting with three or four things I know I want to do, and I hope that everyone else has personal To Do's as well."

    Team-based, high-frequency, real-time strategies are incompat-ible with centralized control. Strategic improvising requires the kind of participative leadership exhibited by Bob Gore. Like a jazz group leader, he does not overdirect. He is able to access the full range of human potential because he expects W.L. Gore's people to think and do on their own, within established strategic parameters.

- *Responsiveness.* The music played by symphony orchestras is ultimately controlled by composers. Conductors choose the music the orchestras play, but once they select a particular composition, the conductors become the agents of the composer. Their role is to eliminate variation and make the performance consistent with the composer's original intent. This goal of consistency supports repetition, not responsiveness.

  Jazz's simple form facilitates the responsiveness of jazz musicians to each other. As musical ideas pop into the heads of jazz musicians, they are able to grab and act on them immediately. When one group member starts a musical idea—for example, the trumpet player may imitate a big-band sound—the other members of the group help to develop it. Jazz groups are able to give the same piece of music a completely different feel simply by varying the rhythms, the notes, and the chords they play.

  Conductors work with their backs to their audiences, and the audiences are constrained by rules of etiquette that define when it is appropriate to applaud. A conductor must finish an entire symphony before knowing how the audience is receiving the orchestra's performance. These protocols limit the responsiveness of symphony orchestras.

  Jazz group leaders face the audience; they play alongside the other musicians in the group. Jazz audiences are rarely placid. They are encouraged to show their approval whenever the music is "hot." This direct contact enables jazz groups to be sensitive and responsive to their audiences. In addition, jazz groups are used to taking audience requests. Jazz musicians are capable of quickly responding to audience requests because they are adept at responding to other group members in real time.

  Individuals who work for organizations that practice strategic improvising are like jazz musicians: they keep their eyes and ears open. They listen to what other individuals and teams have to say, and they watch what those teams do. They are tuned in to new developments in the business environment, which enables them to stay tapped in to an ongoing flow of real-time information and, in turn, heightens internal and external responsiveness.

- *Communication.* Comparisons of symphony orchestras and jazz groups reveal extremely different networks of communication. In orchestras, vertical communications between the conductor and musicians predominate. Section leaders will sometimes listen to what the other sections are playing, but the attention of most of the musicians is riveted on their music stands and the conductor. Orchestra musicians position their music stands just beneath their view of the conductor. As they read their music, their peripheral vision enables them to see the conductor's guiding gestures.

  In jazz groups, the musicians' attention is focused on what other group members are doing, because everyone is expected to respond to each of the other players. For example, we know a jazz trumpet player who studies the recordings of saxophone and keyboard players more than those of other trumpet players. He feels he already understands what his instrument can do, and he wants to learn more about other musicians' skills with their instruments. This knowledge helps him communicate with and respond to them more quickly, and he is able to anticipate how they will respond to him when he takes a piece of music in a new, uncharted direction.

  The lateral communications that characterize jazz groups have clear implications for the design of organizations that practice strategic improvising. Organizations that practice strategic improvising are organized into teams. To accommodate the thick network of lateral communication, they are smaller and flatter than organizations that practice strategic planning.

3. *How do strategic improvising teams act?* We already know some of the characteristics of strategic improvising teams. For example, they are about the size of a jazz group—usually 5 to 9 members, compared to a symphony orchestra's 110 members. They assume strategic responsibilities: much like jazz groups' simultaneous composition and performance of music, strategic improvising teams formulate and implement strategies together in real time. They are self-managing; often, they are led by member-leaders who perform a temporary, rotated role.

Jazz groups, like strategic improvising teams, rotate other roles, beyond the leadership role. Each member of a jazz group has a defined role that complements the roles of the other group members. Their roles overlap: if one group member were to assume a nontraditional role—for example, if the bass player plays melody instead of providing rhythm—another group member could fill in the rhythm. This is analogous to strategic improvising teams' cross-training, in which team members are certified to perform multiple tasks.

The rotation of roles among jazz group members is facilitated by what is called the *bridge* in jazz format. In the most common jazz form, A-A-B-A (two lines of the same melody, a different melody line, then a return to the original melody), the different melody line (B) is the bridge. Bridges perform the same function in a jazz group as huddles perform for unit teams at Hot 'n Now. They are times to shift roles in response to new strategic objectives.

One of the great challenges for both jazz groups and strategic improvising teams is management of the tension between the forces of stability and change. Two different kinds of norms are needed: norms that support group harmony, and norms that encourage experimentation and risk taking.

The behavior of members of jazz groups is affected by norms about the amount of lead time each member should have, how loudly or softly members should play, and how to contribute to and not compete against the ideas of other group members. These norms supersede the preferences of individual musicians because they preserve the harmony of the group. If a group member, even if extremely talented, violates group norms, the other members of the group will adjust temporarily, but if the member does not soon conform to group norms, he or she will be replaced.

It is critical for jazz groups and strategic improvising teams to be creative. Theoretically, the potential variations of a standard jazz tune approach infinity; however, after playing the same tune hundreds of times, jazz groups find it difficult to invent new and exciting ways to play it. The problem is compounded because jazz musicians tend to reinforce each other when they get into ruts. They allow their natural reflexes, not their creative instincts, to guide their playing.

The better jazz groups are aware of this tendency and have established mechanisms for encouraging experimentation and risk taking. Some jazz groups inject new ideas into their music by spending more time jamming together. A similar benefit is realized by strategic improvising teams through brainstorming sessions. Other jazz groups rely on individual members to shake them out of routine. Existing members may consciously force themselves to play the opposite of what they ordinarily play, or new members may be invited to sit with the group temporarily. Strategic improvising teams can access similar benefits by encouraging team members to reconfigure their work or by rotating team membership. However, although variations in behavior are desired, they should be consistent with the established strategic direction.

STRATEGIC IMPROVISING: NOT AN OXYMORON

Several years ago, we attended a conference at which an executive from Ford Motor Company spoke about her company's new employee involvement program. As we listened to her describe the changes at Ford, it became clear that its management was attempting to create a new atmosphere of trust and openness. Executives set the example by speaking extemporaneously and fielding questions off-the-cuff from employee groups. We also observed that Ford was encouraging employee and management teams to do more improvising. When one of us shared this observation with a group of executives, however, they disagreed vehemently. "Ford's employee involvement program is strategic, not improvised," one executive exclaimed. "It's not an anything-goes, winging-it approach to management."

This experience reveals two common misconceptions about strategic improvising. First, most managers think of themselves as reflective, systematic planners, not improvisers. Henry Mintzberg, the Bronfman Professor of Management at Montreal's McGill University, reminds us that managers have always improvised the nonroutine parts of their jobs, and that the image of the rational manager is an artifact of attempts by generations of management scientists to rationalize managerial work. The real facts are that the limited planning that managers do is done implicitly in the context of daily actions; managers are oriented to action, and they dislike reflective activities; they respond in real time to stimuli, preferring live to delayed action.[6] James Brian Quinn adds:

> The processes used to arrive at the total strategy are typically fragmented, evolutionary, and largely intuitive. Although one can frequently find embedded in these fragments some very refined pieces of formal strategic analysis, the real strategy tends to *evolve* as internal decisions and external events flow together to create a new, widely shared consensus for action . . . .[7]

Second, the experience suggests that strategy and improvisation are fundamentally incompatible—that *strategic improvising* is an oxymoron. *Strategic* (from the Greek *strategia,* meaning generalship) suggests to most people a top-down, plan-and-control approach to management, but *improvising* is not the classic nonstrategic response. As we have already learned, it involves freedom exercised within form, not restricted freedom. Jazz musicians are especially frustrated by this misperception because many people, believing there is no form to the music they play, do not consider them true musicians. This misconception persists because, in jazz improvisation, as in strategic improvising, a little form goes a long way.

Strategic improvising is not an oxymoron. Instead, it is a process in which a simple strategic direction provides the limited form needed for team-based improvising. Strategic improvising promotes high-frequency (low-impact) strategic thrusts that are much more effective than low-frequency (high-impact) strategic plans for learning about the rapidly changing business environment. Finally, given the unpredictability of today's global economy, strategic improvising is a much-needed, real-time alternative to front-loaded strategic thinking.

2

A CUTTIN' CONTEST: STRATEGIC PLANNING VERSUS STRATEGIC IMPROVISING

Cuttin' Contest A competition in which two or more jazz bands play segments or variations of a piece back-to-back, with one group cutting in as soon as the other is finished. The volume of audience applause after the cuts determines the winner.

General Electric invented strategic planning in the early 1950s, when it launched significant planning efforts in its Lamp Division and Appliance Division. Strong commitments were made up-front, and only the best and brightest managers and staff personnel were invited to join the planning task forces. In the Lamp Division, the planning effort lasted 15 months; the Appliance Division's task force worked for 18 months. After the plans were accepted, the responsibility for their maintenance and control was turned over to management-research groups.[1]

General Electric's commitment to strategic planning ultimately supported a 350-member corporate planning staff responsible for forecasting and strategy formulation. The staff created voluminous reports proposing strategic ends and detailing the strategic means that GE's stable of businesses could use to achieve those ends.

Under Jack Welch's leadership, however, General Electric abandoned the strategic planning process it had pioneered. The company transferred prime strategic responsibilities to line managers and teams of workers. Currently, each of GE's 13 businesses is expected to develop five *one-page* memos that point to the possible opportunities and obstacles anticipated over the next 24 months.

Why did the company that invented strategic planning abandon it? There was an obvious problem of excess. Jack Welch perceived that the bigger GE's strategic plans became, the less useful they were. More and more hours went into their preparation, and planners began to embellish them with one-upmanship graphics and fancy covers.[2] Instead of a means to an end, they had become an end in themselves. More importantly, Welch—and others—recognized that strategic planning was out-of-step with the demands of the new world economic order.

A similar metamorphosis is slow to occur at other companies; many managers still consider strategic planning a useful discipline. Admittedly, the effects of strategic planning are not all bad. For example, strategic planning makes significant positive contributions to organizational processes. James Brian Quinn has proposed the following list of the process contributions of strategic planning:

1. They create a network of information that would not otherwise be available.

2. They periodically force operating managers to extend their time horizons and see their work in a larger framework.

3. They require rigorous communications about goals, strategic issues, and resource allocations.

4. They systematically teach managers about the future, enabling the managers to calibrate their short-term or interim decisions with more fact-supported intuition.

5. They often create a positive attitude, a comfort factor, concerning the future; managers can look ahead with more certainty, and consequently are more willing to make commitments that extend beyond the near horizons.

6. They often stimulate longer-term "special studies" that can have high impact for specific or critical strategic decisions.[3]

Few managers consciously engage in strategic planning for the above reasons, but the list defines why managers instinctively cling to the process, even when they find the plan increasingly less helpful.

The case against strategic planning, however, continues to build. Although strategic planning served corporate America for several decades, critics are claiming that the global economy has become too complex, too dynamic, and too unpredictable for managers to place their faith in plans. After years of interviewing line managers, Robert Hayes, a professor at the Harvard Business School, reports: "Their [line managers'] complaint . . . is not about the *mis*functioning of strategic planning but about the harmful aspects of *proper* functioning."[4] *Fortune* believes that strategic planning's fall from grace is epidemic:

> At too many companies, strategic planning has become overly bureaucratic, absurdly quantitative, and largely irrelevant. In executive suites across America, countless five-year plans, updated annually and solemnly clad in three-ring binders, are gathering dust—their impossibly specific prognostications about costs, prices, and market share long forgotten.[5]

A BASIC CASE AGAINST STRATEGIC PLANNING

The five most common criticisms of strategic planning are:

1. Because strategic planning overspecifies means, it lacks flexibility and may exclude or postpone a new and better solution.
2. Planning limits innovation by projecting the past into the future.
3. Planning restricts learning because it is an excuse for inaction.
4. When resources are allocated based on plans and not on previous performance, the strategic planning process invites managers to play games.
5. Planning leads to structural, not behavioral, solutions.

A Lack of Flexibility

Recently, we heard a Ford Motor Company executive speak about change at his company during the 1980s. He was in his mid-50s and had been through several cycles of good times and bad times at Ford. He was touting the fact that Ford, once down and out, had risen phoenix-like from its ashes and had become a new, globally competitive company. What was even more interesting than this Ford executive's story, however, was his repeated use of one phrase. Every time he spoke about an unplanned change at Ford he began, "We had to . . . ." From his inflection, we soon got the impression that, although he had accepted unplanned change, he did not embrace it.

It is not surprising that a person who had known Ford in an earlier era would be ambivalent about unplanned change. This executive had inherited the legacy of Robert McNamara, a former Ford president,[6] and the Whiz Kids, about whom it has been said that they tried to impose rationality on an irrational world. Their ultimate goal was to plan everything in enough detail that surprise would be eliminated from business. They took pleasure in gathering and projecting data—"the numbers" were like a theology and formed the basis of the strategic planning system they institutionalized at Ford.[7]

Strategic planning limits a company's flexibility because it locks in one course of action. A means–end shift occurs. Originally the means to an end, the plan becomes the end, and adjustments in the plan are instinctively resisted. The psychology of strategic planning is all wrong for a dynamic business environment because it makes operating according to plan the overriding objective, whether the plan makes sense anymore or not. According to Jack Welch: "Once written, the strategic document can take on a life of its own, and it may not lend itself to flexibility. . . . An organization can begin to focus on form rather than substance."[8]

Robert McNamara, the Whiz Kids, and the managers on whom they left their imprint at Ford were wrong to believe that surprises could be eliminated from business. Every company "has to" change as unforeseen events occur. Unplanned change is inevitable, and inflexible companies that resist change invariably fall behind flexible companies that embrace it.

A Lack of Innovation

Strategic planning is billed as a future-oriented activity, but plans do little more than project the recent past into the future. Strategic objectives that lead to global leadership cannot be planned for; they lie beyond the planning horizon. An unwillingness to pursue strategic ends unless strategic means are well-defined is a definition of short-sightedness. In effect, reinvention is supported and competitive innovation is suppressed.

There is also a tendency for the focus of strategic plans to shift dramatically from year to year, in response to the problems that appear most urgent at the conclusion of each planning cycle. Urgent problems, however, are not always a company's most important concerns; often, they are temporary and, therefore, distractive, and they siphon attention away from more fundamental and lasting problems. The result is a "flavor of the year" planning process that is much more tactical than strategic. In this situation, the focus of innovation suffers more than the rate of innovation. Several unrelated innovations do not create as much competitive advantage as several related innovations because they do not build on each other.

A similar problem is what Charlie Feld, Frito-Lay's former chief information officer, calls the "shifting configuration problem." Shifting configurations occur when businesses create strategic plans only in response to negative information. Because plans focus a business's efforts, most negatives can be turned into positives. Unfortunately, some of the original positives become negatives because they do not receive the ongoing attention they require. The problem with shifting configurations, according to Feld, is that one never knows whether accomplishing plans ever improves the business.

An Excuse for Inaction

A recent cartoon said a lot about strategic planning. In the cartoon, one man suggests, "We ought to start planning ahead." "Why?" asks a second man. The first man answers, "So we wouldn't have to do anything right now." Many companies caught in the planning cycle are more like these two men than they would care to admit. When we consider that the summary figure of the planning model developed by Igor Ansoff, the author of the most influential early book about strategic planning, contains 57 boxes (denoting 57 planning activities), we gain a sense of how long planning can delay action.[9]

Action promotes learning; when plans delay action, they delay learning. Karl Weick, a professor at the University of Michigan, writes:

> Once people begin to act, they generate tangible outcomes in some context, and this helps them discover what is occurring, what needs to be explained, and what should be done next. Managers keep forgetting that it is what they do, not what they plan, that explains their success. They keep giving credit to the wrong thing—namely, the plan—and having made this error, they then spend more time planning and less time acting. They are astonished when planning improves nothing.[10]

The problem for most strategic planners is that they do not realize what they are giving up by delaying action.

The design of the command and control cars for the Rail-Garrison Missile Deployment System, created by Rockwell International's Autonetics Division, is a good example of how action leads to learning that never would have occurred through formal planning. In the Rail-Garrison system, nuclear missiles are deployed on rail cars, in order to disperse them during periods when the threat of nuclear attack is especially high. Ron Kodimer, the Rail-Garrison program vice president, and his team jumped into action by building a mock-up of a rail car. The mock-up accelerated the team's learning about the needs of its customer (the Air Force), the ideal characteristics of the system, and the constraints associated with building the system to fit inside a rail car. As team members developed new concepts for the system, they incorporated them into the mock-up. At an early stage, they invited Air Force representatives and operators from silo-based command and control centers to visit them and react to the mock-up. Feedback and new ideas from these visitors were immediately incorporated into the mock-up. Team members even took turns living in the mock-up so that they could experience what it would be like for a Rail-Garrison crew to live for long periods in cramped quarters.

By using the mock-up as the core concept in an action-oriented approach to designing the Rail-Garrison system, Rockwell International's Autonetics Division encouraged design improvements to bubble up, in an entrepreneurial fashion, from team members and from the customer. The approach provided them with real-time, naturally reoccurring, and readily interpretable design information that never would have been available to paper-and-pencil or computer-assisted design (CAD) professionals, no matter how long or hard they had planned. If the Rail-Garrison team had planned longer and acted later, their learning would have been much slower.

An Invitation to Play Games

The difference between planning and managing is a lot like the difference between campaigning and governing. The individuals who are best at getting elected are not necessarily the best at running a government; similarly, the best planners are not necessarily the best implementers of plans. Whenever organizational resources are allocated based on plans instead of on past performances, there is an attendant risk that the planning process will turn into a game.

At a major defense contractor, for example, the annual operating planning (AOP) process is the primary focus of management activity for three to four months in each of the company's divisions. What is most troubling about the AOP process, however, is not the time and resources it consumes, but the cynicism surrounding it. Most managers view it as a game for gaining corporate support, with the winners able to tell the better stories.

When planning becomes a game, it can send businesses off course. One of the great advantages of plans is that they can be "self-fulfilling prophecies." They instill confidence, and confidence leads to the accomplishment of plans.[11] All the confidence in the world, however, will not be enough for some plans, and businesses can be misled into believing that something is possible for them when it is really impossible. Their plans then become huge black holes into which they throw their resources, thereby robbing current operations of required support.

An Avoidance of Behavioral Solutions

One of the major problems with top-down strategic planning is its overemphasis on quantitative goals and measures; one perspective dominates the strategic planning. Top management should be concerned about the numbers: quantitative measures provide a way of consolidating information and keeping score. Moreover, quantitative goals, like return on investment, mean a great deal to top managers, who are evaluated on their ability to allocate capital efficiently. The problem, however, comes when top managers fail to realize that, although the meanings of quantitative goals and measures are important to them, the individuals and teams working in the trenches of organizations relate better to qualitative goals and measures that pertain directly to the work they do.

According to Robert Hayes, planning-by-the-numbers leads top managers to spend most of their time worrying about structural (rather than behavioral) means for achieving strategic objectives. Their plans focus on investments in new plants and equipment, the introduction of new products, and the redesign of organizational charts, rather than on performance evaluation and reward systems, work-force policies, and management selection and development policies.[12] Efficient markets exist for most structural means—any company can buy and sell them. They cannot offer competitive advantage because, although they may be valuable, they are not unique. Conversely, most behavioral means are firm-specific. They *are* unique and, therefore, they are a potential source of competitive advantage.

One would think that, more than any other industry, the professional services industry should understand the importance of behavioral solutions. After all, there is little debate among professional service organizations, such as law firms and consulting firms, about what differentiates them from their competitors. It is the capabilities of their people. But the tendency of many professional service organizations to rely almost exclusively on a single quantitative measure of firm success—namely, billable hours—has led them to focus on structural, not behavioral solutions.

In the legal profession, firms grow by inviting senior attorneys with established practices—"practices on wheels"—to join them. These "rainmakers" bring new business with them and give an immediate infusion to the firm's bottom line. When law firms focus on acquiring senior attorneys, less attention is paid and fewer resources are devoted to the development of junior attorneys.

At AB&C,[13] a full-service, 50-partner law firm, we saw two effects of the tendency to use structural solutions in the legal profession. First, the senior partners at AB&C were preoccupied with what their competitors were doing and tried very hard to match them move for move. If competing firms hired a new rainmaker, they tried to hire one with a similar practice. This, of course, created a "sellers' market" for rainmakers. The excellent salary deals cut by the new rainmakers created increased dissatisfaction among AB&C's old guard. Many of them threatened to put their résumés out if their compensation packages were not reworked.

The second effect was the falling stock of AB&C's associate attorneys. The firm did not want to invest in them because they were likely to move. Accordingly, the services they provided to clients were less well-developed. This led clients to request more senior attorneys to do their work, further limiting the developmental experiences of the junior attorneys. In spite of the fact that there are currently three partners to every associate, AB&C recently put a hold on the hiring of new associates.

AB&C's senior-named partner pushed the firm toward structural solutions because he had a plan to make AB&C the largest law firm in town, and recruiting rainmakers was the fastest means of growth. The plan's flaw was its failure to recognize that when structural solutions can be acquired on the open market by one firm, they can also be acquired by other firms. There is no possibility of creating competitive advantage. Of more concern is the fact that the forces set into motion at AB&C amplify over time; they are already dangerously close to destroying one of the cornerstones of any professional organization—the development of its young professionals. The only way to reverse the tide *and* create competitive advantage is to reinvest in their development, a firm-specific behavioral solution.

A CASE FOR STRATEGIC IMPROVISING

One of the reasons strategic plans still clutter the boardrooms of most American businesses is that a viable alternative has not been found. Managers assume that planning, even if mostly irrelevant, is better than nothing. Typical reactions are: How else would we guide our companies? How would we provide direction and purpose? What can be done to navigate and safely maneuver our companies through erratic seas of change?

We believe that strategic improvising provides the guidance and direction that managers are seeking, and that it responds to *all* of the concerns being raised about strategic planning. Because strategic improvising is a real-time process, it promotes both flexibility and action-oriented responses. By launching high-frequency strategic thrusts pointed in a well-defined strategic direction, it creates a high rate of focused innovation. High-frequency (low-impact) strategic thrusts are also inherently fairer: individuals and teams prove the value of their ideas through action and experimentation, not through elaborate plans that may not realize their stated goals. Finally, because strategic improvising is a team-based, not a top-down, process, it possesses a built-in bias toward behavioral solutions.

Strategic improvising has even more attractive attributes:

1. It meets the demands of the new world economic order.
2. It promotes the empowerment of individuals and teams.
3. It responds to the shift from routine to nonroutine organizational work.

Strategic improvising thrives in the business environment in which strategic planning failed.

STRATEGIC IMPROVISING AND
THE NEW WORLD ECONOMIC ORDER

In the movie classic *The Wizard of Oz*, Dorothy dreams that a tornado carries her away, in her house, to the mysterious and colorful Land of Oz. Upon landing in the Munchkin village, Dorothy brushes herself off, looks around in amazement, and remarks to her dog, "Toto, I don't think we're in Kansas anymore." American businesspeople are like Dorothy in at least one way: as they look across the evolving global economic landscape, they are genuinely amazed at how much everything has changed. They may be confused about many things, but one reality is clear: They're not in Kansas anymore.

Nothing was more predictable than the old world economic order. In the early 1950s, the United States was responsible for nearly 50 percent of the world's economic production.[14] If U.S. companies could produce it, there was no problem finding someone to buy it. This was the primary reason for the phenomenal success of the U.S. system of mass production and for the popularity of strategic planning, which developed in conjunction with mass production systems and continues to support them.

Initially, planning was focused on plant capacity, investment in new capital equipment, and production volume; later, it was applied across-the-board to the ends and the means of organized behavior. Planning was possible for major U.S. corporations because, as the giants of their industries, they set most of the industry rules and essentially controlled world supply and demand. Forecasts were reliable because the corporations faced few uncertainties associated with serious competition. This is why the reemergence of global competition has been so disruptive to many major U.S. corporations. Suddenly, to be competitive, they needed to foster more rapid technological innovation, stay close to customers, and improve product quality. After decades of unchallenged dominance, they had forgotten how.

George Stalk, Jr. and Thomas Hout propose that strategic eras, determined by innovations in competitive strategy, recur in the business environment. In the ending years of the 20th century, new strategic eras are appearing with increasing rapidity. At the beginning of the new strategic era, executives have two basic choices: Adopt a defensive posture and wait until the value of an innovative competitive strategy becomes clear, or seize the initiative and attack before competitors do. Stalk and Hout note that, at the beginning of new strategic eras, the companies that promptly adopt an aggressive posture generally grow faster and more profitably than the companies that wait.[15]

The idea of strategic eras is similar to Stephen Jay Gould's punctuated equilibria theory of evolution: both suggest that long periods of relative stability are punctuated by short periods of dramatic change. According to Gould, when these periods of dramatic change occur, some species adapt and others do not. The implication is that change is something that species react to but do not initiate.[16]

Occasionally, events affecting industries will kick off new strategic eras; more often, the strategic eras are started by companies. According to Joseph Schumpeter, competitive capitalism is driven by the supernormal profits that he called entrepreneurial gains. These gains motivate some businesses to go toward the challenges posed by innovation. They motivate other businesses to change, creating cycles of "creative destruction."[17] Stalk and Hout are right about the most aggressive companies also being the most successful at the beginning of new strategic eras, but they have overlooked the principal reason for the success. Because these aggressive firms actually launch new strategic eras, they, in a sense, rewrite the rule-book and create an immense competitive advantage for themselves—an advantage that is sustainable until other firms in the industry devise ways to neutralize their advantage.

Strategic eras follow a predictable life cycle (see Figure 2–1). They begin when a company, wishing to acquire industry market share, launches a strategic thrust and punctures the existing industry equilibrium. The purpose of the attack is to destroy the order and discipline of industry competitors; they, in turn, attempt to resist the attack by

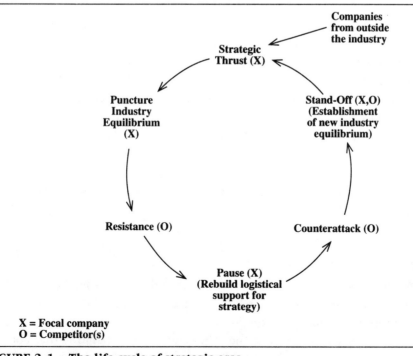

X = Focal company
O = Competitor(s)

FIGURE 2–1.   The life cycle of strategic eras.

retaining their order and discipline. Eventually, the attacking firm must pause to strengthen the systems supporting its strategic thrust or risk overextending itself. This brief pause provides competitors with the opportunity to counterattack. Previously, competitors had focused exclusively on holding themselves together to resist attack. Now, their efforts shift to finding ways to cancel the attacking firm's competitive advantage. A successful counterattack eventually leads to a period of relative stability in which both the attacking firm and its competitors hold their positions. This equilibrium state remains intact until another company, within or outside of the industry, launches a new strategic thrust. At that point, the cycle begins again.

Stalk and Hout are well-known advocates of time-based strategies. The argument they ultimately make is that a new strategic era is launched around time-based strategies, and companies that want to remain competitive must act quickly by adopting a time-based strategy. These authors propose many time-savers, all of which improve a business's response time, but they do not discuss the time-savings associated with real-time strategies. Without intending to, Stalk and Hout's approach misses a significant opportunity to save time because it assumes that time-based strategies should be planned, not improvised.

An understanding of strategic eras is important to strategic improvising because it describes the ebb and flow of the dynamic, competitive environment in which strategic improvising occurs. Early in 1991, Nintendo Entertainment Systems (NES), a company known for its aggressive business strategy, controlled over 80 percent of the U.S. video-game market. The company's name had become a household word in millions of American homes. At the height of Nintendo's popularity, when the giant seemed beyond any challenge, upstart Sega launched Genesis, a video-game system built with a powerful 16-bit computer chip that provided more color, faster action, and better sound than the 8-bit Nintendo system. Nintendo could have easily responded with its own 16-bit system; instead, it waited, because it did not want to upset current NES owners. By the time Nintendo produced Super NES in the fall of 1991, Sega had 150 different 16-bit cartridge games on the market and had sold nearly a million Genesis systems. Sega had punctured the existing industry equilibrium, launched a new strategic era, and shot ahead of complacent—and therefore vulnerable—Nintendo.[18]

The principal lesson of the Nintendo–Sega matchup is that companies gain significant competitive advantage when they puncture existing industry equilibria and launch new strategic eras. Strategic improvising provides maximum leverage to companies because it is preemptive. Within most industry structures, however, more than one company will have preemptive capability. Strategic improvisers are also able to react to the strategic thrusts of competitors, first to limit the damage and eventually to neutralize it.

Nintendo's experience makes another point clear: high-frequency strategic thrusts are a competitive necessity. Given the huge stakes involved in competition for global markets and the growing list of viable global competitors, companies that stand still, even for a moment, will be passed by their competitors. Accordingly, even small traces of complacency and hesitation must be eliminated from people's attitudes because they delay action.

Business is difficult. Given the accelerating competitive cycles in the expanding global economy, business is becoming harder, not easier. Executives, managers, and workers who want to return to the good old days, when conditions were simpler and certainly more predictable, will probably be disappointed by the solutions offered by strategic improvising. It is not a pair of ruby slippers possessed with the magic to return them to Kansas. What strategic improvising offers, however, is a set of tools uniquely designed to meet the challenges of the new world economic order.

STRATEGIC IMPROVISING AND EMPOWERING ORGANIZATIONS

The formula for business success used to be very simple. All anybody needed to do was develop a whiz-bang product or fabulous service, find or create a sizable market niche complete with entry barriers, throw in a little money for good measure, and then sit back and enjoy a sustainable competitive advantage. It was important to plan and control everything from the top, to keep people from messing up the formula. Corporate planners adopted the same philosophy as the engineers in Kurt Vonnegut's *Player Piano:* "If only it weren't for the people, the . . . [°!@&°!] people. If it weren't for them, the earth [and organizations] would be an engineer's paradise."[19]

Two forces—the changing nature of the American work force, and an increasingly complex formula for business success—have profoundly altered the way we think about people in organizations. No longer are a business's people the problem; they are the solution. An empowerment movement has begun in American business: people want less power exercised over them, and more of their own power to accomplish strategic objectives.

History provides perspective on how profoundly the nature of the American work force has changed in this century. Frederick Taylor, the father of scientific management, wrote in 1907 about his ideal worker: "One of the very first requirements for a man who is fit to handle pig iron as a regular occupation is that he more nearly resembles in his mental makeup the ox than any other type."[20] It has been a long time since the American worker accepted such dehumanizing stereotypes. Encouraged by organizational designers bent on removing the imprint of Taylor's scientific management from American business, workers rebel against manual, mindless labor. They want to prove that, when they are allowed more control over the content and context of their work, they can accomplish more for their organizations.

A natural outgrowth of increased global competition is that business is no longer simple. A few key persons at the top of organizations cannot deal with the complexity of the new world economic order. The more people involved in sensing the business environment, the better—as long as they are all turned in the same direction. Reflecting on the increased complexity of the global economy, Jack Welch says: "The idea of liberation and empowerment for our work force is not enlightenment—it's a competitive necessity."[21]

Strategic improvising is what the empowerment movement has been waiting for. Although they have wanted to be empowered for a long time, many people have not known how to become empowered. Empowerment is more than acceptance of responsibility; people must know what they are responsible for. Empowerment is more than the exercising of power; people must know where to concentrate their power. Strategic improvising provides individuals and teams with knowledge of what they are responsible for and where to concentrate their power.

At W.L. Gore & Associates,[22] empowerment and strategic improvising work together. Associates think of their company as a 5,300-member jazz group trying to make music in many different locations simultaneously. Strategic improvising at W.L. Gore begins with the principles of *Freedom* and *Waterline,* which are coordinated to release and concentrate the power of associates.

The Freedom principle asserts that each associate will allow, help, and encourage other associates to grow in knowledge, skill, scope of responsibility, and range of activities. At W.L. Gore, power is always being pushed down to associates, and powerful ideas are allowed to bubble up. The company's philosophy is that problem solving is best sustained by encouraging people to be responsible for themselves rather than by constantly monitoring them. Individuals should be expected—and held accountable by their peers—to do their best to understand what needs to be done, what they can uniquely and realistically contribute to getting it done, and what factors give the greatest value to their efforts.

The Waterline principle, which places boundaries around the exercise of freedom, states:

> Each of us will consult with appropriate associates, who will share the responsibility for taking any action that has the potential of serious harm to the reputation, success, or survival of the company.

In an accompanying analogy, the company is a ship in which holes bored through above the waterline do not lead to serious consequences, but holes made below the waterline could be catastrophic. When associates at W.L. Gore honor the Waterline principle, they keep their actions consistent with the company's strategic direction.

W.L. Gore's strategy is technology-focused. The company was founded by Bill Gore to exploit the properties of Teflon™ as an insulator for electronic wire. In 1969, however, Bob Gore, Bill's son, invented Gore-Tex,™ an expanded form of Teflon. Since then, the company's strategy has focused on exploiting the many potential applications of the Gore-Tex technology. Vascular grafts made from Gore-Tex have been used in millions of surgeries, and Gore-Tex fabrics are used for everything from ski gloves to gym bags and running suits. Much of W.L. Gore's success is attributable to the power and leverage of the thousands of employees who concentrate on discovering new applications of a unique technology.

Strategic planning's top-down orientation is incompatible with an empowered work force. Strategic improvising's team-based orientation is perfectly compatible. Strategic improvising needs an empowered work force to operate and, in the course of operations, empowers a work force.

The U.S. operations of W.L. Gore form two clusters of businesses located near Newark, Delaware, and Flagstaff, Arizona. In 1992, the company was operating 27 different plants in these two locations. It also operates plants in Scotland, Germany, France, and Japan. W.L. Gore keeps its plants small (between 150 and 200 associates per plant). A new business is cultivated within a plant until it is big enough to make it on its own, at which time the new business unit leaves to form a separate plant.

Each plant is remarkably independent of other plants. Plants are organized like lattices: a regular cross-hatching of lines represents an unrestricted flow of communication, with no overlay of lines of authority. The lattice form is quite fluid. Tasks and functions vary with specific problems that require attention and are organized through personally made commitments, not through job descriptions and organizational charts.

Each plant has its own leadership, which tends to evolve naturally. Some associates rise to leadership positions because they are particularly competent; others because they have developed credibility or are perceived as especially caring. Whatever the reason, leaders find a following within a plant and are included in important plant decisions.

Both organizational empowerment and strategic improvising are benefited by free-flowing communications at W.L. Gore. The company has invested in every conceivable communications technology—from electronic mailboxes to plantwide paging systems—to foster the rapid, one-to-one communications needed to formulate and implement competitive strategies in real time. Any associate can ask questions of any other associate. Should an associate mention to a sponsor a concern relevant to another associate, the sponsor is likely to ask, "Have you brought it up with [the other associate] yet?" In other words, sponsors encourage associates to make direct, personal contact; they do not take on the role of intermediary.

The way in which resources are allocated and opportunities are distributed at W.L. Gore is further evidence of a synergy between organizational empowerment and strategic improvising. At W.L. Gore, the greatest asset associates have is their credibility, which is based on their past performance and their ability to keep commitments. Increased credibility provides associates with freer access to resources. It also contributes to heightened visibility: they develop a reputation as problem solvers for future problems, which yields more opportunities for them.

Although everyone is empowered at W.L. Gore, the amount of power each person has is based on what he or she has done lately. This system of allocating power supports strategic improvising for two reasons:

1. It is *not* based on what people plan to do. W.L. Gore has a healthy skepticism for plans and forecasts, as evidenced by the number of jokes told about off-target plans and forecasts.

2. It is self-correcting.

Strategic improvising requires a highly efficient power system to drive high-frequency strategic thrusts. The allocation system at W.L. Gore teaches associates that they have power for a reason: to accomplish strategic objectives. The more strategic objectives they accomplish, the more power they get to tackle new strategic objectives.

STRATEGIC IMPROVISING AND NONROUTINE WORK

In addition to the changes in the American work force during the past century, fundamental changes have occurred in the nature of work. Some of these changes are directly related to the organizational empowerment movement. Job enrichment, for example, is a set of tools developed to respond to fundamental shifts in the growth needs of workers. J. Richard Hackman and Greg Oldham, two of the primary contributors to job enrichment theory, advocate a shift from top-down control to increased self-control for jobholders. One of their key implementation concepts, for example, is *vertical loading,* which involves adding to a lower-level job some responsibilities and controls formerly reserved for higher levels of management. Hackman and Oldham, however, stop short of recommending the vertical loading of strategic responsibilities.[23]

The effects of the new world economic order on the nature of work, however, are even more profound. When global competition was less intense, it was possible for companies to seal off their technological core. The intent was to increase production efficiencies by routinizing work processes. As global industries have become increasingly dynamic, it has become more difficult to protect work processes from the unsettling effects of competition. Companies operating in dynamic industries that cling to established work routines eventually lose their competitive edge.

Figure 2–2 proposes an idealized relationship between organizational work (routine versus nonroutine) and industry structure (stable versus dynamic). Even when businesses operate in highly stable industries, they must perform some nonroutine work. For example, they must fix a

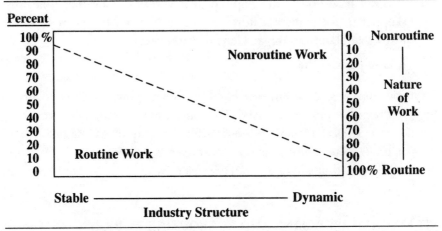

FIGURE 2–2. The relationship between industry structure and routine/ nonroutine work.

machine when it breaks down unexpectedly, or react to unanticipated bottlenecks in a production process. Similarly, some routine work needs to be completed even when businesses operate under highly dynamic conditions. As the industry structures in which businesses operate become increasingly dynamic, there should be an ensuing increase in the amount of nonroutine work (see Figure 2–2).

Traditionally, nonroutine work has been thought of as being most prevalent early in a product's life cycle, when new products are being conceived, researched, designed, or developed. As long as product designs remain relatively open—and, therefore, subject to change—work does not follow a predictable pattern; it is nonroutine. When companies move to dominant designs, work becomes increasingly routinized. The work of many professionals and managers is nonroutine. Nonroutine work is more common in the early stages of organizational development, when structures and systems are not yet institutionalized. For example, it is one of the key defining characteristics of entrepreneurial activity.

Nonroutine work is not necessarily more complex than routine work. For example, an air traffic controller's job is quite complex, but most of the time it is routine. Only when something unanticipated happens—a sudden, severe storm, or a hydraulic landing system's malfunction in an approaching aircraft—does an air traffic controller's job become nonroutine. A defining characteristic of nonroutine work is that it requires people to tackle problems in real time; they must think while they act.

Nonroutine work is the part of a job that can never be explicitly defined in a job description. By definition, it is work that requires individuals and teams to perform extra-role behaviors. People must choose to do nonroutine work; it cannot be required of them. A web of intrinsic commitments to one's organization, profession, co-workers, customers, and so on, fosters nonroutine work much more than extrinsic rewards do. Earlier, we likened strategic eras to Stephen Jay Gould's punctuated equilibria theory of evolution. In reality, however, in a highly dynamic industry structure, strategic eras change with increasing rapidity. Eventually, change overwhelms stability, and strategic eras more closely resemble *punctuated changes*. Under these conditions, an increase of the mix of nonroutine work becomes a competitive necessity.

Other forces influence the shift from routine to nonroutine work. For example, customers are becoming more demanding. As special needs arise, customers expect businesses to respond to them. Because these needs cannot always be anticipated and met with existing routines, they require nonroutine responses.

Organizational designers are making organizational work more interdependent by introducing team-based structures and breaking down functional barriers. Highly interdependent work is successful only when individuals and teams are willing to adjust to each other. Each element of work depends on all the others. Adjustments often require people to work outside of existing routines.

New information technologies and flexible manufacturing equipment are also increasing the mix of nonroutine work. These technologies actually deroutinize work, and, because all businesses have access to them, businesses that do not incorporate them place themselves at a significant competitive disadvantage.

Calvin Pava, of Harvard Business School, suggests one of the more intriguing reasons for a shift from routine to nonroutine work. He argues that new technologies involving networks of smart equipment will regulate more routine work processes automatically. This automation will create a void in the work roles of both factory and office workers, and that void will be filled with nonroutine work. According to Pava:

> Knowledge-based contributions [i.e., nonroutine work] previously defined as tertiary—such as preventive maintenance, system improvements, and training—will become an ongoing, everyday priority for maintaining a competitive advantage.[24]

Returning to Figure 2–2, a point that is often missed is that companies can be proactive as well as reactive. If a company were to change the nature of its work by increasing its nonroutine mix, it would almost inevitably destabilize the structure of its industry. Nonroutine, preemptive moves by one company often require nonroutine countermoves by its competitors.

Both the outside and inside pressures to increase the mix of nonroutine work are profound. When companies respond to these pressures, the effect on strategic thinking is worthy of note. Because the way things were done in the past affects the way they are done in the future, routine work can be planned. This, however, is not the case for nonroutine work. The increasing prevalence of nonroutine work is linked to the decreasing relevance of strategic planning.

Because strategic improvising specifies ends without overspecifying means, it is ideally suited to nonroutine work. There is less investment in front-end loading—that is, trying to anticipate routine events and processes—and more investment in the factors that lead to the successful execution of nonroutine work—general knowledge, a large repertoire of skills, the ability to do a quick study, trust in intuitions, and sophistication in cutting losses.[25]

TWO MODELS

Another way to compare strategic planning and strategic improvising is with models representing the two processes. We highlight the process differences by proposing models with common building blocks. Figure 2–3 represents the strategic planning process. A firm's human energy, capabilities, opportunities in the business environment, and social responsibilities are considered when defining strategic objectives. The strategic objectives combine to form a plan. Because it specifies means, the plan is the hub of the control system for a business's strategy. It directs what action is to be taken.

When we compare Figure 2–3 with Figure 2–4, our model of the strategic improvising process, three differences are readily apparent. First, strategic improvising is much more interactive and dynamic than strategic planning. The basic building blocks are the same, but there are two-and-a-half times as many two-way interactions in Figure 2–4. The strategic improvising process guides strategic thrusts through the continuous push–pull of different perspectives. Strategic improvising's

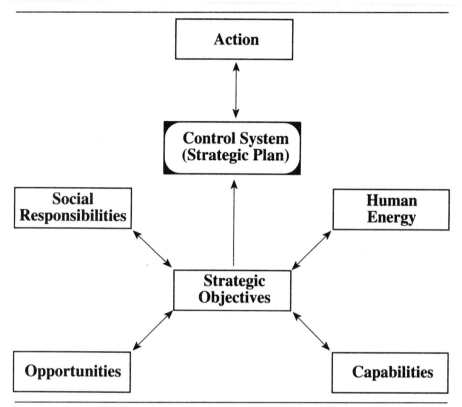

FIGURE 2–3.   The strategic planning model.

trajectory is more uneven than strategic planning's because of ongoing minor adjustments.

The process depicted in the strategic planning model (Figure 2–3) provides almost a stepwise logic to strategic thinking. The strategic improvising model depicts a process a lot like the process of tightening the nuts and bolts that hold a tire on a car. Based on real-time information, a company tightens up one factor as much as seems appropriate, then moves on and tightens up another factor. Once it has tightened the second factor, it can always return to the first and tighten it further, and so on. The highly interactive nature of strategic improvising involves continuous, iterative adjustment. Unlike the nuts and bolts on a tire mount, the factors in the strategic improvising model can always use further tightening.

The second difference between strategic planning and strategic improvising relates to when action occurs. Because action is pulled more tightly into the core or interactive loop, the strategic improvising process involves a continuous flow of thinking and acting. In contrast, strategic

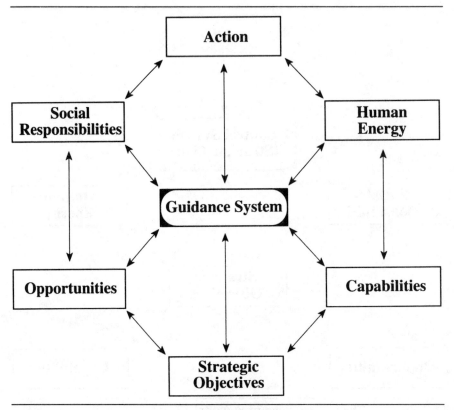

FIGURE 2–4.   The strategic improvising model.

planning involves a series of stops and starts: planning stops when action begins and restarts when action is completed and a new plan is needed. This means that strategic plans proceed unchanged through a planning cycle. Strategic improvising fosters continuous learning and change. Action in the strategic improvising process is a source of real-time information. It provides ongoing feedback about where the strategic thrust is going, and it suggests the next steps for keeping it going in the right direction at the right speed.

Third, at the center of the strategic improvising model is a *guidance* system, not a *control* system. The control philosophy underlying strategic planning is disempowering. Because planners expect people to mess up their plans, they make every attempt to regulate people's behavior. Not only do planners want to control what employees do, they want to control when and how they do it. Guidance systems involve a more interactive decision-making process in which top management provides individuals and teams with general guidelines that are applied, in turn, to team-based decisions. With strategic improvising, it is assumed that real-time information and intense group interaction supplant the need for exhaustive front-end control.

An additional difference exists between the two models. Figure 2–3 can represent a complete corporate or business unit planning process; Figure 2–4 represents a single strategic thrust. Accordingly, Figure 2–4 works only in the context of an established strategic direction, and represents one of several strategic thrusts that occur simultaneously. Once a strategic direction is established, the interdisciplinary team with responsibility for a strategic thrust makes the key strategic decisions.

Figure 2–4 also provides an umbrella for four critical subprocesses: clarifying strategy, building core capabilities inside the unit of competitive advantage, aligning strategy, and finding and creating business opportunities.

Clarifying strategy helps businesses decide what they are in business for. It defines a business's strategic direction, the context for setting strategic objectives. Ideally, clarifying strategy aims businesses in a single direction while still encouraging many and varied activities within it.

Building core capabilities inside the unit of competitive advantage relies on the ability to distinguish among the core work, support work, and nonessential work of organizations, providing them with a distinctive contour and shape. The unit of competitive advantage is important to the design of organizations because it ensures that companies will invest appropriately in the core capabilities needed to accomplish strategic objectives.

The goal of *aligning strategy* is to diminish the loss of organizational energy that normally occurs when organizational structures and systems are misaligned with strategy. Effective alignment releases more of a business's human energy to drive strategic improvising. Because entropy affects organizations in much the same way that it affects matter and energy, aligning strategy is a continuous challenge. Organizations are always falling out of alignment and need to be realigned.

The intent of *finding and creating business opportunities* is to keep businesses open to the changing business environment. When business opportunities are consistent with a business's strategic direction, they inject new momentum into strategic improvising.

Strategic improvising is the warp and woof of these four subprocesses because they depend greatly on its highly interactive, action-oriented nature. It is the four subprocesses, however, that put strategic improvising to work.

3 GETTIN' INTO A BAG: HOW TO CLARIFY STRATEGIC DIRECTION AND STRATEGIC OBJECTIVES

Bag A jazz group's preferred style or genre of performance ("They're into a blues bag now").

The president of a large electronics firm was reviewing his company's performance over the previous five years. The results were outstanding: revenue and profit projections had been exceeded every year. Nevertheless, the president was disturbed as he compared actual results to original strategic plans. Growth and generation of revenues and profits had been according to plan only 50 percent of the time. Many business opportunities that had been expected to contribute significantly had contributed nothing, while unexpected business opportunities had arisen suddenly and had generated significant business. Concerned by what he saw, the president had predicted to a group of senior managers that the company's failure to predict business growth would come back to haunt them.

We interpreted the president's findings very differently; we saw them as a sign of organizational effectiveness, not dysfunction. As strategic plans had failed, the company's ability to improvise strategically had kept it vital. The president may have assumed that the company was just lucky, and that someday its luck would run out, but we found another explanation for its success. People in the company had a clear sense of what the company could and could not do. When new opportunities came along, they knew which ones to select and which ones to reject. Accordingly, they had been able to take advantage of related opportunities without being lured off-track by unrelated alternatives. Their clear sense of what the company

43

was and was not had consistently set them up so that they were in the right place at the right time.

An unusual characteristic of this electronics company—and the trait to which we attribute most of its success—was that it maintained its bearings by acting strategically even in a crisis. The company had held several defense contracts that were wiped out by draconian cutbacks in government defense spending. The most common reaction to a crisis situation is what the company president had thought was happening: "manic panic." Companies throw into the marketplace as many half-baked ideas as they can, hoping to get lucky. Typically, strategic focus goes out the window because, in desperation, companies pursue every perceived business opportunity. The electronics company, however, was able to stay on course because the strategy was clear to the people in the trenches. Their efforts were not spread all over the map; they followed a well-defined strategic direction.

Another unusual twist to this story is that strategy clarification was either bottom-up or inside-out; it was *not* top-down. Top managers, by focusing on overspecified means, had lost sight of strategic direction. They were fortunate, indeed, that the people in the trenches had not fallen into the same trap. When it became clear that plans were not going to work, the crew knew what direction would keep the company on course, even if the officers did not.

Strategic improvising is not a free-form process. Strategy clarification, like jazz format, provides a basic form for strategic improvising. At the very least, it defines limits around what can and cannot be done. As the case of the electronics firm illustrates, strategic improvising can work even when top management has lost its bearings, as long as a strategic direction is clear to the people who are doing the work. Strategic improvising, however, works even better when top managers are not only onboard but are spearheading the strategy clarification process.

Strategy clarification involves two processes: establishing a strategic direction and defining strategic objectives. Establishing a strategic direction is typically a top-management responsibility. It provides the form for strategic improvising by creating a focus for strategic change. Strategic direction defines the nature of the desired relationship between a business and its customers. Within general directional parameters, specific strategic objectives are defined by individuals and teams before strategic thrusts are launched. Through strategic thrusts, key products and markets are defined, and desired relationships with customers are solidified over time (see Figure 3–1).

An example helps distinguish among strategic direction, strategic objectives, and strategic thrusts. For several years, we have worked with Beverly Hills Cards (BHC),[1] which defines itself as "the greeting card company for the rich and famous." It sells limited-edition cards that are actually miniature pieces of art. BHC's cards are ordered through lavish catalogs mailed only to individuals with seven-figure incomes. The company does intensive research on its target customers and is usually the first company to identify new trends in the greeting card business. BHC develops exclusive relationships with artists, to ensure that its products remain unique. Purchasers are given an option of creating their own messages to attach to the artwork they select.

BHC's strategic direction is stated in its self-definition: it is "the greeting card company for the rich and famous." This simple concept provides the umbrella for all of BHC's business activities. Developing new and exclusive relationships with artists and creating new greeting card concepts that appeal to the rich and famous are examples of specific strategic objectives consistent with BHC's strategic direction.

Strategic objectives always define specific foci of activity; strategic thrusts put them into action. Negotiating an exclusive contract with a

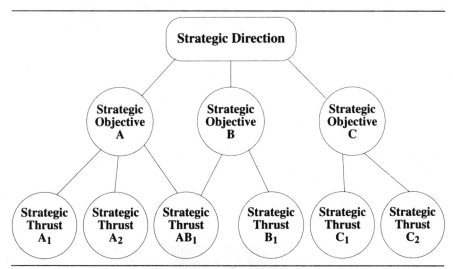

FIGURE 3–1. The relationship among strategic direction, strategic objectives, and strategic thrusts.

talented artist and offering bonus incentives to the creative staff to develop new greeting card concepts would be examples of specific strategic
thrusts.

BHC exemplifies strategic direction as a singular concept that defines the relationship between a business and its customers. Strategic objectives operationalize strategic direction and remain few in number.
Establishing a strategic direction and defining strategic objectives are
simultaneously similar and dissimilar processes. Both emphasize simple,
straightforward strategic thinking. However, strategic direction provides
steady, general guidance to strategic improvising, and strategic objectives
provide flexible, specific guidance. Ideally, strategic thrusts are many
in number, but are constrained by both strategic direction and strategic
objectives.

Establishing strategic direction is not part of the strategic improvising process; it belongs to the strategic thinking that precedes improvising.

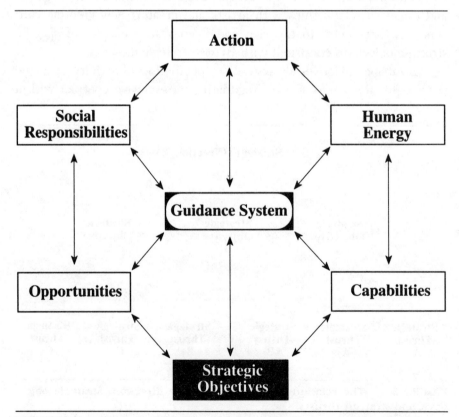

FIGURE 3–2.   Strategic objectives and the strategic improvising model.

The strategic improvising process depicted in Figure 3–2, however, operates within the parameters set by strategic direction. According to Figure 3–2, a strategic objective begins the strategic improvising process. Once the process is set into motion, strategic objectives become part of the ongoing process dynamics and are subject to influence and change.

ACHIEVING STRATEGY CLARIFICATION

When we work with companies, we always state up-front that our approach to strategy clarification is different from that of other consultants. We work with upper-management teams to develop strategies for businesses, but we also encourage the involvement of broader, cross-functional teams composed of workers, professionals, and managers. We do this because we believe strategic thinking should occur at all levels of an organization. Our approach does not mesh well with the view that top managers and their staffs should develop complex, "top-secret" strategies, to be shared with the rest of the organization only on a need-to-know basis.

When we were working with a major fast-food company, we observed that a serious impediment to improving individual store performance was how poorly the store managers and food preparers understood the strategy. When we questioned people at higher levels of the organizational hierarchy, it became clear that the store managers and employees were not the only personnel who were in the dark about the strategy. We had to go all the way up to the corporate executive council before anyone could articulate a strategic direction. Senior managers did not see this as a problem. They believed that people from middle managers on down did not need to understand strategy in order to do their jobs. What could an hourly wage employee do with strategic information that would make a difference?

In answer, we conducted an experiment in which the managers in three different stores were asked to share frequently and consistently a very simple statement of strategy supporting both cleanliness and customer service. After three weeks, the stores had shown significant improvement along both of those dimensions. As we talked with the employees, they explained the changes that had resulted from clarification of the strategy. In the past, they had known all the rules and procedures for working in the store, but now they understood why the rules and procedures were important. Moreover, because they knew the strategy, they could take initiative in helping their store accomplish its strategic objectives.

Secrecy around strategy is often justified by the need to prevent competitors from acquiring strategic information. In top managers' view, the more employees who know about the strategy, the greater the risk that sensitive information will be leaked. Lavell Edwards, head football coach at Brigham Young University (BYU), refuses to worry about another coach getting a copy of one of his playbooks. Edwards believes that another coach could have his playbook, or even his game plan, and BYU would still win the game if his players execute well. In BYU's passing scheme, the receivers are expected to improvise the routes they run, based on the defensive players' moves. For the entire team to execute well, however, all the players need to understand the game plan and the limits within which they can improvise. When organizations keep strategies secret, they lose a clear definition or form within which employees can improvise to create competitive advantage.

We view strategy clarification, which establishes the form for strategic improvising, as a six-step process:

1. Determining current strategic direction;

2. Identifying specific strategic options;

3. Selecting one strategic option;

4. Specifying a strategic direction;

5. Translating strategic direction into a business concept;

6. Identifying specific strategic objectives.

This process does not always proceed stepwise. Three questions commonly asked by strategic thinkers are: Where are we now? Where do we want to go? How do we get there? Because our strategy clarification process is future-oriented, it is focused on the second question—Where do we want to go? (At this point, we mostly ignore the third question— How do we get there?—because we believe strategic means should emerge in the course of strategic improvising.)

The first question—Where are we now?—is sometimes problematic. When businesses do not have a clear sense of where they are currently, they are unprepared to think about where they want to go. This is why the first step, determining current strategic direction, is performed primarily by consultants.

We have done strategy clarification many ways, depending on the cultural norms of different businesses. We like to start the process with a group that is representative of different business interests but weighted toward management. It is especially important for top managers to take the lead and be intimately involved in strategy clarification from the beginning. We do *not* recommend that they go off by themselves to set a strategic direction for the business. It is necessary to include the representatives of different business interests in the group, in order to push strategic thinking beyond management's perspective.

The representative group follows steps 2 through 6 of the strategy clarification process, but it emphasizes steps 2 through 5, giving only cursory attention to identifying specific strategic objectives. At the conclusion of the process, the group reports the results of this first round of strategy clarification to everyone in the business, either in a single large meeting or in multiple small meetings.

Our experience shows that, at this point, strategy clarification takes on a life of its own. The representative group's report serves as a catalyst for the formation of other groups that will both react to the proposed strategic direction and identify specific strategic objectives that fit the proposed business concept. These emergent groups then report back to the representative group, often causing it to revisit issues for which widespread support is critical and around which no clear consensus has emerged. In the midst of this highly interactive and iterative process, the steps of strategy clarification function like a checklist of what needs to be clarified further.

It is important to allow this process to evolve naturally, but it is also important to contain it. Deliberations reach a point of diminishing returns unless people begin to take action. From the action will come new information for making finer determinations of strategic direction and strategic objectives. Therefore, it is necessary to set clear time boundaries at the outset of the strategy clarification process, to establish a deadline for taking action.

STEP 1: DETERMINING CURRENT STRATEGIC DIRECTION

The first decision we make is whether to conduct step 1. In our initial discussions with clients, we learn a great deal about the state of their strategic thinking. We have found it helpful to jump to some rough, imprecise conclusions that enable us to categorize businesses by their clarity or confusion regarding both their current and future strategic directions. An informal rating form is shown in Figure 3–3.

Because we are called on to assist businesses with their strategies, we seldom encounter a situation in which both current and future strategic directions are clear. If, however, we were asked to assist a business in such a situation, we would skip step 1 and likely proceed with steps 2 through 6. Experience has taught us that businesses often overlook strategic options that have a potential for improving their performance. Moreover, even if the businesses ultimately settle on the same strategy as earlier, its nature would likely be clearer after conducting the strategy clarification process.

We often encounter a situation in which a great deal of clarity surrounds current strategic direction, but, because of changes in the competitive environment, there is little clarity regarding future strategic direction. Several of our defense industry clients are in this situation. In such cases we skip step 1, moving directly to step 2.

Whenever there is confusion around current strategic direction, we perform step 1. We encounter some businesses that are clear about where they want to go, but unclear about where they are. This situation typically arises when a business that has meandered strategically suddenly encounters an extremely promising opportunity. The critical question for such a business is whether it is capable of taking advantage of the opportunity.

	Current Strategic Direction	Future Strategic Direction
Business A	X	X
Business B	X	O
Business C	O	X
Business D	O	O

X = Clear
O = Confused

FIGURE 3–3. Knowledge of current and future strategic directions.

Before it can answer the question, it must understand where it is and what it is capable of doing.

In the most common situation we encounter, a business is confused about both its current and future strategic directions. We must then learn something about the business's current directions, in order to decide which strategic options should be considered in the process of specifying a future strategic direction.

Step 1 involves interviewing all the members of the strategy team individually, asking them some variation of the following questions:

1. What is your current business strategy?

2. What is unique about your business?

3. Who are your customers? What markets do you serve?

4. What products or services do you produce or provide?

5. What products or services would you not produce or provide?

6. Are there any recent changes in the business environment that have caused you concern?

7. Who would agree with your views about the business? Who would disagree?

When we ask these questions, we sometimes discover that some strategy team members can provide extremely clear answers, but there is no consistency across team members. At other times, strategy team members are either unable to relate to some of the questions or fail to identify a single, clear strategic direction. We attribute these findings to team members' not having a systematic way of thinking and talking about strategy.

When we give the strategy team feedback based on our interviews, we try to present what we consider to be the majority view of current strategic direction as well as the minority views. We do this without attributing viewpoints to specific strategy team members. As we discuss the different strategic directions, further clarification occurs. Moreover, strategy team members begin to see personal differences in an impersonal way, which clearly promotes more effective team functioning. This helps in two ways: team members no longer attach personal, self-serving motives to the viewpoints of their peers, and they are able to discuss their various viewpoints in a more objective, critical manner.

Determining the current strategic direction of a business also increases our ability to help as consultants. Once we know where a business is at strategically, we are able to provide examples of businesses in similar situations. By tapping in to our experience with businesses that are strategically similar, we can quickly identify the current challenges faced by a new client. For example, we can begin a discussion of the processes most critical to the business's success, and the trade-offs with which it is currently struggling. We can tell whether its current structure is helping or hindering the accomplishment of strategic objectives and what skills individuals need to develop to contribute to the business's competitive strength. We can suggest messages that need to be sent by top managers and reasons why some current messages are not being heard. All this enables us quickly to become "trusted and respected by others"[2] in the eyes of our clients, which significantly adds to our ability to promote positive organizational change.

STEP 2: IDENTIFYING SPECIFIC STRATEGIC OPTIONS

One of the shortcomings of most strategic thinking is that management teams choose a strategic direction without systematically exploring alternatives. The effects of leaping to conclusions are common problems for most groups. Norman Maier, for example, discusses what he calls the "valence of solutions," which is the tendency of groups to settle on the first proposed solution that is minimally acceptable. His research shows that the first solution that receives a positive valence of .15 (based on the algebraic sum of negative and positive comments about the proposed solution) tends to be adopted by group members 85 percent of the time. The problem is that a solution's valence is unrelated to its objective quality. Moreover, once groups jell around one solution, it is unlikely that other solutions, even those of higher quality, will receive appropriate consideration.[3]

One of the keys to avoiding problems such as the valence of solutions is to insist that the strategy team must explore multiple options. We have found that, when multiple options are explored, low-quality solutions are less likely to be adopted. The process makes it legitimate to advocate different options, there is a clearer understanding of the strategic option that is selected, and commitment to the chosen strategic direction is deeper. The rejected options also help clarify what the selected option *is not*.

It is not always easy to persuade strategy teams to explore unfamiliar options. We gain the best results when we use tools that force strategic thinkers to consider clearly differentiated options. This has led to the development of the strategic options matrix shown in Figure 3–4.

The strategic options matrix is based on two assumptions about strategic direction:

1. There are basics that every business must get right, just to keep up with industry competitors. We call these *competitive necessities.* Strategies that focus on competitive necessities can create temporary competitive advantage, but they are better for catching up with competitors than for staying ahead of them.

2. Businesses that aspire to become competitive leaders must do more than perform the basics well. The only businesses that truly distinguish themselves and are able to sustain competitive advantage have a *business focus* that enables them to excel at something. Businesses are excellent only when all employees understand what business they are in and pull together to make the business work.

Before the recent intensification of global competition, providing products or services at a reasonable cost was the only critical *competitive necessity.* The Japanese, however, altered the terms of engagement by making quality, speed, and service equally important competitive necessities (see Figure 3–4). Because techniques for lowering costs, improving quality and service, and increasing speed are well-known and widely used, it has become more difficult for a business to distinguish itself from its competitors based on programs emphasizing these competitive necessities.

	Competitive Necessities			
Business Focuses	**Low-Cost-Anchor**	**Quality-Anchor**	**Speed-Anchor**	**Service-Anchor**
Product/Service Focus				
Customer/Market Focus				
Technology Focus				
Production-Capacity Focus				

FIGURE 3–4. The strategic options matrix.

Strategies that attend to competitive necessities provide businesses with temporary competitive advantages in two ways. First, they apply competitor benchmarking across industries, to determine the best *overall* practices. Typically, competitor benchmarking, a technique that focuses on the competitive necessities presented in Figure 3–4, is used to catch up to industry competitors. It provides a way of determining best *industry* practices. Competitor benchmarking across industries, however, expands the search for best practices. It provides a way for observant businesses to lead: they gain access to best practices and they are the first in their industries to adopt them.

Second, businesses can attain temporary competitive advantages by not treating all their competitive necessities equally. Those who discuss layering competitive necessities[4] miss an important fact: competitive necessities sometimes conflict with each other. A paper manufacturer, for example, was trying to decrease the cost of producing paper while simultaneously trying to improve paper quality. The effects were disastrous because the supporters of improved quality kept tightening the variances which, in turn, increased the cost of production.

With our help, the company's management decided that a strategy for becoming the lowest-cost producer provided the most competitive leverage in the paper industry. Lowering the cost of production was made the anchor for the other competitive necessities. The company was then able to define an appropriate level of quality for its strategy of becoming the paper industry's lowest-cost producer.

A *business focus* defines how a business intends to create industry leadership. While competitive necessities involve options a business must pursue to gain parity with competitors, the intent of a business focus is to create distinctive competencies. A business focus is like a magnet that redirects organizational efforts and the development of individual and team capabilities. A business focus is less limiting in terms of current business activities than future business activities. The intent of a business focus is not to give up existing business, but, over time, to draw together scattered business activities. Distinctive competencies build as the centripetal forces created by a business focus take the development of organizational capabilities along converging paths.[5]

As indicated in Figure 3–4, the four most common business focuses are: product/service, customer/market, technology, and production-capacity (for characteristics of business focuses, see Table 3–1).

Table 3–1. The Characteristics of Business Focuses

Business Focus	Characteristics
Product/Service	Focus is on specific product or service
	New products/services resemble present products/services
	New products/services evolve from existing products/services
Customer/Market	Focus is on a group of customers
	Customer needs are monitored and determined
	Products are developed to satisfy customer needs
	Success depends on customer satisfaction and loyalty
Technology	Focus is on the development of valuable and unique technological capabilities
	New products are derived from technological expertise
	Technological solutions are looking for new applications
Production Capacity	Focus is on keeping the production system running at full capacity
	Economies of scale are employed to reduce unit cost and increase profits

An example of a product/service-driven business is the Chevrolet Division of General Motors. The Chevrolet Division, which makes cars, vans, and trucks, measures its success in terms of the total number of new vehicles sold by its dealers in a given reporting period. Its efforts are focused on supporting the effective development, production, promotion, sale, delivery, and servicing of its vehicles.

A customer/market-focused business is American Hospital Supply. It sells products such as tape, toilet paper, bandages, and similar products, but only to hospitals. American Hospital Supply concentrates its efforts on high-quality service to one customer group—hospitals.

Monsanto Agricultural Company ("Monsanto Ag") is an example of a technology-focused business. Monsanto Ag leverages its technological leadership in biological engineering to create agricultural products that are effective and environmentally safe. For example, Roundup, Monsanto Ag's best-known product, is an effective herbicide that is environmentally safe because it kills unwanted weeds and grasses by dramatically altering their rate of growth. Moreover, its effective life is only two weeks.

An example of a production-capacity-focused business is Georgia-Pacific Paper (G-P). Instead of building new mills, G-P has used a strategy of buying mills, repairing and improving operations, and then pushing production to the limit. A paper mill in Monticello, Mississippi, purchased by G-P from St. Regis Paper Company Ltd., expanded its capacity from 1,500 tons to 2,700 tons of paper per day. According to a former G-P executive:

> The basic philosophy is: Make the product as inexpensively as you can, ram it into the marketplace as expensively as customers will buy it, and keep your mills going. God forbid that any sales manager shuts down a mill. No one will challenge him if he doesn't get an extra $20 for a ton of paper. But God save him if he doesn't make the sale.[6]

After we have provided clients with examples of businesses with different business focuses, we have returned to the strategic options matrix. We help the strategy team to choose several options that they want to investigate further—for example, the product-focused (quality-anchored) option; the customer-focused (quality-anchored) option; the customer-focused (low-cost-anchored) option; and the technology-focused (speed-anchored) option. The choices we make are based on our understanding of current strategic direction (we want to explore strategic options the business is capable of doing) and on our desire to upset the applecart and challenge traditional ways of thinking about the business (we want to drive thinking beyond the conventional wisdom of the company and industry).

We divide the strategy team into *advocacy teams* and assign them to investigate and report back on what the business would look like if it were to pursue their strategic option. These reports are based on answers to two questions:

1. What products would you produce if this option were selected?
2. What customers would you serve or pursue?

To facilitate this process, we provide each advocacy team with articles about businesses that are pursuing their strategic options. By reading these articles, members of the advocacy teams gain a sense of the range of possibilities associated with each strategic option.

Advocacy team members are assigned strategic options, rather than allowed to choose them, to encourage the championing of positions other than their own. They are also expected to look for flaws in the strategic options being explored by other advocacy teams. Assigning champions results in a significant increase in the range of issues considered.

STEP 3: SELECTING ONE STRATEGIC OPTION

Before the advocacy teams present their ideas about what their business would look like if they pursued their strategic option, we announce that both research and our experience indicate that high-performance businesses pursue only one strategic option. The choice of a strategic option will vary from business to business. For some businesses, choosing among options is a toss-up; in all cases, it is important to narrow strategic direction down to a single option.

This announcement shocks some participants, and, because it imposes limitations on their strategic decisions, there is initial resistance to the idea. People say: "If I narrow my focus, I may miss some attractive opportunities." Moreover, they might be concerned that putting all their eggs in one basket is riskier than spreading their eggs around. For example, when the customer-focused (quality-anchored) option is chosen, businesses become dependent on serving a specific customer type in a specific way, despite the risk that the demands of their customers will inexplicably change.

We do not minimize the risk associated with choosing a single strategic option, but we explain that such risks are inevitable in business and that much greater risks result from being spread too thin. We share a Chinese proverb—"If you chase two rabbits, both will escape"—and we explain that one of the purposes of strategy clarification is to ensure that businesses will not try to run in two different directions. Strategy clarification focuses attention on a single strategic option because businesses, like people, inevitably fail when they try to be everything to everybody. Andrew Grove, Intel's CEO, has said: "I'd rather have all my eggs in one basket and spend my time worrying about whether that's the right basket, than try to put one egg in every basket. Because then you have no upside."[7]

An example from political campaign strategy makes the point even clearer. Fred Frankhopf, the chairman of the Republican National Committee from 1983 to 1989, summarizes his political strategy in three words: Target, Target, Target. He tells how Richard Nixon promised to visit every state in the union in 1960. During the last few weeks of the campaign, Nixon concentrated on fulfilling that promise instead of focusing his efforts on the states with the most electoral votes, where the race was still close. Michael Dukakis made a similar pledge in 1988, and Frankhopf claims he knew instantly that George Bush would be the next President of the United States.

For Frankhopf, the formula for success in a presidential election is simple. There are 25 states that cast 362 of the 538 electoral votes. Those are the states where campaign efforts should be concentrated. Moreover, in most states, 40 percent of the people consistently vote for Republicans and 40 percent consistently vote for Democrats. Of the 20 percent swing vote, 5 percent tend to vote Republican and 2 percent tend to vote Democratic. The key to success, therefore, is to influence the remaining 13 percent. Frankhopf calls this the 13 percent solution of presidential politics—a solution based on the assumption that *efforts must be concentrated if they are to make a difference.*

We also explain to clients that, although questions about such limitations are natural, there are dangers associated with continued resistance. Indeed, the benefits of narrowing strategic direction to a single option never materialize when people pay more attention to what they are giving up than to what they are gaining. We warn clients to avoid what we call the "cow-grazing phenomenon."

One of us, as a teenager working on his uncle's dairy farm, noticed that when cows were moved to a new pasture that had not been grazed for a while, an interesting thing happened: the cows would eat only the grass along the inside of the fence. When all the grass inside the fence was eaten, instead of turning around and eating the tall grass in the middle of the pasture, the cows would maneuver their heads through the fence and eat the grass just outside it.

A corporate example of the "cow-grazing phenomenon" occurred in the satellite business of a major defense contractor. The business lost a contract that management had counted on for significant bottom-line contributions over a 10-year period. The cancellation created a crisis because it was unclear whether the business could survive without somehow replacing the lost income. Senior managers spent a year desperately looking for new business opportunities. They were unsuccessful because they had no focus. Recognizing the problem, the president convinced his people that the business would have no chance of survival unless they clarified their strategy. The president met with the senior managers to establish a strategic direction. After several marathon sessions, they agreed to exploit the business's expertise in electro-optics technology.

Two months after the agreement was reached, senior managers reassembled for a progress review. One manager described a program he was supporting, which involved building small satellites with payload capacity to hold rats for scientific research. After he described the project—

affectionately called "RatSat"—one of his senior management colleagues questioned how it related to electro-optics. The manager quickly answered, "All we need to do to make it fit is to cut out holes in the satellite for windows, so the rats can look out. It may not be electro, but it certainly would be optical."

People in organizations naturally resist the imposition of boundaries. The lesson of the "cow-grazing phenomenon" is that people fail to see a lot of opportunities because they think the grass is greener just outside the fence. By focusing their attention on the barrier instead of the space within it, individuals and teams are turned the wrong way and they miss many opportunities they could easily have.

The loss of freedom from narrowing strategic direction to a single option is inconsequential, if people realize all the freedom they still have. The gains to strategic thinking from the resulting discipline are invaluable. Frequently, business units begin with a single product serving a single market. As growth starts to taper off, businesses look for new ways to continue growing. Growth opportunities are found by discovering new markets for existing products, by developing new products for existing markets, or by doing both. If the realm of strategic possibility is not narrowed, however, the search for growth opportunities tends to shift back-and-forth until all sense of strategic direction is lost. Ultimately, a business's combinations of products and markets can all trace their genealogy to a common ancestor, but they share little else in common.

A lack of commonality becomes especially critical when resources become scarce. There is no way to leverage resources: the benefits of funding one product area do not overlap into other product areas. Rather than make the tough choices in what has developed into a zero-sum game, managers opt for partial funding of all product areas. The result is an across-the-board loss of competitive advantage.

Disciplined growth eliminates this problem by ensuring commonality across product areas. When resources are tight, it is obvious to managers where the available resources can be allocated to create the greatest leverage. Even when ample resources exist, there is an allocation logic for creating maximum competitive advantage. Moreover, when there is commonality across product areas, individuals and teams focus their efforts on finding ways to share resources rather than on competing against each other for their ownership.

After we have made a case for narrowing strategic direction to a single option, we listen to advocacy team presentations and we begin the task of deciding which of the several options being considered makes the most sense for the business. We use Figure 3–5 to move the decision-making process forward. The value of Figure 3–5 is that it keeps team members focused on the consistency between the current organizational capabilities and the opportunities in the business environment. A high level of consistency is important during this step of the strategy clarification process because its purpose is to make a ballpark estimate of strategic direction. Current capabilities clearly influence the development of future capabilities, and the success of a firm depends on what it can do with the opportunities it confronts. Businesses may never find opportunities they can turn into successes if they choose an option that is unrelated to what they currently do best. Therefore, some strategic options are ideal, but others are seductive, difficult, or foolish.

It is important to choose a strategic option that builds on current capabilities that are *valuable, unique,* and *difficult to imitate.* Again, a strategic option is two-dimensional for two purposes: to reach parity with competitive necessities, and to create distinctive competencies with business focuses. Current capabilities that are valuable, unique, and difficult to imitate are the bedrock of distinctive competence. Therefore, they contribute more to the competitive advantage of a business than current capabilities that are worthless, common, or easily imitated.[8]

Usually, the presentations themselves eliminate one or two of the strategic options because participants quickly see a lack of consistency

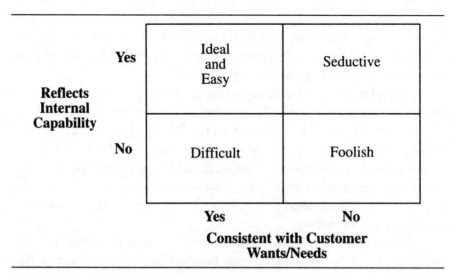

FIGURE 3–5.   Selecting a viable strategic option.

between the company's current capabilities and the opportunities in the business environment. Further considerations are future-oriented. Team members ask: How much future promise do the remaining strategic options offer? As teams present their analyses of products that can be produced and customers who can be served or pursued, the implications for future business opportunities are considered. Although it is impossible to predict with precision what the future holds, it is possible and necessary to make predictions, however imprecise they may be. Rough approximations provide adequate precision to narrow strategic direction to one option.

Finally, team members consider which of the remaining strategic options creates the most energy and excitement. The commitment and support of individuals and teams for a strategic option are so critical to the success of strategic improvising that people's *feelings* about two equally viable and promising strategic options provide the final tiebreaker.

STEP 4: SPECIFYING A STRATEGIC DIRECTION

Narrowing strategic direction to a single strategic option is not the same as establishing a specific strategic direction; however, some of the preliminary work involved in specifying a strategic direction is accomplished when current and prospective products and customers are identified. The biggest challenge associated with step 4 of strategy clarification is refining the thinking done in step 3. Participants need to be tough-minded about establishing directional parameters—choosing the two- to three-degree arc to which they will confine their business operations—while at the same time finding expansive ways to think about their business. Accordingly, this is a convergent process that immediately begins to diverge when focus is achieved.

Jan Carlzon, the CEO of Scandinavian Airlines Systems (SAS) and author of *Moments of Truth*, provides an example of a specific strategic direction. SAS is clearly a customer-focused (service-anchored) business: it aspires to be the preferred airline for frequent business travelers. This goal translates into three service priorities: safety, punctuality, and other services. According to Carlzon, "If you risk flight safety by leaving on time, you have acted outside the framework. . . . The same is true if you don't leave on time because you are missing two catering boxes of meat."[9]

We have identified three ways to facilitate the thinking necessary to specify a strategic direction: asking what the business is not, discovering sources of distinctiveness, and redefining the dominant design.

Asking What the Business Is Not

Participants have already taken a first cut at defining what the business is, but additional understanding always comes from defining what the business is *not*. The critical questions are: What products would you *not* produce? What customers would you *not* serve or pursue? These questions are especially useful in focusing the business. Paradoxically, by asking what a business is not, participants open up to new and creative ways of thinking about what the business is.

3M is a good example of a company where people understand what their business is *and* what it is not. The culture of 3M is entrepreneurial, but all new-product ideas must pass through a grueling review process. Decisions about whether to fund new-product development depend on the strength of the idea and on whether it fits 3M's technology-focused (quality-anchored) strategic direction, which focuses on the development of new coating and bonding technologies.

At 3M, a story is told about an engineer who wanted to develop a business around optical laser disk storage technology. Because 3M encourages all its engineers to devote 15 percent of their time to special projects of their own choosing, the engineer was able to develop a prototype of the optical laser disk. He received only a lukewarm response from management during the preliminary stages of the new-product approval process. One of the engineer's colleagues asked him how he had held the prototype disk while he was making his presentation. The engineer explained that he had held the disk vertically, to let everyone see what it looked like. The colleague suggested that he should hold the disk flat on his fingertips. He explained that 3M was in the business of making flat products, not round products. The engineer changed the way he held the laser disk and it sailed through the remainder of the product review process.

Two companies that are equally clear about what they do and do not do are Japan's auto giants, Toyota and Nissan. Both companies are product-focused; their early strategies involved establishing a beachhead in low-cost, economical automobiles. The model lines offered by both companies have expanded over the years to include better appointed, higher-quality cars, but, until recently, neither company considered itself in the high-cost, luxury-car business. It was so clear to Toyota and Nissan that they were *not* in the luxury-car business that, when they finally decided to enter that business, they created the Lexus and Infiniti nameplates and have continued to operate them as separate businesses.

Discovering Sources of Distinctiveness

Many companies do not realize that they possess unique competitive advantages. A significant benefit of strategy clarification is that it leads businesses to uncover previously unrealized sources of distinctiveness. When businesses discover new sources of distinctiveness, they improve the focus of their strategy and introduce new ways of identifying strategic opportunities.

A giant chemical company ran a polypropylene plant that was struggling just to break even. The demand was high for the polypropylene produced by the plant, but intense price competition in the industry was eating away profits. Believing that a new strategy was needed, the plant's management invited us to help. In the process of doing strategy clarification, we realized that the plant produced the highest-quality polypropylene in the world because it used the purest resins. We began a process in which we identified higher-end uses of polypropylene, such as disposable cups, plates, and hospital products, which required the plant's superior-quality product. Participants also decided that they needed to create more awareness of the superiority of their polypropylene in the marketplace, to encourage customers in need of a purer product to come to them with their business. Moreover, because the current plant was nearing full capacity and a decision about future plant expansion needed to be made, strategy clarification helped participants decide to build a new plant that would use lower-grade resins and manage it as a separate business emphasizing low-cost, high-capacity production. The current plant could then increase profitability by concentrating on expanding the higher-quality, higher-margin side of the polypropylene business.

Redefining the Dominant Design

The most important information companies can gather about competitors deals with what their competitors do *not* do well. Information about the limitations of a dominant competitor's product line, for example, may be a reason for an upstart company to change the terms of engagement. By refusing to accept a dominant competitor's definition of industry and segment boundaries, new competitors can rise up and literally redefine industry standards.

This was certainly the case in the battle Canon waged against Xerox for control of the global copier business. When it invented the concept of distributed copying, Canon challenged Xerox's entrenched position in centralized copying for corporations. Xerox was powerless to stop Canon's redefinition of the copier business, because Xerox could not challenge Canon without undermining its own line of large, expensive copiers. In redefining the standards of the copier industry, Canon introduced several reinforcing product and concept innovations. For example, it offered low-cost liquid toner as an alternative to Xerox's high-cost dry toner. Canon used standardized components; Xerox built its machines with custom components. Canon's copiers were priced so that even small business customers could purchase them; Xerox leased its copiers. Finally, Canon channeled sales and service through office products dealers; Xerox continued to maintain its expensive direct sales and service network. Industrial giants like IBM and Kodak had failed in their attempts to challenge Xerox. Canon was successful because, at every turn, it neatly converted Xerox's competitive advantage into a competitive disadvantage.

STEP 5: TRANSLATING STRATEGIC DIRECTION INTO A BUSINESS CONCEPT

Strategic improvising involves a series of strategic thrusts launched within directional parameters. Confining strategic thrusts to strict directional parameters ensures that they are closely related. Translating strategic direction into a business concept is an effort to clarify further the relationships between individual strategic thrusts. A business concept also suggests ways to broaden strategic direction over time.

A business concept cuts across strategic objectives. It is common to all strategic thrusts and connects them to a superordinate intent. Linkages among strategic thrusts are sadly lacking in most strategic plans.

While attending a strategy review for a division of a Fortune 500 company, we witnessed a type of performance that is repeated in many strategic planning presentations. The division president spent four hours reviewing detailed charts on the 40 market segments the division was pursuing at the time. Each market segment was analyzed for its market size, growth potential, and competitor strength. The market position of the division in each segment was described, and an assessment of the probability of improving market position was presented. The detail and sophistication of the analysis were impressive, by any measure. The division president and his staff had done their homework and were making a good impression among the corporate attendees.

Looks, however, were definitely deceiving. Operating without a clear sense of strategic direction, the division was firing in all directions and hoping that an opportunity might get in the way. There was little or no relationship connecting the market opportunities the division was pursuing. Each business decision, when analyzed separately, seemed to make sense, but the combination of decisions did not add up. There was no underlying concept to tie all the division's activities together. It was unclear how learning from one activity could be leveraged to another.

In Figure 3–6, each of the circles represents a strategic objective. Although separate, each of these strategic objectives is also part of the business concept. With a clear business concept, learning from one strategic thrust can be leveraged across all the other strategic thrusts. This leveraging of learning is critical to the development of core organizational capabilities.

Jon Younger, our partner at Novations Group, Inc., tells a story from the oil industry that illustrates how learning occurs across strategic thrusts when they are linked together by a business concept. During the oil bust of the mid-1980s, a medium-size oil company was forced to cut back its exploration budget. The company's vice president of exploration had planned to develop four different basins. The budget reductions meant the company could either drill fewer wells in each basin or drill in fewer basins. The vice president and his staff agonized over the decision for several days until they finally decided to spend all their exploration budget drilling in one basin. When questioned about putting all his eggs in one basket, the vice president revealed the reasoning that had driven the decision.

He explained that the exploration wells, called wildcats, have only a one-in-ten chance of hitting oil. They are not drilled to discover oil, but to learn about the geology of an area where oil is likely to exist. By drilling several wells in the same basin, the company would be able to learn a great deal about that basin and would be in a position to make better

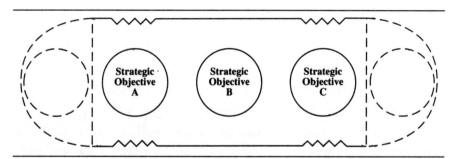

FIGURE 3–6. A business concept.

decisions about developing it in the future. The information gained from each well would benefit the subsequent drilling operations. If the company drilled in all four basins, a dry hole would be a failure; however, each dry hole drilled in a single basin provided information for drilling other wells.

When strategic thrusts are linked to other strategic thrusts within a business concept, they serve the same purpose as a hole drilled in a single basin in conjunction with other holes. They add to and build on the learning of related strategic thrusts, to help businesses zero-in on success.

Translating a strategic direction into a business concept is a simple process. It involves little more than looking in a different light at the work already done to clarify strategic direction. We ask strategy team members to look at the connections among the decisions they have already made about products, customers, and markets. What cuts across all the independent strategic decisions that they have made? Their answer is their business concept.

Business concepts are accordion-like—they can expand to provide space for new strategic objectives. In Figure 3–6, the spaces defined by dotted lines represent areas for expansion of the business concept. Space can also be created between current strategic objectives, to accommodate new strategic objectives.

When a business is clear about its business concept, a significant benefit is the creation of a logic for broadening strategic direction over time. For example, when a business is customer-focused and defines its business in terms of servicing a specific group of customers, knowledge about its business concept will help to identify new, related customer groups or to refine the definition of current customer groups.

New, related customer groups are identified by broadening the customer concept based on:

1. Common need (rental car companies, trucking companies, and the U.S. Postal Service all need to maintain large fleets of vehicles);

2. Common end user (airlines, hotels, and cellular telephone companies all serve business travelers);

3. Common input (hydrocarbons are a basic raw ingredient for plastic manufacturers, herbicide producers, and soft cookie makers);

4. Common functionality (materials used to insulate homes can be produced by fiberglass, cellulose, rock wool, or styrofoam producers).

A customer-focused business serving one customer group may easily broaden its business concept to include another customer group with common needs, common end users, common inputs, or common functionality.

STEP 6: IDENTIFYING SPECIFIC STRATEGIC OBJECTIVES

This final step in strategy clarification is also the first step of strategic improvising. Because strategic objectives operationalize a business concept, they come and go rapidly. Once specific strategic objectives are identified, strategic thinking is no longer stepwise; it becomes a highly interactive, nonlinear process. As strategic objectives are pulled into this process, they become subject to dynamic influences that are likely to change them over time.

Identifying strategic objectives involves exercising freedom within form. Therefore, every strategic objective should reflect a business's concept. For example, if a business concept is to provide world-class service to a specific customer group, then every strategic objective should resonate to that common theme.

Because strategic direction defines the nature of the desired relationship between a business and its customers, objectives are only strategic when they lead to outcomes that are recognized by customers. Strategic objectives, therefore, are always externally focused. Internal objectives—creating better employee involvement, or becoming one of the best places to work in America—do not qualify as strategic objectives unless they create changes that are recognized by customers. Businesses should not neglect internal improvements, but, in order to be strategic, internal improvements should be directed at improving performance in ways that are noticeable to customers.

Strategic improvising encourages the rapid-fire creation of new strategic objectives. Strategic improvisers are expected to generate and regenerate strategic objectives that will renew and revitalize their business concept. They should not abandon strategic objectives before they are fulfilled. Once a strategic objective is identified and a strategic thrust is launched, strategic improvising requires staying power. Nevertheless, strategic improvising is principally a creative process. The best strategic improvisers, like the best jazz musicians, possess restless spirits. They are constantly searching for new meanings to guide what they do.

WHY YOU CAN'T BE EVERYTHING
TO EVERYBODY

We were invited to discuss strategy at an afternoon session with the board of directors of a small company. The chairman of the board sent us some background material to read in preparation for the meeting. The company's annual report was the most revealing document he sent. It presented a strategy that was all over the map.

The company was started in 1979 to develop a low-power laser device that could be used to reduce swelling and pain associated with infirmities such as rheumatoid arthritis. Unfortunately, the low-power laser technology developed by the company never received approval for commercial distribution from the FDA. Eventually, the FDA did approve the use of low-powered lasers in advanced research at major universities, but the company could not build a business around such a restricted market. It was forced to search for new product ideas.

The company discovered that many of the products used by chiropractors and physical therapists had not been improved for several decades. The company developed a new focus: employing modern technology to improve existing devices used by chiropractors and physical therapists.

Because the company did not have the resources to service all the needs of these two customer groups, initial development work focused on a single product—an advanced electrotherapy device. The device was an instant hit with both chiropractors and physical therapists and led immediately to positive bottom-line results.

By listening to chiropractors and physical therapists who were using its electrotherapy devices, the company discovered that it had made a better machine but it still had not dealt with the major problem associated with the use of electrotherapy equipment—the specific targeting of electrical impulses to the point of injury. This insight led to the development of a high-end electrotherapy device that incorporated an innovative touch-screen targeting feature. This second electrotherapy machine was even more successful than the first and established the company as the leading maker of electrotherapy equipment. It even attracted attention from physicians practicing rehabilitative medicine, who felt more comfortable providing targeted, rather than untargeted, electrotherapy treatment.

This success, however, was the company's high point. Instead of focusing on the development of a line of electrotherapy equipment or a specific customer group, the company believed it could be everything to everybody. Lacking a specific strategic direction, its product development efforts began to drift. First, it developed testing and rehab equipment, which was at least somewhat related to its electrotherapy devices. Then, however, it moved into developing software to help private physicians manage their patient files. People at the company began to talk about becoming the WordPerfect of the medical software business. The company even considered managing a new venture involving tourist-attraction movie theaters within its existing structure, but then decided to manage it as a separate business.

The customer concept was expanded to include family practice physicians, podiatrists, osteopaths, and occupational medicine physicians.

While the company was continuing to expand its vision of products and customers, a competitor introduced an electrotherapy device that offered most of the features of its high-end machine at a price competitive with its low-end machine. Moreover, the company's attempts to serve all kinds of medical practices were seriously hampering its ability to be responsive to the needs of any of them.

Strategy clarification is important: it focuses a business's efforts. One of the company's officers proudly observed that the company was fortunate in that it had always had plenty of opportunities to pursue. We felt obliged to tell him that having a lot of opportunities can be both a blessing and a curse. He did not understand why, until we explained something about the *unit of competitive advantage*.

THE FRONT LINE: CORE CAPABILITIES, SUPPORT CAPABILITIES, AND THE UNIT OF COMPETITIVE ADVANTAGE

4

Front Line The melody instruments of a jazz group: trumpet, trombone, clarinet, and so on. Front-line musicians generally stand or sit in front and are backed (supported) by the rhythm section.

A manufacturing company created several "Centers of Excellence," to focus attention on making corporate functions world-class. The underlying assumption was: if all of the parts are world-class, then the whole will also be world-class. Five years after the program was launched, the company collected feedback. Customers were asked to rate it relative to its competitors on several dimensions, including: product quality, responsiveness to customers, and understanding of customer requirements. The results were surprising. The company expected that customers would describe areas where it was stronger or weaker than its competitors. What it got instead was a consistent pattern of sameness alongside the competition. There were no glaring weaknesses, but nothing set the company apart. A concurrent study that examined the organization's culture revealed similar findings: employees reported that nothing about the organization made it distinctive, and, therefore, there was little they felt proud about.

The "excellence movement" of the early 1980s produced its share of winners and losers. It provided a battle cry for organizations to look seriously at improvement, but it created an unintended consequence: some organizations treated everything equally. Gradually, it has occurred to managers that global competitive leaders focus on only a few core capabilities that they do exceptionally well. In contrast, "excellence in everything" is a misleading and potentially dangerous management oxymoron.

There were at least two flaws in the manufacturing company's reasoning. First, it ignored the interdependence among the processes. A basic premise of systems theory, for example, is that optimizing the parts suboptimizes the whole. Second, the organization operated under real resource constraints. When decisions had to be made about how to allocate resources, there was no rationale for selecting one area of excellence over another. Accordingly, limited resources were spread equally across the functions. When budget cuts occurred, they were also made across-the-board. Little wonder that this manufacturer was saddled with "excellence mediocrity."

To be competitive leaders, companies do not need to be world-class at everything. In fact, when a company tries to do everything well, it becomes a jack-of-all-trades and master of none. One of the chief reasons strategy clarification is so important is that it establishes a basis for building organizational capability by providing a framework for deciding which capabilities to master.

One of the major weaknesses of competitive strategies based on microeconomic theory is their treatment of organizational capability. In standard microeconomics textbooks and some strategy texts, companies have an infinite range of capabilities from which they can choose. Moreover, previous choices do not constrain future choices. Because the realities of internal organization are never seriously considered, "the sky's the limit" in terms of strategic possibilities, and "bygones are bygones."

In our approach to competitive strategy, company history and current capabilities influence the choice of strategic direction. Changes in strategic direction are difficult and costly; once they are made, companies enter into de facto long-term commitments. A commitment to a strategic direction defines the boundaries of strategic improvising, and an important part of strategic improvising is the focused acquisition, development, and bundling together of organizational capabilities.

A strategic approach to building organizational capability assumes that the capabilities companies need are not necessarily the ones they currently have. A recent consulting experience demonstrates how restrictive strategic thinking becomes when current capabilities are the only ones being considered by companies as they explore their options.

We were invited by the top managers of a division of a major U.S. defense contractor to help them with their strategy.[1] Because opportunities in the defense industry were drying up, they wanted to move vigorously into commercial markets, but they were confused about the best direction for them. We spent several months on strategy clarification—exploring different strategic options and then choosing one strategic direction. The division's technical leadership in satellite-based navigation systems was both the key source of competitive advantage across all its defense-related products and a technology with numerous potential commercial applications. We identified several specific applications in the commercial aircraft, automobile, trucking, and shipping industries, and framed them as potential strategic objectives. Next, we gave the team of managers an assignment to be completed before our next consulting visit: To develop a list of the business capabilities they believed were necessary to accomplish each strategic objective.

When we returned a few weeks later, the team of managers was visibly discouraged. To develop a list of necessary capabilities, they had gone down the list of strategic objectives we had identified together. When they determined that they did not currently possess all the capabilities necessary to accomplish a strategic objective, they crossed it off the list. They had exhausted the existing list of strategic objectives and had devised a new list, but the results were the same. They were discouraged because they had concluded from the exercise that their strategic options in commercial markets were extremely limited.

Strategic thinking about core capabilities involves much more than taking an inventory of current capabilities; if it did not, existing capabilities would always determine strategic objectives, and organizational growth and development would essentially be stopped in their tracks. Strategic improvisers formulate and implement strategies in real time by looking at the road ahead, not the rearview mirror. They focus on the capabilities or combinations of capabilities that they do not presently have but will need in order to accomplish their strategic objectives. Current capabilities should not be ignored, but once they have influenced strategic direction, they should not constrain further strategic choices.

Strategic improvising is a process that depends on a simple form in which freedom, imagination, and creativity can be exercised. In practice, strategic direction constrains strategic choices. When a company's attention focuses on building organizational capability, a parallel form is required to help the company decide:

What to do themselves;

What to do with someone else;

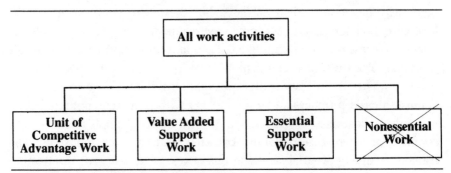

FIGURE 4–1. The four categories of work.

What to contract others to do;

What not to do.

As we have worked with organizations, we have developed a vocabulary to help our clients differentiate among the various types of work, and, in turn, make decisions about building organizational capability. As shown in Figure 4–1, the four categories of work that we have identified are:

1. *Unit of competitive advantage (UCA) work,* or the work and capabilities that create distinctiveness for the business in the marketplace;

2. *Value-added support work,* which facilitates the accomplishment of the UCA work;

3. *Essential support work,* which neither creates advantage nor facilitates the work that creates advantage, but must be done if businesses are to continue to operate;

4. *Nonessential work,* or activity that has lost its usefulness but continues to be done because of tradition.

THE UNIT OF COMPETITIVE ADVANTAGE

Despite their sophistication in dealing with other aspects of business, most managers have archaic views of the different types of work. Most of their models for characterizing work have come from a finance or accounting orientation. Accounting terms such as overhead, direct labor, and indirect labor may be useful as a way to report costs, but they provide little understanding about the relative strategic importance of the work.

Yet, these classifications are frequently used to determine how work is organized and where resources are allocated.

In a division of a large aerospace firm, the managers' way of thinking about work had led them to treat their research and development (R&D) as a flexible pool of "indirect work." They saw R&D as either a way to keep technical people busy between "direct work" assignments, or as work that was easily eliminated when performance problems associated with "direct work" required budget cuts to meet profit goals. After five years of this practice, the business found itself in a noncompetitive state. It had just lost the follow-on contract to its core business and had few if any unique technical skills on which to build new business opportunities.

We can only speculate about whether thinking of R&D work in a different way would have prevented the decline of the division. Still, from talking to people at the division, we concluded that the way they had classified R&D work had led both the management and the technical staff to treat it as work from which little was expected; people were held less accountable for results, and insufficient continuity existed.

The concept of *unit of competitive advantage* (UCA) helps to explain why some organizations, like the aerospace division described above, either emphasize the wrong capabilities or deemphasize the right capabilities. UCA also explains why some forms of improvement lead to competitive disadvantage, and why some businesses consistently outperform their competitors by gaining greater leverage from their competitive advantages.

The UCA includes the critical processes that create distinctiveness within an established strategic direction. It is based on the premise that businesses create competitive advantage when they focus their attention on a few key processes and implement those key processes in world-class fashion. For example, continuous improvement is a popular management program that assumes benefit from any kind of ongoing improvement. Our experience, however, is that only when an organization defines a strategic direction, clarifies strategic objectives, and determines its UCA, will continuous improvement programs be effective at creating competitive advantage. These crucial prerequisites tell where continuous improvement efforts should be focused, to create maximum leverage. They suggest what kinds of work to improve interdependently, what kinds to improve separately, and what kinds not to waste time on. They even signal when continuous improvement is more likely to create competitive disadvantage rather than competitive advantage.

A large printing press supplier identified its strategy as driven by a core set of technologies. The competitive advantages it was trying to create in the marketplace included a reputation as a world-class provider of technology, an ability to find market applications for its technology, and an ability to quickly translate technology advances into viable products. As the printing press supplier evaluated its business, four processes were identified as fitting within its UCA: technology development, applications engineering, business development, and preliminary design. All of these processes were directly related to the continuous improvements that were most needed.

In addition to identifying the processes in its UCA, this business explicitly defined processes *not* in the UCA—detailed design, manufacturing, sales, and post-sales service. Exclusion of these processes from the UCA did not mean they were unimportant; if done poorly, they would lead to competitive disadvantage. However, the company recognized that becoming world-class in the non-UCA processes would not increase its ability to create competitive advantage with its technology strategy.

As we have studied different businesses, we have found that there are some consistencies across the UCAs of companies that have the same business focus. The UCA we have consistently observed in high-performing, product-focused businesses is represented by the boxed area in Figure 4–2(a). The included activities are: develop the product specifications, design the product, manufacture the product, and service the product. The activities not highlighted represent support work: identify the customer requirements, develop the technology, sell the product, and deliver the product. For product-focused businesses, the processes that end up in the UCA are those that usually have the biggest impact on superior product quality, product innovation, and superior post-sales service.

Successful customer-focused businesses have UCAs that differ from the UCAs of product-focused businesses in significant ways. As indicated in Figure 4–2(b), the sequence of activities is: identify the customer requirements, develop the product specifications, design the product, and sell the product. The support activities in customer-focused businesses are: develop the technology, develop the manufacturing process, manufacture the product, deliver the product, and service the product. Again, an identification as support work does not mean that the work is unimportant.

The printing press supplier described earlier is an example of a business that is technology-focused. In high-performing, technology-focused businesses, the activities generally are as shown in Figure 4–2(c): develop

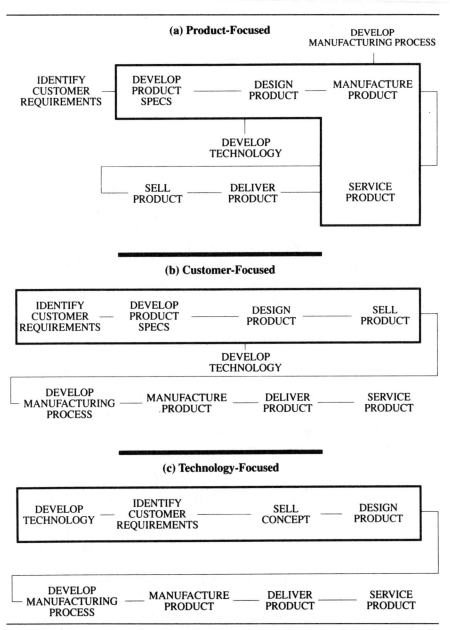

FIGURE 4–2. Potential units of competitive advantage (UCAs) for high-performance businesses.

the technology, identify the customer requirements, sell the concept, and design the product. The UCA creates competitive advantages around superior technology, quick transfer of technology to product application, and new market creation. The support activities of technology-focused businesses include: develop the manufacturing process, manufacture the product, deliver the product, and service the product.

Although a business focus indicates what should be included in the UCA, a specific strategic direction guides how the UCA is managed. Only a specific strategic direction can show what specific core capabilities are needed in the UCA in order to accomplish strategic objectives.

One of our clients, Harley-Davidson, is a product-focused business. Harley's strategic direction is established around its major product category—the Harley Lifestyle, which includes motorcycles, clothing, accessories, and participation in Harley-sponsored events and rallies. Like all product-focused businesses, Harley is most concerned about identifying product specifications, designing and manufacturing products, and providing post-sale support. Because Harley's product is a style of living, however, these UCA processes are quite unique.

For example, the company's vice president, William ("Willie") G. Davidson, exemplifies Harley's biker image. He wears bikers' attire and learns firsthand about the Harley Lifestyle by associating with other bikers. By observing how bikers modify their motorcycles, Davidson learns whether a subtle change in styling is consistent or inconsistent with the Harley Lifestyle. He says about bikers:

> They really know what they want on their bikes: the kind of instrumentation, the style of bars, the cosmetics of the engine, the look of the exhaust pipes, and so on. Every little piece on a Harley is exposed, and it has to look just right. A tube curve or the shape of a timing case can generate enthusiasm or be a total turnoff. It's almost like being in the fashion business.[2]

Harley is unique in the nature and intensity of its post-sales support. Because the company is selling the Harley Lifestyle, its post-sales support is support of a way of living. This is why Harley has developed unique core capabilities around the Harley Owners Group (HOG), which sponsors some kind of motorcycle event almost every weekend from April to November, all over the country. In many respects, HOG's 100,000 members have become a huge, unpaid national sales force. They sell the Harley Lifestyle.

As a product-focused business, Harley grows by attracting new customers to the Harley Lifestyle. Another of the company's unique core capabilities involves fine-tuning an image that attracts customers as diverse as members of hard-core biker clubs and corporate executives. The company is especially good at turning a Harley-Davidson motorcycle into a symbol of American individualism. To draw people from mainstream America into Harley's biking culture, the company sponsors events for charitable causes. Harley's recent 85th birthday celebration involved a lot of wild fun, but participating bikers had to contribute $10 to Harley's favorite philanthropic organization, the Muscular Dystrophy Association. The event raised more than $500,000 for the charity and attracted 40,000 bikers of all ages and backgrounds.

Harley-Davidson also exemplifies an important role for *competitive necessities* outside the UCA. In the mid-1970s, Harley, then a subsidiary of AMF Corporation, was in trouble. The quality of its motorcycles had deteriorated; they were no match for Japanese high-performance bikes. By 1980, the company's share of the big-bike market had dropped from 75 percent to less than 25 percent. By early 1981, AMF had lost interest in keeping the business. AMF accepted an offer from Vaughn Beals, Harley's president, and 12 other executives, who took over the business in an $81.5 million leveraged buyout.

The attention of Harley's new owners first turned to manufacturing. The company had just completed the development cycle of a new family of engines that could compete with the performance of Japanese engines and still meet federal noise and emissions standards. However, to restore the company's reputation, it needed to produce engines that had the same high quality as the Japanese. Harley's management introduced a just-in-time inventory system, promoted greater worker involvement on the plant floor, and taught workers statistical methods for monitoring and controlling the quality of their work. It also helped its suppliers to adopt similar methods.

Although the improvements in the quality of manufacturing enabled Harley to catch up to Japanese competitors and regain a 50 percent share of the big-bike market, they were not unique and they did not create competitive advantage. They were already in place among Harley's Japanese competitors. Improvements in the quality of manufacturing at Harley were outside its UCA because they were made to keep up with the Japanese; a secondary effect was to attract new customers to the Harley Lifestyle. Quality manufacturing eliminated competitive disadvantage and made significant contributions to Harley's competitive position because it responded to a competitive necessity.

Competitive necessities are associated with processes both inside and outside the UCA. No matter where they are, competitive necessities are magnets for the attention of individuals and teams, more because they can eliminate competitive disadvantage than because they create a temporary competitive advantage. Situations often arise when businesses, like Harley-Davidson, need to eliminate competitive disadvantage before they can create competitive advantage. In those situations, competitive necessities—even non-UCA competitive necessities—should become top-priority strategic objectives.

While working with a company that was technology-focused, we observed that its customer service was horrendous. Some customers continued to stick with the company because of its superior technology, but its customer base was rapidly eroding. Improving customer service was a competitive necessity—for this business, it was a means of eliminating competitive disadvantage, not creating competitive advantage. Nevertheless, we advised the company to define a strategic objective and launch a strategic thrust to improve customer service. Given the company's strategic direction, it was still more important to be world-class at technology development than at customer service. We never even mentioned becoming world-class at customer service; but if the company did not improve its customer service immediately, it was going to lose customers for its world-class technology.

HOW THE UCA AFFECTS THE DESIGN AND MANAGEMENT OF ORGANIZATIONS

The unit of competitive advantage has important implications for the design and management of organizations. First, the processes and skills in the UCA cannot be managed separately. The traditional approach of assigning to different functional areas the responsibility for a given process, and then expecting them to complete it independently, prevents businesses from maximizing the potential of the UCA. The UCA is, after all, a *unit*. As the term implies, in the unit of competitive advantage, the interactions between processes are just as important as the processes themselves.

Because it is product-focused, GE Aircraft Engine must look at the interaction between the design of an engine and the business's ability to manufacture the engine and to service it once it is mounted on an aircraft. It is difficult to imagine how such a technologically sophisticated product could be designed, manufactured, and serviced if all three processes were considered separately. Moreover, thinking about UCA processes separately would severely limit learning opportunities. For example, GE Aircraft Engine's designers get many of their ideas for new products and product enhancements through frequent interactions with people in their field service shops.

What happens when UCA processes are kept separate? Costs increase, and quality, service, and speed decrease. A field service representative for a telecommunications switch supplier had an idea for adapting the company's switch to handle both incoming and outgoing calls. The representative could never get the design organization to listen to the concept. By the time the designers were ready to begin exploring the concept, the company's major competitor had already developed a new product that incorporated the concept. While the company waits to introduce its product, its competitor is winning all the new business requiring the application.

The second implication of the UCA deals with competitive leverage—businesses gain maximum leverage by improving UCA processes. An example is the benefits associated with improving the speed of UCA processes. We have found that speed is most critical in the UCA and that the rest of the organization should be designed for its maximization. This means that, within the UCA, there must be an obsessive search for and a removal of any hurdles or barriers that obstruct the natural work flow.

North American Aircraft, a division of Rockwell International, discovered many different kinds of hurdles and barriers that were slowing down work in the UCA of its military aircraft modification business. Some of the barriers were tangible and obvious. The structure of the business had historically been functional: people with similar skills were organized and physically located together. A matrix structure then allowed the company to assign specific people to a project on a temporary basis. This structure was very effective at maximizing the utilization of technical people and helped to maintain a high level of functional expertise.

As management examined the UCA, however, it became clear that the structure created multiple handoffs, caused discontinuities within the UCA, resulted in a long cycle for the development and implementation of new modifications, and produced significant costs associated with maintaining acceptable levels of quality. Frequently, because requirements from customers were not clarified until well into the actual modification process, significant design changes and reworking of the modifications were needed. The business was losing money because it was operating inefficiently under fixed-price contracts; its customers were dissatisfied because they wanted quick turnaround on their aircraft.

Subtler problems within North American Aircraft's UCA were equally serious. Manufacturing engineers were viewed as second-class citizens by design engineers. The design engineers all had undergraduate and graduate degrees; many of the manufacturing engineers had no college training. This disparity led to two consequences. First, the design engineers, who saw manufacturing as the black hole of an engineer's career, avoided involvement with manufacturing at all cost. Second, the manufacturing engineers felt that they had important knowledge to contribute to the design process but, because they were being treated poorly by the design engineers, they were reluctant to approach them with their ideas.

North American Aircraft recently gained significant competitive leverage by reorganizing its military aircraft modification business into multidisciplinary teams. Design engineers and manufacturing engineers were assigned to the same teams. Each team was responsible for a major phase of the UCA. Although there are still handoffs and fumbles in the UCA, their number has been reduced significantly. Smooth transitions in the UCA are facilitated because a small, core group of people moves from each phase of a project to the next. This forces design engineers to expose themselves to the manufacturing phase, while eliminating the career-threatening stigma previously associated with such a move. The design engineers are also gaining a new appreciation for the knowledge of the manufacturing engineers as they work together on the teams and develop a common language for sharing their expertise and knowledge.

A third implication of the UCA deals with the relationship between UCA work and non-UCA work. Non-UCA work should be organized so that it does not dilute the competitive advantage of UCA work. The purpose of non-UCA work is to support the UCA, and it should be managed with that perspective clearly in mind. When trade-offs need to be made, they should be made in favor of UCA work.

When companies fail to give priority to UCA work, the results are detrimental to their competitive advantage. A major fast-food company had grown rapidly over a three-year period. As the company grew, so did the amount of reporting imposed by headquarters on store managers. Every week, a store manager was required to take inventory, reconcile both the labor report and the bank account, and then send information reports to the corporate accounting group. What began as a halfday activity evolved into a 12-hour chore as the accounting group demanded more and more detailed information. Adding insult to injury, store managers were required to complete an equally detailed monthly report by the last day of each month. During one week out of every month, store managers had to spend half their time on reporting and reconciliation.

A frustrated store manager suggested an alternative method of reporting that involved changing to a four-week reporting cycle (a total of 13 reports annually). Store managers would not have to do double reporting in the same week; instead, they could use the last of the weekly reports as their monthly report. After studying the proposal and concluding that it would raise costs, the accounting group rejected the proposed change.

The accounting group had failed to realize that its role was to support the store managers and to conform its routines to their wishes. Store operations were part of the UCA; the reporting and control system was not. Because it had assumed its role was central and its costs were the most important, the accounting group had failed to consider the impact of extensive reporting and rigid scheduling on the ability of individual stores to serve customers. Every hour that store managers spent completing reports was one less hour they had to train their crew, develop subordinate managers, and visit with customers.

Gerard Closset, vice president of corporate technology at Champion International, sponsored a five-year change effort at the company's Technology Center. When asked about the most significant outcome of the change effort, Closset is emphatic: it is the shift from valuing technology development for its own sake to valuing it only for what it contributes to increased production capacity and lower costs in Champion's paper mills. In other words, Closset has redefined the role of the Technology Center as supporting the UCA of Champion, a production-capacity-focused (low-cost-anchored) business.

The human resources department of Esso Resources Canada is another good example of a support organization that chose to subordinate its own functional interests so it could better attend to the company's UCA. The merger of Esso Resources Canada with Texaco Canada provided a perfect opportunity for the human resources staff members to reevaluate their role in the corporation and to organize themselves in a way that would support the competitive advantage of the core business. The human resources staff first spent time with internal customers, understanding business unit strategies and how their department fit into the overall corporate strategy. Brian Hallamore, the manager of human resources, and his staff made an early decision about their philosophy: they were going to assume that they would be out of the human resources business in five to 10 years. Therefore, they needed to create the kinds of systems that would make a corporate human resources staff unnecessary, and to develop in the core businesses the kinds of capabilities that would continue their ongoing functions.

This underlying philosophy changed the way the human resources people thought about their work. First, the systems they developed had to be simple and user-friendly so that they could be used eventually by their internal customers. Second, their focus had to be on developing the human resources capabilities of their internal customers rather than on refining their own capabilities. Their success would be measured in terms of how little, not how much, their customers needed them.

By preparing to be out of business in five to 10 years, Brian Hallamore and his staff actually made themselves more valuable to the organization. Their philosophy led them to create a unique organizational arrangement for some of the more traditional human resources support work. Rather than organize around compensation, benefits, recruiting, relocation, and so on, they structured their new organizational arrangement around employee joining, employee staying, and employee leaving. Each of the new groupings has the relevant capabilities embodied in the old groupings, but each is now made relevant to a particular stage in an individual employee's career. Now, when managers have new employees joining their department, they need only access the employee-joining systems that Hallamore and his staff have developed for assistance with compensation, benefits sign-up, new employee orientation, and relocation. When employees retire or take an overseas assignment, the employee-leaving team jumps into action to ensure that all needed assistance is provided. This makes each interaction with the human resources department one-stop shopping for managers and their subordinates.

MANAGING CAPABILITY OUTSIDE THE UCA

One of our strongest held beliefs is that companies should own and control the processes within their unit of competitive advantage. Because the processes within the UCA are the basis of a company's distinctive competence, sharing them is tantamount to losing the company's competitive edge. Moreover, the only way to ensure the integration of UCA processes is to own them.

Knowing what to do with UCA work, however, does not resolve what to do with non-UCA work. Is it important to own all kinds of support work, or can managers outsource some of it? A few companies have concluded that they should not own the support work if it's cheaper to buy it. Berrett-Koehler Publishers, for example, plans to outsource many of its traditional publishing activities to various business partners. Activities to be outsourced include: all the production components—copyediting, design, typesetting, and proofreading; printing and binding; warehousing and shipping; trade sales to bookstores and other retail outlets; printing and mailing of promotional brochures and catalogs; publicity; and international marketing and distribution. Given the extent of its outsourcing, Berrett-Koehler is obviously operating without precise decision rules about which support activities to own or buy. Accordingly, there is no way of determining whether its outsourcing strategy will create competitive advantage or competitive disadvantage.

Our partner, Jon Younger, has developed a way to consider the different options for managing non-UCA work. It is based on two key considerations:

1. Is the non-UCA work value-added or is it essential support work?

2. Does the company use proprietary or generic capabilities?

Value-added support work helps the UCA run more smoothly, faster, and more cheaply. It facilitates work within the UCA. Essential support work needs to be done for companies to stay in business, but it does not facilitate UCA work. A good example of value-added support work comes from American Hospital Supply. Technology development is not a part of American Hospital Supply's UCA because the company is a customer-focused organization. Nevertheless, when the company developed computer systems and placed them in the hospitals it served, work within the UCA was facilitated. The on-site computer systems performed value-added support work in two ways. First, they helped hospitals with inventory control so that the hospitals knew what and when to reorder. Second, because the computers were linked to American Hospital Supply, they provided hospital workers with quick access to supplies and ensured that the supplies would be ordered through American Hospital Supply.

One of the best examples of essential support work is the preparation of reports to the Internal Revenue Service (IRS). Companies have to file corporate tax returns or risk getting into deep trouble. Therefore, it is work they must do, but doing it does not create competitive advantage. Companies can be world-class at filing IRS forms, and still be uncompetitive.

Companies also determine how to deal with non-UCA work by considering whether capabilities are proprietary or generic. Proprietary capabilities are either firm-specific, involving work that is unique to a specific firm, or they are developed when work involves unsecurable, proprietary information. In both cases, firms are forced to do the work themselves. Generic capabilities exist both inside and outside a firm: they are firm-nonspecific. When generic capabilities are involved, there are no constraints dictating who does the work. Firms have a choice about whether they do it themselves or outsource it.

The two criteria—whether non-UCA work is value-added or is essential support work, and whether it requires proprietary or generic capability—are the basis of Figure 4–3, which proposes four options for managing non-UCA work: provide, maintain, broker, and contract out.

To *provide* involves both owning and developing support capabilities that are proprietary and add value to core capabilities inside the UCA. The *maintain* option also involves owning, but downplays the improvement of non-UCA capabilities. Because the support work is essential, it must be done. It is done inside the firm only because it either

	Proprietary Capability	**Generic Capability**
Value-Added Support Work	**Provide** (Develop Best Internal Capability Possible)	**Broker** (Develop Ongoing Access to Best Capability Possible)
Essential Support Work	**Maintain** (Manage Internal Capability to Meet Cost and Quality Standards)	**Contract Out** (Monitor to Secure Compliance)

FIGURE 4–3.   **Options for managing non-UCA work.**

requires firm-specific capabilities or involves unsecurable, proprietary information. When companies *broker* non-UCA work, they outsource it; however, because it is value-added support work that does not require proprietary capabilities, they spend a lot of management resources ensuring it is done as specified. The final option, to *contract out*, applies to essential, generic support work. When companies contract out non-UCA work, they enter into a contractual relationship but do not maintain close ties with the provider. Companies continue to be satisfied with contractual relationships as long as interruptions in the flow of work are kept to a minimum and an acceptable standard of work is maintained.

There is one other kind of non-UCA work: nonessential work (see Figure 4–1). This work is done just because companies have always done it. Nonessential work neither provides nor supports competitive advantage. It is work that clutters up the attics of most organizations and is the major target of programs like General Electric's Work-Out. In other words, it is work that should be worked out of any organizational system. By eliminating nonessential work, companies prevent many common bureaucratic diseases.

Once companies have eliminated nonessential work and have either brokered or contracted out generic support work, they can turn their attention to how to manage proprietary, value-added, and essential support work. Something we have discovered through our consulting is that value-added and essential support work should be organized separately. Whenever value-added and essential support work are organized together, the essential work drives out the value-added work, thus eliminating the benefits that value-added work brings to the UCA. Value-added support work should be performed as close as possible to the UCA; essential support work should be kept as far away as possible.

Companies that are organized functionally tend to mix value-added and essential support work because people with the same educational background can do both. Human resources departments are notorious for this problem. For example, the people assigned to do benefits administration are also assigned human resources development responsibilities. They spend all their time doing benefits administration because it involves short, well-defined tasks, and they forget the longer-term, more ambiguous responsibilities associated with the development of human resources.

The experience of a major energy company demonstrates the benefits of being clear about what is value-added and essential support work, and then managing them separately. The company's information systems

group realized that it was spending about 80 percent of its time and resources updating the accounting and financial records systems. Realizing
this was essential support work and not value-added support work, they
asked what kind of information system their internal UCA customers really needed. Asking this question helped them realize that the information system that would provide the most leverage in facilitating UCA
work was one that would help geologists and geophysicists to integrate
the data they were collecting to exploit energy resources. Because they
were expending so much effort supporting the accounting and financial
information systems, however, only 15 percent of their effort was supporting the geologists and geophysicists.

The information systems group realized that they were being viewed
by management as an overhead cost because most of what they were doing
was providing essential support work. Over a two-year period, they implemented dramatic changes in how they performed their support role. They
divided into two groups, one to do value-added support work and the
other to do essential support work. Gradually, resources shifted in favor of
value-added support work. The group in charge of essential support work
eliminated nonessential work and contracted out generic support work.
They also streamlined their procedures so people in the UCA had to
spend less time filling out reports. The information systems group realized they were making significant progress when management, for the
first time in five years, concluded during the annual budget review process that the company was not spending enough on information systems.

CORE CAPABILITIES AND
VALUE-ADDED SUPPORT CAPABILITIES

As indicated in Figure 4–4, considerations about organizational capabilities—especially core capabilities and value-added support capabilities—
are critical to strategic improvising. With the launching of different
strategic thrusts, the *development* and *acquisition* of core capabilities and
value-added support capabilities, along with the creative *bundling* of core
capabilities, become critical to the accomplishment of strategic objectives.

Development

A common challenge associated with strategic improvising is the development of world-class core capabilities. Core capabilities are of primary

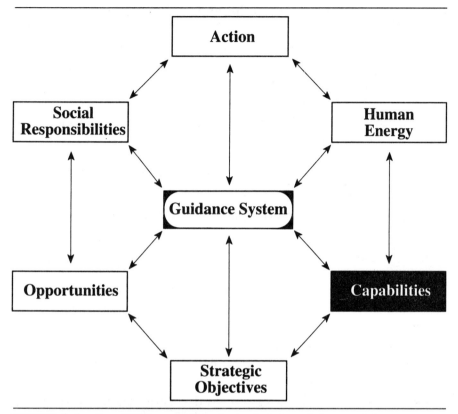

FIGURE 4–4.   Capabilities and the strategic improvising model.

importance because they provide the most leverage to strategic thrusts. The only place to develop core capabilities is within the UCA. Because the UCA is defined by a business's strategic direction, concentrating on the development of core capabilities also ensures that strategic thrusts remain inside established directional parameters.

Because value-added support work facilitates UCA work, new value-added support capabilities also offer significant leverage to strategic thrusts. Accordingly, it is important for businesses to develop value-added support capabilities.

Value-added support capabilities, however, should always take a back seat to core capabilities. Because strategic improvising encourages so much exercising of freedom and initiative, there is a real danger that strategic thrusts will sometimes drift away from their original objectives. This tendency is especially pronounced when, in the process of developing value-added support capabilities, individuals and teams forget that everything they do should facilitate UCA work.

A major defense contractor found itself losing competitive bids because its costs were 20 to 25 percent higher than the competition. To reduce costs, the company decided to launch a strategic thrust to consolidate the manufacturing capability of its three divisions. Over several years, each division had developed its own manufacturing capability; in some cases, multiple manufacturing capabilities had been developed within the same division—in fact, there were seven manufacturing facilities across the three divisions. Consolidation made strategic sense because:

1. The manufacturing capability provided value-added support in this technology-focused business.

2. The manufacturing capabilities were similar across the three divisions.

3. Significant costs could be trimmed by eliminating duplicate capabilities and jobs.

An interesting culture began to emerge in the consolidated manufacturing organization. Driven by its new charge to decrease manufacturing costs, and reinforced by a measurement-and-reward system that made the people in manufacturing accountable only for manufacturing results, the manufacturing organization began to make decisions to maximize its own results. A single manufacturing process that permitted the scheduling of long, uninterrupted runs best maximized results. Standard procedures were developed to reduce engineering change requests and last-minute scheduling changes. The people in the consolidated manufacturing organization even began talking about an emerging new age in which they were no longer at the mercy of the divisions that were known to "screw up" their numbers and make them look bad.

The only problem with these changes was that they were not in harmony with the strategic needs of the divisions. Each division had multiple manufacturing requirements to support the different customers it served. One division, for example, required two manufacturing capabilities: to produce sophisticated products with full government specifications, and to produce low-cost electronic assemblies with few government requirements. Because the single manufacturing capability approach adopted by the consolidated manufacturing organization ignored these differences, many of the division's requirements were left unmet.

A year after the consolidation occurred, corporate management evaluated its impact. Manufacturing costs had been reduced, but less than expected. The disturbing news to corporate management was that each division's customer response capability had been severely compromised. A small reduction in cost had come at the expense of responsiveness to customer needs. Because the tail (value-added support work) was wagging the dog (the UCA), the strategic thrust failed to accomplish its strategic objectives and even created competitive disadvantage.

Acquisition

Recent thinking about competitive strategy mistakenly concludes that capabilities are not easily acquired—instead, they must be developed.[3] The UCA, however, brings to strategic improvising a way of thinking about when it is appropriate to acquire core capabilities. It makes the acquisition of core capabilities a viable alternative to internal development.

C. K. Prahalad and Gary Hamel suggest, in a recent *Harvard Business Review* article, that we should view multidivisional corporations as portfolios of capabilities. They believe that capabilities should be considered corporate property, not owned by individual business units, and that rich horizontal communication should be encouraged to facilitate the sharing of capabilities across business units.[4] This suggests that, when a business is part of a multidivisional corporation, the first place to look for new capabilities is inside other corporate businesses.

The problem with Prahalad and Hamel's view is their belief that the assembly of a corporation's portfolio of capabilities should be orchestrated from the top. This is inconsistent with our view of strategic improvising. Strategic thinking can occur at several levels in a corporation. Corporate-level strategic thinking, for example, should set a strategic direction for the entire corporation and provide an umbrella for decisions about strategic direction in individual business units. However, there is a huge difference between our approach to guiding and their approach to orchestrating the exchange of core capabilities.

Our view is that the exchange of core capabilities between individual business units should occur naturally when business units develop UCAs consistent with *their* strategic direction. As corporate strategic direction influences the strategic directions of individual business units, they form similar UCAs. Many linkages between core capabilities are possible when individual business units have similar UCAs. Accordingly, the exchange of core capabilities between business units does not need to be orchestrated by corporate management. It will be initiated between individual business units whenever they believe that an exchange is in their mutual self-interest.

In the case of dissimilar UCAs, capabilities can still be acquired by one business unit from another, but only to support its UCA. For example, core capabilities from one business would become value-added support capabilities in another, dissimilar business. Because of the highly integrative nature of UCA work, capabilities from dissimilar UCAs are extremely difficult to assimilate.

A second place to look to acquire core capabilities is outside the corporation. The success of major Japanese corporations—such as NEC, Honda, and Sony—at acquiring core capabilities by forming joint ventures with Western partners is well-documented. The single most important reason the Japanese have been successful in exploiting joint venture relationships is that, unlike most of their partners, they have started with a crystal-clear understanding of both the capabilities they wanted to acquire and the capabilities they did not want to share. The Japanese were very willing to share their value-added support capabilities in exchange for core capabilities they could ultimately integrate into their UCA. At the same time, they carefully protected their own UCA.

An understanding of the UCA provides important insights about how to manage strategic partnerships. Strategic partnerships appear to work best when companies manage non-UCA work together and UCA work separately. A joint venture involving General Mills and Nestlé provides a useful illustration. General Mills' UCA centers around new product development, production, and understanding consumer preferences. Nestlé's UCA includes core capabilities in product marketing and distribution. The partnership enables each company to bring unique strengths to the relationship without having to compete with similar strengths or being forced to coordinate highly interdependent core capabilities that are best managed separately.

Bundling of Core Capabilities

One of the most powerful ways of creating competitive advantage involves the bundling of core capabilities into unique combinations. Again, Japanese companies are exemplars of this variation in strategic thinking. Canon's core capabilities in optics, imaging, and microprocessor controls have enabled it to enter, then dominate markets as diverse as copiers, laser printers, cameras, and image scanners. Casio bundles together capabilities in miniaturization, microprocessor design, and ultrathin precision casing to make miniature card calculators, pocket TVs, digital watches, and miniature radios.[5]

There are two different approaches to bundling core capabilities. The most common approach is for a business unit to start with a strategic objective, then develop and acquire new capabilities to bundle together with current capabilities as part of launching a strategic thrust. This approach is both forward-looking and longer-term. It is most successful when companies accurately anticipate future market trends.

We have found that charts similar to the one shown in Figure 4–5 are particularly helpful with this first approach to bundling core capabilities. Each column represents a distinct strategic thrust; the rows represent different core capabilities. The Xs indicate the core capabilities needed to accomplish strategic objectives that are already housed in the UCA, and the Os indicate core capabilities that still need to be developed or acquired. The chart offers a way of keeping track of *all* core capabilities in the UCA and of progress in acquiring the new core capabilities needed to sustain strategic thrusts. It also provides a feasibility sieve for determining which strategic thrusts are possible. Businesses do not want to launch strategic thrusts that require over half of the required core capabilities to be new.

The second approach is more opportunistic. It involves solutions seeking problems, and it requires individuals and teams to be constantly on the lookout for opportunities they can exploit with different combinations of current capabilities. Because only capabilities within the UCA are used,

Core Capabilities	Strategic Thrusts					
	A_1	A_2	AB_1	B_1	C_1	C_2
1.	X	X		X		X
2.			X	X	X	
3.		O	O	O		
4.	O		O	O		O
5.	X	X	X	X	X	X
6.	O				O	

FIGURE 4–5. **Bundles of core capabilities that support strategic thrusts.**

this approach ensures that, when strategic thrusts are launched, they are consistent with strategic direction. This approach is also quite dynamic. Although current capabilities are used, they typically change when they are bundled together in unique combinations. The principal advantage of this second approach is its requirement of very little start-up time. It facilitates quick response to unanticipated and narrow windows of opportunity.

ALIGNING THE UCA

After our many years of consulting experience, only a few managers with whom we worked have continued to inspire us. One of them is Gene Hendricksen, the manager of Tektronix's Forest Grove, Oregon, plant. Hendricksen is one of the most participative managers we know. He wants everyone in the plant to have a voice and, either directly or through elected representatives, to participate in all plant decisions. He shows incredible patience with his people as they improvise strategies within the plant's established strategic direction.

The Forest Grove plant produces circuit boards; it is not on the cutting edge of new technology development. Its strategic direction is production-capacity-focused (low-cost-anchored). Hendricksen and his people have decided they want their plant to become the world's "best cost" producer of circuit boards. Given this strategic direction, it was important to include both manufacturing engineering and manufacturing in the UCA.

Decisions about the UCA affect decisions about how people should work together. For better alignment of manufacturing engineering and manufacturing, it was decided at Forest Grove that the manufacturing engineers would move down to the plant floor, where they would work more closely with manufacturing teams. The engineers understood the reasons for the move and—reluctantly—agreed to do it. After several weeks, however, they still had not moved. The manufacturing teams were being deprived of the hands-on engineering assistance they sorely needed to increase production capacity and lower costs.

Although the manufacturing engineers always seemed to have a valid excuse for not moving at the appointed time, it eventually became obvious to everyone at the Forest Grove plant that they were stalling because they did not want to leave their professional enclave in engineering. After giving them every opportunity to complete the move, Hendricksen finally ran out of patience. Without conferring with the engineers, he hired movers to come in on a weekend to move the engineers' desks down to the plant floor. Hendricksen never offered an explanation for his action to the engineers, and none of them asked for one. Both he and the engineers knew that their reluctance to move out of the engineering department and co-locate with manufacturing teams was impeding the plant's progress in accomplishing its strategic objectives.

Besides translating strategic direction into a way to organize work, the UCA indicates which strategic alignments are most critical to organizational success. Given his commitment to participative management, Gene Hendricksen would not have done what he did to the manufacturing engineers without a compelling reason. He did not have the UCA concept to guide his actions, but he knew intuitively that tightening the alignment between the manufacturing engineers and the manufacturing teams would provide more leverage for accomplishing strategic objectives than almost anything else he could do.

IN THE GROOVE: ALIGNING ORGANIZATIONS TO CONSERVE HUMAN ENERGY

5

In the groove A phrase introduced in the Swing Era to describe a settled, swinging, blended way of playing that becomes infectious to the audience, which often responds with head nodding or upper-body swaying in acknowledgment of the rhythm.

In almost every company with which we have worked during the past four or five years, we have seen evidence of the "empowerment trap." An empowerment trap is set when senior executives, often presidents or general managers, are persuaded by popular writers or consultants that the only way to become more competitive is to empower their people. They appoint a steering committee to oversee the task because, they have been told, decisions about *how* to empower their organizations should be made participatively.

The steering committee appoints a task force, composed of a representative cross-section of employees, to propose what to do. The task force conducts interviews and distributes attitude surveys to identify key issues. From this effort emerges a set of issues that always seems to include: improving customer service, increasing the level of quality awareness, broadening career development options, increasing teamwork, increasing work across functions, and transforming managers into leaders.

The steering committee compliments the task force for its careful work, then appoints several smaller task forces to gather more information about each of the key empowerment issues. Assigning a task force to gather information about an issue leads to two important outcomes: task force members really learn about the issue, becoming in-house experts; and members become advocates as their commitment to the issue deepens and they invest in the development of relevant expertise. As task force members read books and articles, attend conferences, and meet international experts, they begin to believe they are dealing with an issue of paramount importance. When they propose an implementation plan to the steering committee, there is tremendous energy behind their recommendations.

The problem is that there are multiple task forces and each has tremendous energy for its own particular issue. The steering committee does not need to hear all the task force reports before it realizes it is caught in an empowerment trap. All the reports have a familiar ring: they propose a training solution as a first step, and they justify the investment in training with promises of dramatic improvements in business performance. The catch is this: the business can do something but it cannot do everything, and it lacks criteria for deciding what it should do. Its dilemma is compounded by the fact that each rejection of the recommendations of any of the task forces will likely leave members feeling disempowered and enervated.

Both irony and tragedy are associated with the empowerment trap. The irony is that a process designed to empower people ultimately disempowers them. The tragedy is that human energy, once lost, is difficult to recover.

As indicated in Figure 5–1, human energy is an important element of strategic improvising. Strategic thrusts require human energy to drive them; without it, strategic thrusts are likely to fall short of accomplishing strategic objectives.

Organizations are open systems. This trait has both positive and negative implications for human energy. On the positive side, there are many ways to introduce new energy into organizations; on the negative side, there are many ways to lose it. Accordingly, people in organizations must be concerned about both acquiring and preventing the loss of human energy.

Most managers believe that infusing their organizations with new human energy is the only way to raise the level of organizational performance. The intent of employee motivation programs, for example, is to encourage people to expend more effort at work than in other settings. The desired outcome is a net increase in human energy that raises the level of organizational performance.

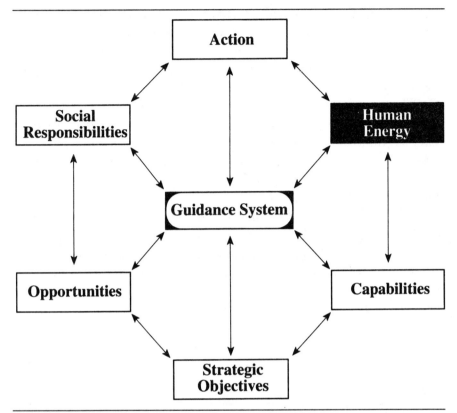

FIGURE 5–1. Human energy and the strategic improvising model.

Another popular way to release greater human energy is to increase employee commitment. When employees are committed to an idea, a strategy, or a company, they are much more likely to work above and beyond the call of duty or to go a second mile to please a customer. Moreover, commitment provides a second line of defense: it maintains the release of human energy when traditional efforts to motivate employees fail.

Interestingly, one way to deepen employee commitment to an idea or a strategy is to encourage improvisation. Our partner, Gene Dalton, has written: "Where internalization [i.e., a deepening of commitment] occurs, typically the guidelines are general enough that the person being influenced is forced to improvise."[1] Improvising specific actions after receiving general instructions helps individuals make something their own. For example, at an automobile assembly plant studied by Robert Guest, supervisors were impressed with a more participative approach to management that was introduced and modeled by the new plant manager, but they had to study his approach, modify it, and then improvise to make the new approach work for them in their own unique situation.[2]

Some managers, believing that human energy reserves are tapped out, look to new technologies either as alternative sources of energy or as ways to leverage existing human energy. The recent interest in building flexible factories that rely on robotics technology is driven by a desire both to replace human workers with machines and to gain maximum leverage from those employees who remain on the factory floor. Businesses are willing to make enormous investments in flexible factories because of their potential for providing new sources of energy that will yield higher levels of performance.

All possible ways of acquiring new energy should be explored, including increasing employee motivation and commitment and introducing new technologies. However, we choose to focus on a specific way of reducing human energy losses: strategic alignment. Our view is this: the only thing that matters is the net increase in human energy, regardless of whether that increase comes from acquiring more energy or losing less. Because the conservation of human energy provided by improved strategic alignments has been mostly ignored, we believe it offers the greatest *untapped potential* for increasing energy to drive strategic thrusts.

CONSERVING HUMAN ENERGY
THROUGH STRATEGIC ALIGNMENT

Misaligned businesses are a lot like cars with front wheels out of alignment: people, the wheels of industry, work against each other, promoting unnecessary wear-and-tear and a loss of energy due to friction. In essence, their efforts cancel each other out. Over time, effort diminishes because few things are more frustrating to people than working hard to improve something, only to have the efforts undermined by actions taken by others.

Several years ago, while we were facilitating quality control circles in a plant that manufactured gas turbine engines, we saw a graphic example of energy loss in a misaligned system. A quality circle with which we were working was trying to solve a balancing problem that occurred when rotors were attached to the engines. It frequently took hours, even days to balance the rotors before engines could be moved to final assembly.

The quality circle, using all the quality techniques its members had learned, worked for three months to devise a solution. When the members of the team made their final presentation to plant management, they were proud of what they had accomplished. The solution they proposed was both workable and low-cost. As they completed their presentation, a man near the back of the conference room raised his hand. He was the chief engineer for the gas turbine engine project. He praised the team members for their efforts, then advised them that their solution would not be needed because his engineering team had just completed a redesign of the engine that eliminated the need for manual balancing of parts during assembly.

The misalignment at the gas turbine engine plant was between two parallel teams, and the obvious solution to the problem was to improve organizational communications. Often, however, obvious solutions are not the best solutions because they deal only with obvious problems. For example, improved organizational communications would have informed the quality circle about what the design team was doing, but the less obvious, more important question of who should be doing what would not have been answered. Improved organizational communications might have left the two teams better informed but still misaligned.

The problem goes deeper: even if the two teams could have managed to align themselves to each other, it is unlikely that they would have been aligned to the rest of the plant. Improved organizational communications, a necessary solution, was insufficient to the alignment problem because it lacked a common reference point. Communicating better is not going to solve a problem unless there is also a way of resolving differences.

George Labovitz's work on superordinate goals suggests what is needed. Labovitz contends that either increasing interactions between groups or sponsoring meetings between the leaders of groups will often increase, not decrease intergroup conflict. If groups are to put their differences behind them, they must realize that they need each other. Superordinate goals are goals, set by each group, that cannot be accomplished without another group. The groups are able to align their activities and cooperate because superordinate goals provide a common reference point.

Strategic alignment occurs only when strategy provides a common point of reference. Everything in an organization is aligned to everything else because all elements are aligned to strategic objectives, and they, in turn, are aligned to a strategic direction. Our acid test for an aligned organization is whether representatives from a team or functional area will voluntarily give up resources to another team or functional area because, given their understanding of the business's strategy, they realize those resources can be put to better use elsewhere. The few businesses that pass our acid test waste little human energy.

In a typical empowerment trap, the steering committee gets stuck because it did not begin the empowerment process with a strategic direction. The work of the various task forces has been allowed to wander, unguided by strategic considerations. Recommendations have not been strategic because they were not originally anchored to strategy.

In a company that had adopted "Workforce Empowerment" as its slogan for the 1990s, we interviewed a cross-section of employees. They believed that empowerment was a state of complete freedom in which they could pursue their individual interests. When managers attempted to impose restrictions on employee freedom, their actions were seen as signs of a lack of commitment to the empowerment process. Our experiences with both successful and unsuccessful empowerment processes have taught us that empowerment is not synonymous with complete freedom. The only way for organizations to avoid the empowerment trap is to insist that empowered individuals and teams align their recommendations to the business's strategy. The only organizations that gain more power than they lose through employee empowerment encourage freedom exercised within the form provided by strategic direction.

IDENTIFYING MISALIGNMENTS

Misalignments are to nonroutine work what variations are to routine work. W. Edwards Deming, the father of the quality movement, calls variation the enemy of quality. He attempts to identify two types of variation based on whether it results from "common" or "special" causes. Common causes are difficult to identify because they are inherent in the system; special causes are the product of temporary glitches in a system. An important goal of Deming's philosophy and statistical teachings is to achieve predictable results in processes by pinpointing the common and special causes of variation. Deming considers a system under control only when the common and special causes of variation are identified and are in the process of being eliminated.

Deming's obsession with common and specific causes of variation is not particularly helpful to the continuous improvement of nonroutine work because of a principal characteristic of nonroutine work: it seldom happens the same way twice. The work is not out of control, as a follower of

Deming might presume; rather, the work requirements are constantly changing in response to multiple and competing inputs and outputs.

Our concept of misalignments accounts for the nonrepeating nature of nonroutine work. As the proportion of nonroutine work increases in organizations, so does the potential for misalignments. Misalignments, therefore, are not the enemy; they are inevitable by-products of nonroutine work. It is important to identify misalignments because they provide ongoing opportunities to learn about what causes them and to make adjustments that might prevent them in the future.

We are as intent about eliminating misalignments as Deming is about eliminating variations. The major focus of strategic alignment is energy conservation, and misalignments are significant energy wasters. The elimination of misalignments is never considered permanent; individuals and teams engaged in nonroutine work should expect to be making adjustments all the time, in a continuing effort to eliminate misalignments. This means that people cannot simply get caught up in a flow of routine and allow the work to manage them. Everyone needs to be informed about strategic direction and involved in developing strategic objectives, in order to know what adjustments to make as nonroutine work is performed in real time. The mutually adjusting nature of strategic alignment, occurring within a preset strategic direction, gives strategic improvising its similarity to jazz improvisation.

Because of the dynamic nature of nonroutine work, a *reactive* approach to the elimination of misalignments is the only available method for aligning organizations. Under stable circumstances, it would be possible to *anticipate and prevent* misalignments; furthermore, by refining alignments over time, progressive improvements could be made. In the case of nonroutine work, however, individuals and teams can only react to misalignments. Moreover, because reaction time is critical, early detection of misalignments is critically important. When misalignments are not identified and eliminated, their negative effects typically compound over time.

The key to early detection of misalignments is knowing where to look for them. Misalignments occur between the cracks of organizations, along a wide range of interfaces. We have identified five distinct types of misalignment for discussion here: the misalignment of strategy, organizational design, and culture; the misalignment of self- and organizational interests; vertical misalignment; horizontal misalignment; and temporal misalignment. Although certainly not comprehensive, this list of misalignments will help individuals and teams to start looking in the right places.

Misalignment of Strategy, Organizational Design, and Culture

Organizational misalignment of strategy, organizational design, and culture is common because these elements tend to evolve separately and because different groups of people consciously attend to one and not to the others.

Why do most off-the-shelf solutions to organizational problems seem to create more conflict than they solve? Because their impact on the alignment of strategy, organizational design, and culture is not considered. Currently, an off-the-shelf intervention that is popular with organizational development specialists is sociotechnical redesign. A classic means–ends inversion occurs with most sociotechnical redesign efforts, which, in turn, misaligns strategy, organizational design, and culture. Because team-based structures are the preferred means of organizational redesigners, many of them forget that their goal is improving organizational performance, not organizing into teams. Some misalignments result when the prevailing cultural assumptions, values, and artifacts do not support individuals working together as a team. Other misalignments occur because efforts to organize into teams draw attention and resources away from more urgent strategic concerns.

Procter & Gamble (P&G) is one of the leading corporate innovators in sociotechnical redesign; over nearly two decades, team-based structures have been woven tightly into P&G's corporate culture. Misalignments between organizational design and strategy, however, have a long history at P&G. The Modesto, California plant, for example, was one of the first places in which sociotechnical redesign was tried. At the time, redesign efforts were focused on maintaining balance between social and technical considerations, but the Modesto design team clearly emphasized the social side, measuring their successes in terms of the level of satisfaction and happiness of team members. Because strategic factors were never considered in the redesign effort, the plant gradually became more like a country club than a competitive business.

After business results for several successive months continued to drop, the plant manager abruptly canceled the intervention and, in the process, alienated the majority of the plant's work force. When P&G tried to reintroduce the team concept several years later, most of the workers at the plant resisted, claiming that they would rather work under an autocratic system because they knew what to expect.

The misalignment between strategy and organizational design at P&G's Modesto plant wasted energy in at least two ways. First, the country club atmosphere created an illusion among workers that their satisfaction was more important than their productivity. When such perceptions are common, workers are more likely to seek satisfaction through self-indulgence than through self-challenging and productive work. Second, energy was wasted on creating a noncompetitive system at the Modesto plant. Because organizational design efforts were not aligned with strategy, they did not contribute to the accomplishment of strategic objectives.

Misalignment of Self- and Organizational Interests

Akio Morita liked to call Sony, the company he founded, a "fate-sharing vessel." What he tried to create at Sony was a system in which everyone's individual interests were tied to the interests of the whole. As a result, Sony's people developed a strong identification with the organization—business successes were synonymous with personal successes, and vice versa.

Morita intuitively understood that the basis of worker–management trust is belief in a common ground where individual self-interests and business interests overlap. Unfortunately, in many organizations, the common ground is undermined and trust collapses. These organizations are crippled by irreconcilable differences; they limp along, enduring chronic misalignment of self- and organizational interests.

At a major business school, a significant strategic thrust involved redesigning the MBA program. A senior faculty member with a national reputation in his research specialty was appointed by the dean to be the new program director and was immediately commissioned to design a program for the 1990s. The new program director brought substantial energy and influence to the assignment. With a group of senior faculty, he created a new vision for the program and began to implement it. The vision involved breaking down functional boundaries to build a truly integrative approach to management education. Implementation in the classroom involved building cross-functional faculty teams who could encourage students to analyze cases from several different functional perspectives.

During the first year of the new program, a great deal of excitement was generated among both junior and senior faculty. The best and the brightest professors were anxious to join cross-functional faculty teams and learn from their colleagues. Classroom results were sometimes mixed, because of the radical departure from previous roles, materials, and methods, but student feedback was extremely positive. Indications were that the changes were moving in the right direction and that significant progress was being made.

When faculty members were invited to participate during the new program's second year, however, a serious problem surfaced. Several of the professors who had contributed heavily to the new program's success chose different teaching assignments. Because they had devoted so much time and effort to improving the MBA program, their research productivity had dropped off from previous years. Their department chairs, who controlled annual performance reviews and salary increases, refused to give them credit for their contributions to the MBA program and ranked them lower than colleagues who had better research records. The common feeling among these professors was that they had worked harder during the past year than they had ever worked before, in order to contribute to one of the school's most critical strategic objectives, and they had been punished for it.

Inevitably, systems lag behind strategies. The consequences of the misalignment between the self-interests of professors and the interests of the school of business were unintended, but some form of misalignment should have been expected. It is difficult to predict exactly where misalignments will appear or to prepare for their natural consequences. An obvious solution is to decrease response time by more quickly aligning systems to strategies. When systems cannot be changed fast enough, leaders should be encouraged to make exceptions, ensuring that early supporters of strategies for change are rewarded, not punished, for their efforts. Again, the goal is to conserve, not destroy, the human energy needed to drive strategies for change.

Vertical Misalignment

Organizations throughout the world are delayering to become more competitive. Beyond the obvious cost benefits that come from delayering, there are benefits to strategic alignment. The probability and severity of vertical misalignments decrease significantly as the number of organizational levels decreases. This decrease occurs mainly because there are significantly fewer alignments to make. In addition, the fewer levels through which a strategic direction must be communicated, the lower the possibility that inconsistencies will arise, interference will build, and/or noise will distort the signals being sent.

Because of the central role of strategy in the strategic alignment process, vertical misalignment most commonly occurs when strategic direction, strategic objectives, and strategic thrusts do not match up. Vertical misalignment has many causes. Jon Younger tells of an experience he had at Exxon Chemicals, in which a policy forgotten by top management but remembered by middle management was misaligned with proposed changes in strategic direction. In the early 1980s, the president announced that he wanted Exxon Chemicals to change from a production-capacity-focused to a customer-focused strategy and that new development efforts should concentrate on specialty chemicals. After a year, however, little progress had been made in the development of specialty chemicals and Exxon's commodity business was dying. Quite bewildered, the president gathered his managers together in an attempt to understand what was going on. Eventually, he discovered the cause. In 1975, an internal audit team had concluded that the company was giving away too much product to customers, and a corrective policy was established: no one should share more than a gallon of product with customers. This policy was inconsistent with the new strategic direction set by the president; for Exxon's people to develop specialty chemicals with customers, they needed to be able to share a lot more than a gallon of product.

At Esso Resources, vertical misalignment occurred for a different reason. One of the primary products of Esso Resources is bitumen, or heavy oil, which, if not upgraded, is used for asphalt on roads. Historically, the company had followed a "volume at any cost" strategy because management had believed that everything the company produced could be sold. More recently, management had realized that a new competitive reality had arisen—low-cost production had become a competitive necessity because bitumen could not be differentiated except by price. The previous emphasis on "volume at any cost" needed to be replaced by a production-capacity-focused (low-cost-anchored) strategy. The development of new process efficiencies was critical to selling product profitably.

After several months, process efficiencies had not improved, and managers were beginning to sense significant employee resistance to the change in strategic direction. At a meeting called to discuss the problem, a welder stood up and said to the district manager, "For all the talk about the importance of costs, you sure act hypocritical. Everybody knows that the weekly volume sheet [a form that compared production volumes across operating facilities] is what's really valued around here." The district manager was both startled and embarrassed when he realized why the new strategy and employee behavior were misaligned. The weekly volume sheets had not been modified to reflect new concerns about the costs of production. Therefore, no matter what he said, employees still believed he wanted volume irrespective of cost. A new system for eliminating the volume report and for distributing unit-cost information was implemented within a month.

Because human energy drives strategic thrusts better when it is converging, the primary purpose of strategy clarification is to get everyone in a business pulling in the same direction. In the cases of Exxon Chemicals and Esso Resources, vertical misalignment defeated the purpose of strategy clarification. Human energy diverged because no common strategic direction had existed in the minds of each organization's people, and strategic objectives and strategic thrusts went in a lot of different directions.

Horizontal Misalignment

As more companies move toward team-based structures, the possibility of vertical misalignment decreases and the possibility of horizontal misalignment increases. Horizontal misalignment occurs within teams (between individuals), between teams (both functional and cross-functional teams), and between teams and their suppliers and customers. Several of these horizontal misalignments were represented in a cross-functional team assigned to a project designated OJ-663, at Division 1D of the Hughes Ground Systems Group.

In March 1990, the management of Division 1D decided that the division needed to develop a concurrent engineering capability and chose to test the concept on the OJ-663 project, which involved the design, development, and manufacture of a graphics display for the U.S. Navy. Members of the OJ-663 team were pulled from 15 different functional areas and assigned to the team on a temporary full-time or part-time basis. Because of the size of the OJ-663 team and its commitment to concurrent engineering, it was necessary to break it up into several subteams. Given this initial design, the potential for horizontal misalignment was seemingly endless.

At the most basic level, there were misalignments among the individual members of the team. Coming from 15 different functional areas, team members had varied backgrounds, orientations, and perspectives. Mark Booth, the OJ-663 team leader, ultimately concluded that the technical wizardry of team members was of secondary importance to their ability to work hard and get along. After the experience was over and he had suffered a series of misalignments involving team members' personalities, Booth recommended that teams institute a 60-day probationary period during which team leaders could either accept or reject team members based on their ability to work with the team.

Several horizontal misalignments involved the OJ-663 team's triadic relationship with team members and their functional areas. Generally, a tension existed among the strategic objectives of the OJ-663 team, the ongoing responsibilities of the functional areas, and the needs of individual team members. This tension and its potential for horizontal misalignment required the constant attention of the OJ-663 team leader. For example, some functional areas were more committed to and supportive of the project than others. This, in turn, affected both the attitudes and the availability of team members from the different functional areas. There were misunderstandings about the roles and responsibilities of the functional areas and of the individual team members. Issues related to performance evaluations, rewards, and career impact, which were significant for team members, created a series of horizontal misalignments until differences between functional heads and the OJ-663 team leader were satisfactorily resolved.

There were also horizontal misalignments between subteams and between the OJ-663 team and the subteams, when they attempted to work concurrently. Many horizontal misalignments between the team and its customers were averted by adding counterparts from General Electric (the primary contractor) and the Navy to the team.

When the OJ-663 project was completed, Mark Booth wrote a widely circulated internal memo titled: "Helpful Tips on Concurrent Engineering Team Formation and Project Leadership (aka 'Diary of a Madman' as recollected from the OJ-663 Team Experience)." What had driven Booth crazy and taken most of his energy were all the horizontal misalignments he had to deal with as the OJ-663 team leader. He was successful against difficult odds because the division's strategy was on his side. The OJ-663 project was a high-priority strategic objective at Division 1D because it provided both technical know-how and learning about

concurrent engineering. By consistently leveraging the strategic importance of the project, Booth was able to achieve a favorable resolution to
most horizontal misalignments.

Booth, however, had clearly been on the hot-seat: as long as misalignments had lasted, they had depleted the human energy of the team.
By dealing with the misalignments head-on, Booth and his team had acquired significant knowledge about a core technology and concurrent engineering. Therefore, as they made the needed adjustments to reduce
horizontal misalignments, they both reduced human energy losses and
added new organizational capability.

Temporal Misalignment

Edward Luttwak, a noted military strategist, tells a simple story about the
effort of three families to drive to the beach together. The families intended to meet at a predetermined place at 9:00 A.M., leave immediately
to take advantage of the light traffic, and reach the beach at 11:00 A.M.
The first family, however, was delayed 15 minutes by a child's announcing
that he needed to go to the bathroom. The second family forgot an essential tackle box, turned around midway to the rendezvous to retrieve it, and
was nearly 45 minutes late. The third family created the longest delay because their car would not start. A neighbor graciously loaned them a car,
but after unloading one car and reloading the other, even a fast and impa-
tient drive to the meeting place could not make them less than an hour
late. By this time, some of the children who had been waiting for more
than an hour needed to visit the bathroom. When the three-family cara-
van finally departed, the traffic had increased. Instead of two hours, the
trip lasted over three. The beach was finally reached, over two hours later
than the families had intended.[3]

The point of Luttwak's story is that, in activities involving multiple
participants, *friction*, a Murphy's Law that destroys time schedules, is inevitable. Because friction is inevitable, it should be an expected characteristic of strategic improvising. It is important to use time wisely, but cutting
things too close, by not accounting for friction, ultimately wastes more
time. In other words, minor temporal misalignments are not only tolera-
ble, but desirable; they reduce the incidence of major temporal misalignments. Luttwak's analysis confirms this point:

> In my example, the plan was very simple with its one starting point, sin-
> gle route, and fixed destination, but it was badly flawed in failing to

anticipate that a 9 A.M. starting time would not allow enough leeway to avoid the rush hour on the highway to the beach.[4]

Temporal misalignment occurs when the concurrent activities of individuals and teams are out of sync. Human energy is wasted because somebody is waiting for somebody else to catch up. The more complex and interdependent activities become, the greater the likelihood of temporal misalignments. Luttwak, for example, posits that, if the scenario he created were expanded to involve two dozen families, they would likely never arrive at the beach.[5] Applied to strategy, this means that cutting out the fat in organizations can be both underdone and overdone. Leaner organizations are also simpler, which reduces the likelihood of temporal misalignments. If managers obsessed with efficiency make cuts all the way to the bone, however, there will not be enough slack to accommodate friction. By eliminating minor temporal misalignments, they increase the probability that major temporal misalignments will occur.

Just-in-time (JIT) inventory systems, for example, are a great idea that can become a bad idea if they are overdone and cause major temporal misalignments. GE Appliances learned, from its experience with JIT techniques, that not all the parts need to be ordered just-in-time, to effect cuts in inventory costs. At the GE Appliances plant in Louisville, Kentucky, analyses showed that only 20 to 30 percent of the parts in any appliance are unique to a specific model, and less than 5 percent of the unique parts are complex and costly. Major temporal misalignments are avoided by having only the complex and costly parts delivered just-in-time by suppliers, while maintaining a buffer stock of the rest.

Organizations have only a fixed amount of time each day to convert the potential energy of their employees into kinetic energy. When that time is not used wisely, human energy is wasted. Seiuemon Inaba, the founder and CEO of Fanuc, a Japanese manufacturer of robotics equipment, felt so strongly about the value of time that he placed on the wall of his product development lab a clock that runs at ten times normal speed.

Organizations that waste the least human energy, however, are not necessarily those that run at the fastest rate of speed. Stopping and starting organizational processes burn up the most energy, and organizations that try to perform complex, highly interdependent work at maximum speeds are much more likely to shut down because of major temporal misalignments. They burn still more human energy getting back up to speed—an argument for persons working at a controlled, even pace. Although there will still be minor temporal misalignments that waste human energy, the best way to conserve energy is to have organizations run smoothly.

STRATEGIC ALIGNMENT TOOLS

During the past several years, we have been involved in the strategic alignment of several organizations. A few of the organizations with which we have worked have a long enough history of aligning themselves that we can visit them with new clients and conduct observation tours, to exhibit what the process looks like when it is ongoing. As we have done this, we have taken note of what people remember and find useful long after our involvement with them. These recollections help us to determine which of our many recommendations made a significant difference and to refine our strategic alignment tools accordingly.

Strategic alignment tools are ideas or ways of thinking about organizations that help individuals and teams fix misalignments once they are identified. We have learned a lot about strategic alignment tools, but the most important lesson is that, despite our initial intentions to give more, we are able to provide organizations with only a starter set. As with most starter sets, the tools in them are ultimately found wanting and are then replaced. The only purpose of a starter set is to get people started. As they become more skilled at strategic alignment, they will acquire new strategic alignment tools as needs arise.

We initially resisted this lesson because we did not like being told that the strategic alignment tools we were providing to organizations had become obsolete. Nevertheless, it was difficult to interpret what we heard and saw in any other way. People still thought in terms of aligning their organizations, and they continued to use strategy as a reference point for alignment of everything else. They were even using pieces of the tools we had provided them, but most of our original tools were forgotten and had been replaced by other tools. Even the pieces of tools that survived were being used by individuals and teams in very different ways than we had initially intended.

As we continued to observe this phenomenon, we wondered where these tools were coming from. People at all organizational levels told us that they were tuning in more to information: now that their learning had a purpose (a strategic objective), they were turning on to the world of ideas. They were putting their antennae out to look for better ways to align their organizations because misalignments made them uncomfortable. Sometimes, useful information came from discussions with other people, from both inside and outside their organizations. At other times, deciding to watch a management program on television or attending a training seminar on a relevant topic had proven valuable. Often, they wandered through bookstores looking for titles that were germane to their perceived needs. As they browsed, they were quickly able to differentiate between good and bad books: good books provided ideas they could forge into strategic alignment tools.

Our philosophy of strategic alignment and the way we view our role as consultants have changed since these revelations. We have cleaned out our strategic alignment toolboxes to make them look more like starter sets, and we use these starter sets to help individuals and teams begin to think about strategy in terms of strategic alignment. Our most common starter set includes five tools, each specially designed to fix one of the five misalignments discussed above:

1. Trade-offs (misalignment of strategy, organizational design, and culture);

2. Strategic reward systems (misalignment of self- and organizational-interests);

3. Up-close-and-personal contact (vertical misalignment);

4. Meetings for a strategic purpose (horizontal misalignment);

5. Search-and-rescue teams (temporal misalignments).

We make it very clear to individuals and teams that it is their responsibility to fill up their toolboxes by discovering, reshaping, and creating their own sets of strategic alignment tools.

Trade-Offs

We had an interesting experience when we took a group of Chicago- and Houston-based Amoco people to New York to observe the strategic alignment results at Champion International's Corporate Technology Center. After meeting with several teams at Champion, the people in the Amoco group were skeptical; it all seemed too good to be true. Everyone they talked to was excited, empowered, and engaged in strategic alignment. They requested to meet with a team in which strategic alignment was not working, and were perturbed when they were informed that no such teams existed.

During a break, a maintenance engineer from Champion entered the room and began to fix something. One of the people from Amoco-Houston noticed that the maintenance engineer's name tag read: Tex. He struck up a conversation with him, figuring he was a fellow Texan, but was disappointed to learn that Tex was not from Texas. Then he asked: "Well, Tex, what do you think of all this strategic alignment stuff?" Tex said, "I think it's great." The Amoco manager decided to play along, assuming that Tex knew little about the process. He explained to Tex some of the specifics of their situation, paying particular attention to Amoco's culture and organizational design. Then he asked Tex for his advice. Tex responded matter-of-factly: "I haven't heard you say anything about strategy yet. Do you know what your strategy is? You can't do anything if you don't know your strategy." The Amoco manager smiled, then shook his head in amazement. The strategic alignment process must work, he concluded, if Corporate Technology's maintenance engineers were thinking strategically.

Tex, and everyone else at Champion International's Technology Center, had been schooled in *trade-offs,* one of the strategic alignment tools in our starter set. A basic tenet of strategy clarification is: companies cannot do everything. A related tenet underlying trade-offs is: companies cannot have it both ways.

We use trade-offs to resolve misalignments of strategy, organizational design, and culture in organizations. Trade-offs involve a balancing of factors, all of which are not attainable at one time. When making trade-offs, we believe, it is especially important to remember that strategy is the common point of reference. Although strategic issues can be traded-off against organizational design and cultural issues, it is important that organizational design and culture both align to strategy. If they don't, then trade-offs of strategy, organizational design, and culture are made in a political free-for-all, and the outcomes of negotiations sometimes will and sometimes will not be aligned to strategy.

In recent efforts to cut the fat out of organizations, we have observed the effects of not being clear about how to make trade-offs among strategy, organizational design, and culture. Cutting corporate fat often begins with impassioned speeches by senior managers about the need to eliminate excess and waste. They make it very clear that lowering costs is a competitive necessity. The effect, however, is similar to crash dieting. There is an immediate loss of excess weight, but once the pressure to reduce fat is lifted, new fat is added gradually until organizations are fatter than they were before. Because the strategy does not offer a common point of reference for making trade-offs, concerns about organizational design and culture ultimately reassert themselves and undermine long-term strategic impact. People do not purposely set out to sabotage the strategy, but they gradually lose strategic focus because they are not disciplined about making the tough day-to-day decisions.

When we talked about trade-offs at Champion International's Technology Center, we used a more complex model to identify potential misalignments of strategy, organizational design, and culture: McKinsey's 7Ss Model. We realized, however, that two drawbacks were associated with relying too heavily on the 7Ss Model. First, because the model is often assumed to be complete, individuals and teams fail to think outside it, thereby limiting their thinking about potential trade-offs. Second, individuals and teams feel as though they always need to go through the entire model to complete each iteration of strategic alignment. This repetition becomes especially time-consuming and tedious around highly politicized trade-offs; essentially, strategic improvising goes into gridlock. If strategic alignment is to be consistent with the spirit of strategic improvising, it should not delay action. When we revisited Champion with the Amoco group, we discovered that individuals and teams had varied their use of the 7Ss and were only using four of them in making trade-offs: strategy, structure (organizational design), shared values (cultural assumptions), and systems (strategic reward systems).

Strategic Reward Systems

Intel PCED, located in Beaverton, Oregon, is one of the most dynamic, high-energy businesses we have ever observed. As the sole retail division of Intel, PCED sells personal computer enhancements such as expanded memory boards. Starting with only a few million dollars in seed capital from Intel, a young group of intrapreneurs grew PCED into a business that currently generates annual revenues of several hundred million dollars.

Walking into PCED is a visual feast. Hundreds of cubicles are housed in a large warehouselike building. Streamers flow out of the middle of the ceiling creating a tentlike effect over one of the cubicles. Ant farms, posters, and toys personalize every open space. Written in large block letters on a distant wall is "The Far Side," and on a wall next to the main entrance is written "The Near Side." Employees at PCED (average

age: 32 years) have a history of weekly water fights. They protect their PCs and important papers with sheets of plastic, arm themselves with super soakers, and play.

A few years ago, we invited Steve Kassel and Greg Hayes, PCED's comanagers of new product development, to visit 3M's corporate headquarters in Minneapolis to discuss how 3M continues to excel at new product creation. The PCEDers were surprised by 3M's culture—people were older, wore suits *and* socks, and acted a lot like the rest of corporate America. Still, 3M was highly innovative and had sustained a variety of high-growth businesses. Because the PCEDers had always credited their success at innovation to their distinctive culture, they found it difficult to believe what they were seeing at 3M. As they shared their confusion with one of 3M's senior managers, he remarked: "It's not the clothes or the offices that generate the energy to have fun and develop new products. The secret is getting everybody involved in contributing to what the business needs, when it needs it. At 3M, people get involved because the reward systems link together their needs with the needs of the business."

Strategic reward systems are formal tools for aligning individual interests with organizational interests. They ensure that people focus their energy on the accomplishment of strategic objectives. Strategic reward systems contribute to strategic alignment by rewarding people for (1) developing capabilities consistent with strategic objectives, and (2) working to accomplish strategic objectives. The key idea behind strategic reward systems is that the rewards are contingent on the contributions people make to strategic objectives.

The story of Art, a middle manager at a client's R&D Center, demonstrates the power of strategic reward systems. At the Center, every individual and team was contributing to the accomplishment of strategic objectives except Art. Art did not want to change the way he had always done things, and everything he did reflected his resistance to change. Art's boss was at his wits' end about what to do with him. He liked Art, but because his work was misaligned with everyone else's work at the Center, a lot of energy was being wasted and people were always complaining about having to work around him.

After much discussion, Art's boss decided there was one more thing he could try before he either transferred or fired Art. He could hit Art where he would feel it most, in the pocketbook. When annual bonus checks were distributed a few weeks later, Art's was only a small fraction of what he expected.

Suddenly, Art's attitude took an about-face. He was not exactly sure what he should do, but now he wanted to do it. He had a reason to change. Art went to his boss and pleaded for help. He explained that he initially resisted the changes because he was convinced they were the "flavor of the month" and would soon go away. When they did not go away, he panicked because he did not see where he fit in the overall scheme of things. He did not understand his role in accomplishing strategic objectives.

Consultants have an inside joke they sometimes tell on themselves. Simulating what they might tell a prospective client about a change process in order to sell it, they come to the point where they cannot predict what will happen next, then spread their arms like a televangelist and pronounce, "And then the miracle happens." When we use strategic reward systems, we know exactly the moment of the miracle: when people (1) understand that the change in strategic direction is permanent; (2) become clear about what they can do to help accomplish strategic objectives; and (3) have a reason to change. In other words, when their self-interests are aligned with strategic objectives, the miracle happens: suddenly, they are empowered to benefit both themselves and the organization.

Up-Close-and-Personal Contact

It is tough to send a message from the top of an organization all the way to the bottom, but the level where most messages are lost is neither the top nor the bottom. It is in the middle. Top managers would never have gotten where they are if they had not had their ears to the ground, picking up and responding to the distant din of change. When they are tuned in, they can hear the most remote or imperceptible messages. In the trenches of organizations, informal networks are immensely efficient at getting the word out. If only one person hears something, everybody soon knows it. The middle of organizations, however, is an impermeable, soundproof mass. In some organizations, it is called the concrete layer; in others, the brick wall. Some consultants have argued for strategic alignment tools that resemble bulldozers and jackhammers. They insist that powerful messages need to be sent frequently and consistently, to penetrate the concrete layers and brick walls that plug up the middle of organizations.

Our approach is different. Irresistible forces often work, but there are times when they meet immovable objects. Therefore, the only way to ensure that a message reaches its targeted listeners is to go around the barrier and meet with them up-close-and-personal.

Jack Welch, General Electric's CEO, is a master of up-close-and-personal contact. He relishes the time he spends engaging GE's employees in rough-and-tumble debate in the Pit, the main amphitheater at GE's Management Development Institute in Crotonville, New York. The Pit offers Welch a forum for communicating directly with a remarkably large number of GE's people. Before the Welch era, Crotonville was attended exclusively by high-level GE executives. Welch, however, was quick to broaden its mission by inviting everyone hired as a manager or promoted to that rank to attend the Institute. He annually receives as many as 5,000 GE employees in the Pit.

It was after an especially invigorating session in the Pit that GE's Work-Out program was spawned. Welch was flying from Crotonville to GE headquarters in Fairfield, Connecticut, with the Crotonville director, James Baughman. He was excited about what had just happened and told Baughman, "We've got to find a way to take this thing and transfer it out into the businesses." Work-Out, which Welch likens to a New England town meeting, is fundamentally a forum in which GE employees meet up-close-and-personal with their bosses. It is a business-level tool that imitates the function served by the Pit at the corporate level: it opens up direct lines of communication between the top and bottom of the organization, facilitating the vertical alignment of strategies.

Ideally, up-close-and-personal contact promotes two-way communication that fosters both upward and downward strategic alignment. Unfortunately, some senior executives, like Martin Marietta's corporate management team, do not always listen to what is being learned at the business level. In the process of making Titan missiles, Martin Marietta's Astronautics Group had developed a wide variety of new technologies and skills that had potential applications in the commercial marketplace. For example, to appease Colorado's environmentalists, the Astronautics Group had pioneered a waste treatment technology that was far superior to any commercial methods. Martin Marietta's corporate management, however, refused the Astronautics Group's request to develop commercial applications of the technology because it believed the corporation should restrict itself to the business of making long cylindrical objects that go into space.

The Astronautics Group's proposed venture into waste treatment may have been unwise. It might have been managed as a separate business, but it clearly did not fit the Astronautics Group's current strategic direction. The point here is that the decision not to pursue commercial applications of the waste treatment technology was a secondary problem. The real problem was the process that led to the decision. There was certainly enough up-close-and-personal contact with Martin Marietta's corporate officers as the Astronautics Group pleaded its case, but there was a lack of two-way give-and-take. The corporation simply stuck to its missiles, refusing to learn from one of its businesses anything that might cause it to rethink its strategy.

It does not take a rocket scientist to figure out that Martin Marietta is in trouble. Given recent pressures to downscale the defense and space industries, the market for long cylindrical objects that go into space is not what it used to be. The best evidence that its corporate strategy is too restrictive is the consistent pattern of layoffs affecting all its divisions— including the Astronautics Group—over the past four years. Just because the Astronautics Group's business strategy is aligned with Martin Marietta's corporate strategy does not mean the alignment is favorable. If the two groups are ever going to move to a more favorable alignment, the terms of up-close-and-personal contact need to be redefined.

Meetings for a Strategic Purpose

People in most companies have a bad attitude about meetings—they think they are a waste of time. We cannot defend the way meetings are conducted in most organizations, but we believe that (1) the only way to resolve horizontal misalignment is for people to meet and (2) meetings improve significantly when people *meet for a strategic purpose.*

People at Division 1D of the Hughes Ground Systems Group met a lot—and always for a strategic purpose—to bring the OJ-663 project to completion. There were formal off-site meetings to establish strategic objectives, define member roles, and set a schedule. Meetings were held by team leaders with functional and lab managers, to share corporate expectations and obtain the managers' commitment and backing. An initial meeting was held with the administrative services people to solicit their support for the project and team.

The core team of the OJ-663 project met daily to focus everyone on strategic objectives, on the task, and on sharing information. The chairing of these meetings was rotated, to encourage everyone's participation; early on, explicit norms were established to discourage any individual from dominating the meetings. The core team had an assigned room (called the "war room") in which members could always meet. The walls of the "war room" were generously appointed with whiteboards and corkboards for posting schedules, meeting minutes, and any other pieces of information that needed to be shared. Also posted on the walls of the "war room" were a statement of the team's strategic objective, team slogans and values, and *The Deadline*. In addition to the "war room," several "design rooms" were assigned to the OJ-663 project.

Subteams were expected to meet daily during critical periods. In every way, subteam meetings were treated similarly to core team meetings. If possible, strategic objectives were stressed more in subteam meetings than in core team meetings, to ensure coordination and avoid horizontal misalignments.

Formal meetings were clearly the anchor of the OJ-663 project, but they were only half of the story. Informal meetings were popping up all the time, to deal with horizontal misalignments as they arose. In these informal meetings, strategic improvising was accomplished literally in real time.

Three factors made these informal meetings successful. First, because core team members were co-located, calling a meeting at a moment's notice was as easy as wandering down a corridor. Second, core team members had pagers to summon them to informal meetings when they were not in their offices. Finally, informal meetings, like formal meetings, were always held for a strategic purpose.

Search-and-Rescue Teams

Managers at companies that have moved to self-directed production teams have learned that, although team-based structures are in many ways more flexible than the assembly lines they replaced, they have less flexibility when a bottleneck hits. When a bottleneck occurs on an assembly line, workers beyond the bottleneck who are left with little to do can be shifted up the line to help correct the bottleneck.

The kinds of bottlenecks that people on an assembly line are so good at fixing seldom occur when individuals are organized into teams. Equipment failure, however, the most common cause of bottlenecks, is as likely to create serious temporal misalignments for production teams as for people on an assembly line. Moreover, because production teams and assembly lines are equally dependent on outside suppliers, another common bottleneck for production teams results from temporal misalignments with suppliers. The problem for production teams is not that they experience more bottlenecks than assembly lines, but that, when they do experience a bottleneck, they are seldom able to fix it by themselves. Human energy is wasted; team members end up sitting around and waiting for someone to fix a problem they cannot fix.

When temporal misalignments create bottlenecks for self-directed teams and they are unable to fix them by themselves, our strategic alignment tool-of-choice is *search-and-rescue teams*. Search-and-rescue teams are assigned to self-directed production teams. Like members of a volunteer fire department, search-and-rescue team members drop what they are doing and go to the rescue, when the production teams to which they are assigned experience bottlenecks. They search out the causes of bottlenecks, which are commonly temporal misalignments, then rescue production teams by figuring out a way to unplug the bottleneck.

At many production facilities, self-directed teams display flags to signal how they are doing: green flags mean they are on schedule; yellow flags indicate they are behind schedule but the work is still moving; red flags signal that production is stopped. As long as a green flag is displayed, search-and-rescue team members concentrate on their own work. When a yellow flag is raised, they are put on alert. Finally, with the posting of a red flag, they spring into action.

When we discussed temporal misalignments, we warned against removing all the slack from the timetables associated with highly complex, interdependent tasks, because friction is inevitable. We noted that it is better to accept the waste associated with minor misalignments than to risk major misalignments. Because search-and-rescue teams can move at a moment's notice to study the causes of temporal misalignments and can then work at restoring operations, organizations equipped with these teams can tighten things up more than organizations not equipped with them. It is still better to leave some slack in the system, to ensure smooth operations. Because search-and-rescue teams provide damage control for major temporal misalignments, individuals and teams can be encouraged to experiment more with tightening minor temporal misalignments.

EXTERNAL STRATEGIC ALIGNMENT

Businesses conserve human energy by aligning themselves internally. External alignments between businesses and their environments, however, are also critical to strategic improvising. Organizational capabilities and human energies are only valuable if they are aligned to existing or potential business opportunities.

A business with an advanced external strategic alignment process is Frito-Lay. The snack food giant, a division of PepsiCo, has been a pioneer in applying leading-edge information systems technologies to understanding its customers better—and more quickly than its competitors. Its 10,000 salespeople all carry hand-held computers that transfer information nightly to computers in Plano, Texas. This information is shared with delivery people, who are able to advise retailers about how to stock their shelves for more profitability.

Frito-Lay has learned from its experience that all information about customers is not created equal, and the importance of information depends on the business's current strategic objectives. Some information should be ignored because it is strategically unimportant. The result at Frito-Lay has been a businesswide effort to use strategic objectives to highlight a few critically important measures. The information they generate is then used to track progress toward the accomplishment of strategic objectives.

State-of-the-art management information systems, like Frito-Lay's, become precision tools for aligning a business to its external environment. When they are anchored to the business's strategy, they help people think strategically about external alignments and provide them with a way to keep their attention riveted on the information that matters most.

6 HEP TO THE JIVE: THE OUTER GAME OF STRATEGIC IMPROVISING

Hep to the Jive In common terms, aware, informed, or worldly-wise.

Andy Garcia, the founder of SeLaVi Corporation,[1] had a unique idea: he wanted to start a company to provide marketing services to new start-ups in the medical products industry. Garcia had over 20 years' experience selling disposable medical products to doctors and hospitals, and he believed he could leverage his know-how and industry connections in helping young companies grow.

Garcia traveled extensively for several months in search of new companies he could assist. He came close to cutting several deals, but always walked away empty-handed. Several medical products entrepreneurs acknowledged that he could help them, but they were reluctant to sign up—at least, under terms Garcia considered fair and reasonable.

At a point when Garcia was beginning to doubt himself and his original idea, a different kind of opportunity presented itself. The inventor of a luggage carrier that mounted on the back of vans and mini-vans heard about Garcia through a friend and approached him about marketing his product. Through their discussions, Garcia learned that the inventor was willing to enter into a royalty contract that would give Garcia exclusive rights to manufacture and sell the luggage carrier. Garcia jumped at the opportunity. The members of SeLaVi's board of directors cautioned him against the sudden move, but he maintained that the luggage carrier was

123

a "sure thing" that would quickly generate the cash flow needed to drive his original business plan.

That was over three years ago; to date, SeLaVi Corporation has sold only a handful of rear-mounted luggage carriers. The product has generated significant interest when shown at recreational vehicle and boat shows, but Garcia has been unable to develop a marketing and distribution system to sell the product. The major problem is that Garcia's understanding of marketing and distribution systems for disposable medical products did not transfer to the luggage carrier business. At every turn, there were obstacles that Garcia, with all his experience, had not previously encountered. He learned quickly how to overcome them but, in retrospect, there is no way he could have learned quickly enough. Although the opportunity was attractive, Garcia was not capable of exploiting it. He learned the hard way that the real value of opportunities depends on what a company can do with them.

Andy Garcia probably thought he had set a strategic direction for SeLaVi Corporation; at least, he had a vision of a new service and potential customers. However, he had not participated in a formal strategy clarification process. If he had, SeLaVi's strategic direction would have been more explicit and his decisions would have had more consistency and discipline. He would have declined the luggage carrier opportunity, realizing that it would take him in a very different strategic direction. Instead, he would have realized that if he wanted to create competitive advantage he needed to focus on opportunities that aligned with *his* unique capabilities.

A company's business concept establishes parameters for both the inner game (related to capabilities and human energy) and the outer game (related to opportunities and social responsibilities) of strategic improvising. A clear business concept also helps companies decide when the capabilities they have developed internally match opportunities available in the business environment. This is another dimension of the discipline provided by strategic improvising.

A clear business concept would have helped Andy Garcia understand that, although SeLaVi provided a service, it was *customer-focused:* only businesses interested in selling medical products to doctors and hospitals would find SeLaVi's services valuable. A customer-focused business looks straight ahead at customers. Environmental scanning is confined to a single class of customers. Its people learn everything about the relevant business environment through customers—including what they need to know about competitors.

Product-focused businesses concentrate on information about competitive products. They pay close attention to the activities of direct competitors so that they are not surprised or upended when new products hit the market. Related products developed by competitors may create new opportunities for product-focused businesses.

Technology-focused businesses look straight ahead for new opportunities to apply their technological know-how. They also look for opportunities to combine their technology with related technologies. The consistent purpose of their environmental scanning is to find ways to increase the leverage of existing technologies.

Because the business concept associated with *production-capacity-focused* businesses is less confining, they view the business environment through a wider-angle lens. They search for any developments in the business environment that would affect the shape of the demand curve for their products or the supply of inputs necessary for production. These might include any actions by customers, present and potential competitors, suppliers, and others, that affect their ability to move their product out the door.

THE OUTER GAME OF STRATEGIC IMPROVISING

Strategic improvising is a process for guiding strategic thrusts within a preestablished business concept, not a process for redefining the business concept. As seen in Figure 6–1, equal attention is paid to the inner game and the outer game of strategic improvising. The interactions that characterize strategic improvising, however, take place within directional parameters. Attractive business opportunities might redirect individual strategic thrusts, but they should not redefine the business concept.

This means that the goal of the outer game of strategic improvising is very different from the goal of industry and competitor analysis, which attempts to relate a business to its environment. Industry and competitor analysis leads to recommendations about positions in the industry where businesses can best defend themselves against competitive forces. The primary goal of the outer game of strategic improvising is more modest and, in our view, more realistic: to find and create opportunities in the relevant business environment that align with a business's existing capabilities.

Industry and competitor analysis attempts to provide an up-front, comprehensive picture of the business environment; the outer game of strategic improvising concentrates on real-time monitoring to provide

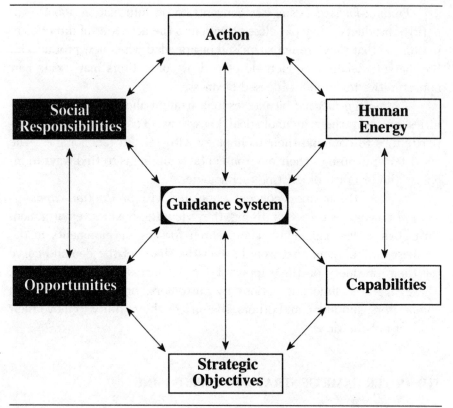

FIGURE 6–1. Opportunities, social responsibilities, and the strategic improvising model.

information about the *relevant* business environment. The outer game of strategic improvising has been influenced by the views of John Wooden, UCLA's legendary basketball coach, on scouting other teams. Wooden downplayed scouting reports because he wanted his players to focus on their strengths, not continually adjust to the strengths of competitors. He assumed that any necessary adjustments could be made during the game, in response to what the other team was doing. According to Wooden, such real-time adjustments were the essence of effective coaching.

What is relevant to businesses that practice strategic improvising is what is straight ahead of them. They are like race horses: without blinders on, they tend to look from side to side and get distracted. This affects their form, which, in turn, affects their speed of execution. The paradox of wearing blinders is that, by restricting their angle of vision, businesses actually improve visual acuity straight ahead.

An explicit business concept functions much like a set of blinders in the outer game of strategic improvising. When members of *self-directed teams* have their blinders on while they engage in strategic improvising, their energy is extremely concentrated. Moreover, they are able to get a detailed look at the competitive space directly in front of them.

Wearing blinders also has a downside. Because members of self-directed teams do not look from side to side, there is great potential for horizontal misalignments. Inevitably, self-directed teams act in ways that interfere with the work of other self-directed teams. The problem for members of self-directed teams who are wearing blinders is they do not see the interference coming as they are running at full speed. For this reason, it is necessary to play the outer game of strategic improvising as though it were a series of one- or two-furlong races punctuated by horizontal realignments. By stopping briefly and looking from side to side at what other self-directed teams are doing, strategic improvisers both correct and prevent horizontal misalignments.

Industry and competitor analysis is a highly sophisticated process performed by well-trained strategic planning staffs who serve top executives. Conversely, the outer game of strategic improvising relies on the wisdom of the masses. It is successful because many individuals and teams have their noses up against the glass, sensing and interpreting the environment. It also works because people actively share their learning about the environment with co-workers. In many respects, information about the business environment is like irrigation water—maximum benefit is realized only by spreading it around.

Because the outer game of strategic improvising involves a lot of people doing a lot of different things and inventing many of them in real time, it has many variations. There is no stock set of tools and techniques for playing the game. As with the strategic alignment process, we can only offer a starter set, knowing that people will find and invent their own sets of techniques. We have developed a starter set with techniques designed both for *finding* and *creating* business opportunities.

FINDING BUSINESS OPPORTUNITIES

The starter set contains four techniques for finding business opportunities—one technique is designed for each of the four types of businesses, as identified by their business focuses. The first technique, *acquiring a deep understanding of customers* helps customer-focused businesses play the outer game of strategic improvising. Product-focused businesses benefit from *high-frequency (low-impact) product introductions,* the second technique in the starter set. *The 15 percent solution,* the third technique, is specifically designed for technology-focused businesses. The final technique in the starter set, *entering new markets,* is designed for production-capacity-focused businesses.

Acquiring a Deep Understanding of Customers

This technique, designed for customer-focused businesses, is very helpful for finding opportunities in the business environment that align with current capabilities. A deep understanding of customers involves more than meeting customer needs. Customer-focused businesses must open their borders and invite customers in, then provide opportunities for employees to develop close relationships with them.

Hillenbrand is the parent corporation of the Batesville Casket Company, which is the largest producer of caskets in the world. Batesville has honed to perfection the technique of acquiring a deep understanding of customers.

Batesville owns Jawacdah Farms, a recreational property. In any given year, 10 to 15 percent of all the funeral directors in the world come to Jawacdah Farms and spend a week being wined, dined, and entertained by rotating groups of Batesville employees. A healthy dose of business is always mixed in with pleasure. As Batesville employees participate in activities with the visiting funeral directors, their conversations naturally drift to the funeral business and ways in which Batesville can better serve its already immensely loyal customers. In these informal conversations, funeral directors do not talk about the same things they would address on customer satisfaction surveys—timeliness, quality of product, and customer service, for example. Rather, they talk about how the funeral business could be improved, where they see the funeral business going in the future, and what they are looking for in future products and services. From these informal conversations, a deep understanding of customers develops—an understanding that makes Batesville's employees keenly aware of new and emerging opportunities in the casket business.

It was after participating in discussions with funeral directors at Jawacdah Farms that the management of Batesville Casket Company decided to go into the insurance business. The funeral directors were concerned about the spiraling costs of funerals. They wanted to offer potential patrons an insurance policy that guaranteed a certain kind of funeral. They believed such a policy had two major advantages. First, it was a unique product offering that would attract and secure more business. Second, it was a more delicate way to handle a sensitive time in the lives of surviving family members. Spiraling funeral costs were catching many survivors off-guard and were adding to the stress of losing a loved one. It would be unnecessary for funeral directors to discuss financial arrangements with owners of an insurance policy guaranteeing a certain kind of funeral.

Today, the Forethought Group, owned by the Batesville Casket Company, is the largest provider of funeral insurance in the world. Moving into the insurance business was a big step for a casket manufacturer, but the move was consistent with its customer-focused strategy. Pursuit of this opportunity required Batesville to acquire and develop a new set of capabilities, but some existing capabilities could be used because the company continued to serve the same group of customers.

High-Frequency (Low-Impact) Product Introductions

High-frequency (low-impact) product introductions rely on keeping the speed of iteration and cost of new products down. Each new product introduction varies one or more features of the product design, giving a product-focused business the chance to learn from the marketplace how it can better align internal capabilities with opportunities.

According to Gary Hamel and C. K. Prahalad, "[A] company with a 12-month iteration cycle will be able to close in on a potential market faster than one with a 36-month cycle." By keeping the costs of each new product introduction low, businesses are able to sustain a blistering pace. Toshiba, for example, has been able to explore every possible niche in the laptop computer market. Between 1986 and 1991, Toshiba launched 31 different laptop computers; by March 31, 1991, the company had discontinued 12 of them. In the process, Toshiba learned more about the laptop computer market than any of its competitors. Not only did the company have 19 successful laptop models—more than any of its competitors—it had dramatically improved its hit rate.[2]

An American company, not a Japanese company, is the champion at introducing rapid-fire products. Rubbermaid, the Wooster, Ohio, manufacturer of dish drainers, dust pans, and plastic containers, was voted the second most admired company in America in *Fortune's* 1991 and 1992 annual surveys. A major reason for Rubbermaid's most-admired status is the visibility it receives through its products. For example, Twin Valu, a Cleveland mass merchandiser, dedicates 10 of the 100 aisles in each of its stores to nothing but Rubbermaid products. Wal-Mart is experimenting with all-Rubbermaid selling areas in its stores. In 1992, Rubbermaid's goal is to introduce a new product *every day*.[3]

The rapidity with which new products can be introduced is different for every business. Compared with one of Rubbermaid's red soapdishes, it will always take a lot more time to develop, launch, accumulate market-place insights on, and then rework and relaunch one of Toshiba's laptop computers. Comparisons among businesses' speeds of interaction are only relevant within industries. However, all companies—including Rubbermaid and Toshiba—can pick up the pace of new product introduction. If a new product fails, what does it matter when it is only one of many? The important step is to get the product in the hands of customers and monitor carefully what happens. New products are like space probes: they send back up-close, detailed information about what was previously unknown. Some space probes fail, but others perform far beyond expectations. Even a failure can teach something important and increase the probability of future successes.

The 15 Percent Solution

This technique is designed for technology-focused companies playing the outer game of strategic improvising. At 3M, for example, research scientists can use up to 15 percent of their time on their own projects. Post-it Notes may be the most famous product developed under 3M's 15 percent solution, but it is one of hundreds of other successful products. The 15 percent solution works because it engages more people in the search for opportunities to use existing technological capability. In this way, technology-focused businesses gain maximum leverage from their technologies.

DuPont is another technology-focused company that employs the 15 percent solution. One of the technique's most dramatic successes involved Jay Daigle, a production worker, and Mal Smith, a research chemist, in the creation of a new business with potential annual sales of $200 million.

Jay Daigle decided to raise crayfish part-time, to provide some extra income for himself and his family. Raising crayfish took a lot more time than he had anticipated because none of the crayfish baits available on the market lasted more than a few hours. He constantly needed to reset his traps. His problem, however, gave Daigle an idea: Why couldn't DuPont's polymer technology be used to create a binder that would make crayfish bait last longer? Daigle contacted Mal Smith to help him with his idea.

Smith thought Daigle's idea had merit, and he decided to bootleg the project under DuPont's 15 percent solution. Smith began to experiment with different polymer-bonded crayfish baits in the lab and received encouraging initial results. When Smith had developed a bait that lasted five to seven days under a variety of conditions, he and Daigle decided to share their idea with Smith's supervisor and others at DuPont. Initially, people were skeptical. But when Smith and Daigle explained that the popularity of Cajun cooking had created a tremendous demand for crayfish and discussed the size of the potential market for the bait, people started to get interested. Smith and Daigle were given funding and permission to form a team to pursue the project.

After several months of field-testing the product, Smith and Daigle approached DuPont's Agricultural Products Group to propose that the bait be marketed. The Agricultural Products Group, however, concluded that crayfish bait did not fit into its product line. Smith and Daigle decided to pursue an alternative path. They made large quantities of the bait and began giving it away to crayfish farmers in order to create demand. Word that farmers badly wanted the bait eventually came back to the Agricultural Products Group through DuPont's sales representatives. People from the Agricultural Products Group approached Smith and Daigle and asked to join their team. The success of DuPont's long-lasting crayfish bait has led to the development of new baits (also using polymer technology) for the crab and lobster industries. DuPont's 15 percent solution allowed two employees to test a unique application of the company's technological know-how and eventually to align it with a huge new business opportunity.

Entering New Markets

Production-capacity-focused businesses are highly efficient operations that attempt to run as close to full capacity as possible. They are driven by market demand because no matter how efficient they become, they must still have a market for their products. There are two basic approaches for finding new business opportunities available to production-capacity-focused businesses.[4] The direct approach is by entering new markets; the indirect approach involves making improvements in process technologies that will lower prices, increase quality, or decrease time-to-market, thereby enabling businesses to enter new market segments.

Vanport Manufacturing, a small lumber company located 30 miles outside of Portland, Oregon, used both the direct and indirect approaches to enter the Japanese finished lumber market. The only thing Vanport had going for it in its conquest of the Japanese market was that it had no choice—the company's future was jeopardized by federal regulations prohibiting the cutting of whole logs from national forests for shipment to Japan. The company's survival depended on sales of finished lumber to Japanese lumbermen and construction firms. The only way to enter the Japanese market, however, was to satisfy Japan's finicky customers by cutting lumber to exacting traditional Japanese specifications. According to Adolf Hertrich, Vanport's co-owner and CEO, the decision was simple: "We could go out of business, or we could remodel our sawmill to meet their [Japanese customers'] needs."[5]

Hertrich led the charge by traveling extensively throughout Japan to meet with potential customers and inspect the facilities of Japanese lumber suppliers. He took pictures and careful notes at each facility he visited. When he returned to Oregon, he involved everyone in redesigning the mill from head saw to edger to trim saw. Vanport's log carriage was computerized to accommodate metric measurements, and company foremen were instructed by Japanese specialists on the complex lumber-grading systems that are based on such aesthetic factors as color and graining.

It took Vanport's people two years to become fully confident about impressing potential Japanese customers. To make their point, they built a traditional Japanese guest house from their own lumber and invited overseas guests to spend the night there.

Vanport's strategy has paid handsome dividends. While many local mills are idle, Vanport's 170 nonunion workers labor at double shifts. Once it entered the Japanese finished lumber market, the production-capacity-focused company found plenty of opportunities. Today, 90 percent of its business comes from Japanese customers.

CREATING BUSINESS OPPORTUNITIES

In addition to *finding* opportunities, businesses can use their imagination to *create* opportunities that align to their present capabilities. It is difficult to keep secret the best places to find opportunities. Businesses with focused strategies are a step ahead of their competitors, but they will always be pursued or travel in a pack when they choose a strategic direction that is opportunity-rich.

David Maister, a consultant to professional services firms, tells a story that shows how strategic plans inevitably lead firms to swarm in areas that are opportunity-rich. He had an opportunity to examine the strategic plans of most of the major competitors in a given professional service area. Each firm, after performing a thorough analysis of the marketplace, had identified which client industries were most attractive, based on factors such as growth, profitability, and need for services, and which services were most in demand among these large clients. Each firm had written a strategic plan stating: "Our strategy is to target the following clients in the following designated industries and serve them with the following key services." What shocked Maister was that every firm had exactly the same list of target clients, industries, and key services.[6]

A second problem is that opportunities go in cycles. It is difficult for a business to choose a strategic direction that will always have enough opportunities to sustain it. At Hughes Aircraft, for example, people talk about the way things used to be in the defense industry and compare them to the way things are. In the good old days, almost anything the company did hit a window of opportunity. Presently, the talk is about doing everything they possibly can to ensure success and still missing the target as often as they hit it.

The number of opportunities can vary significantly during different business cycles. In the defense industry, sustained periods of peace, combined with pressures to reduce the federal deficit, create significant pressures to reduce the number of opportunities available to defense contractors. The opportunity structure would change overnight, however, if a war were to break out.

Businesses that possess the ability to create opportunities are less vulnerable to the cyclical nature of business opportunities. They become the masters of their own fate.

Four techniques for creating business opportunities can be added to the starter set of techniques for playing the outer game of strategic improvising. Like the techniques for finding business opportunities, the techniques for creating business opportunities are designed for businesses with a specific business focus. The techniques are:

1. Creating new customer demand (customer-focused businesses);

2. Redefining products (product-focused businesses);

3. Expanding the portfolio of technical capabilities (technology-driven businesses);

4. Benchmarking noncompetitors (production-capacity-focused businesses).

Creating New Customer Demand

Customer-focused businesses define their strategic direction in terms of serving a specific group of customers. Their principal technique for creating new business opportunities involves creating new demand among existing customers. It is important that the principle of mutual self-interest guide the use of this technique. Customer-focused businesses will eventually destroy the good will existing between themselves and their customers unless their self-interest is secondary to an interest in how new products and services benefit customers.

One of the best examples of a business that created new opportunities by creating new customer demand is seen in the relationship between Pitney Bowes Inc. and the United States Postal Service (USPS). The USPS has tried for 30 years to avoid fostering a private-sector monopoly, but it has been unable to break Pitney's lock on the postage-meter business. The fact is: Pitney Bowes and the USPS need each other.[7]

Pitney creates new customer demand by influencing the USPS's strategy. The major reason for Pitney's ability to do this is its incredible attentiveness to the USPS. Pitney employs a full-time director of postal relations in a Washington office a block from USPS headquarters. The director's sole responsibility is to get all the information possible about the USPS, to prevent any surprises. The director of postal relations is so effective that some USPS officials admit to initially hearing about internal USPS matters through Pitney's Washington office.

Realizing that the USPS was pushing efficiency, Pitney created new opportunities by transforming the postage business into a mailing business. The company developed new "smart" mailing systems that print, fold, and stuff envelopes; weigh each piece of mail; and print out appropriate postage. Some systems even "read" addresses against data bases for accuracy; others help a company centralize accounting of mailing costs.

Pitney also saved the USPS $3.3 million annually with its "remote meter reset" systems, which enable postage meters to be refilled with postage over telephone lines. In the process, and in spite of the USPS's intention to do otherwise, Pitney created a new market for itself that it serviced uncontested for nearly a decade.

One of the keys to the success of Pitney Bowes is that it has never been content to rest on its laurels or on the strength of its current relationship with the USPS. It is continuously trying to improve itself *and* the USPS. Despite remarkable success between 1986 and 1990, Pitney raised R&D outlays an average of 15 percent annually. The company acquired 103 patents in 1990, compared with 69 in 1986. These patents both directly and indirectly benefited the USPS because they improved overall efficiency and lowered costs. One postal official has admitted: "There is no stomach here to fight Pitney Bowes. Ours is an extensive and wide-ranging relationship. We don't want to jeopardize it."

Redefining Products

Figure 6–2 illustrates how product definitions develop naturally. In the beginning, the definition of a product is open—it diverges, testing the limits of a chosen strategic direction. In time, however, a product definition closes as a dominant definition emerges. When this happens, product-focused businesses use little imagination in creating opportunities; based on tradition they pursue only those opportunities that are straight down the middle. When businesses break free of tradition by redefining the business they are in and the products they produce, new opportunities are created. As Figure 6–2 illustrates, these opportunities can come about through natural overlaps with related products and industries, which occur as strategic directions diverge.

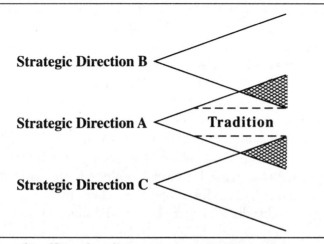

FIGURE 6–2. The effect of tradition on strategic improvising.

The National Basketball Association under the leadership of David Stern is a classic example of a business that turned itself around by continuing to produce essentially the same product, but redefining it. Before Stern became commissioner, the NBA was on the ropes. During the 1980–1981 season, 16 of the 23 NBA teams lost money, and overall attendance was averaging only 58 percent of capacity. Finances were so bad that, in 1982, a committee was established to study how the NBA would survive if it were to lose up to six nonviable teams.[8]

Stern redefined the NBA as part of the entertainment business. According to Detroit Pistons guard Isiah Thomas: "David [Stern] came in and looked at the NBA and saw something more than just sports. It's really just entertainment. It's a Michael Jackson tour, a Rolling Stones tour. He saw it as an NBA tour." One of the models that Stern used, to help NBA owners rethink the business, was Disney. "They have theme parks," Stern told the NBA owners, "and we have theme parks. Only we call them arenas. They have characters: Mickey Mouse, Goofy. Our characters are named Magic [Johnson] and Michael [Jordan]. Disney sells apparel; we sell apparel. They make home videos; we make home videos."

David Stern is also creating new opportunities for the NBA by redefining it as an international, not a national, product. The Seattle SuperSonics and Houston Rockets, for example, opened the 1992–1993 basketball season with games in Tokyo and Yokohama, Japan. Currently, the 60-minute, 90-minute, and uncut versions of the NBA Game of the Week are sent to over 77 countries. The NBA even televises 10 games a year in China. The performances of the Dream Team in the 1992 Summer Olympic Games further expanded the NBA's exposure on the international scene, and supported its claim of offering the best basketball in the world. Stern is also planning the McDonald's Open, modeled after soccer's World Cup, in which the NBA champions will compete against the champions from every other major league in the world.

Stern's efforts to redefine the NBA and create new opportunities have had fabulous bottom-line results. Under Stern's leadership, the NBA has broken its attendance record for eight straight years. Gross annual revenue, which includes gate receipts and TV money, soared 437 percent, from $160 million to $700 million. The average worth of an NBA franchise has more than tripled, from $20 million in the early 1980s to $65 million a decade later. NBA Properties, which handles all licensing of NBA-logo merchandise, generated over $1 billion in gross retail sales in 1991.

Expanding the Portfolio of Technical Capabilities

A technology-focused business is a composite of its portfolio of technical capabilities. Some of its technical capabilities may be unique; others are not. The uniqueness and value of each technical capability, however, matters much less than the uniqueness and value of the entire portfolio. For example, 3M leverages a portfolio of widely shared technical capabilities in substrates, coatings, and adhesives into an extensive range of products that include magnetic tape, coated abrasives, photographic film, pressure-sensitive tapes, and, of course, Post-it Notes. Interaction effects are associated with technology-focused businesses. What creates competitive advantage is the technical leverage generated when technical capabilities are mixed together.

This interaction suggests another technique for creating new opportunities; it involves a little more give-and-take between opportunities and capabilities than other techniques. The idea is to exercise existing technical capabilities by mixing them with other, preferably easily accessible, technical capabilities so that new opportunities can be created for technology-focused businesses.

Kodak realized that the future of its core business—manipulating images—lay as much in electronics technology as in film technology. Because many of the leading electronics labs were concentrated in Tokyo suburbs, the U.S. company decided to build a research facility there. Kodak hired internationally known researchers and recruited young graduates of first-rate universities like the Tokyo Institute of Technology.[9]

Full-scale operation of Kodak's Japan Center began in October 1988. The primary mission of the research facility is to acquire technological building blocks in electronics and materials science. Today, Japan is the center of Kodak's worldwide efforts in molecular beam epitaxy, a method of growing crystals for making gallium arsenide chips. Also, Kodak's Japan Center has developed a system, now being sold worldwide, for sending fax images to multiple locations directly from a computer.

According to Tom Kelly, the head of Kodak's Japan Center, the company's move to Japan literally opened the floodgates of technical information. By moving into Japan, the company learned that it is actually easier to gather technical information in Japan than in the United States. Japanese companies announce new technical developments in both the popular press and the trade press faster and more consistently than U.S. companies do. Moreover, Kodak's people receive a constant flow of technical information when they are out drinking or playing tennis with friends from university days or from previous employers, customers, and even competitors. When interpreted through the lenses of Kodak's technology-focused strategy, this technical information creates many focused opportunities for the company.

Benchmarking Noncompetitors

We have consulted with several production-capacity-focused businesses in the oil and gas, chemicals, and forest products industries. This may not be our favorite business focus, but it is often the only one available to businesses that have operated for many years in capital-intensive, mature industries. It is simply too risky and too expensive for some production-capacity-focused businesses to pursue other strategic options.

Production-capacity-focused businesses present special challenges when we try to improve how they play the outer game of strategic improvising. Because they emphasize efficiency so much in their headlong pursuit of production capacity, they neglect effectiveness. This creates a built-in resistance to change and often means that they are out of touch with their industry's changing opportunity structure. Even when current patterns of operating create significant competitive disadvantage, production-capacity-focused businesses are reluctant to change them.

Competitor benchmarking is a well-known technique for unfreezing organizations. It provides the impetus to improve competitive necessities, such as quality, speed, and service. At Xerox, for example, every department is expected to find the competing company or organizational unit that performs its function the best. The competitor's performance level then becomes the target for the Xerox unit.[10] The problem with competitive benchmarking is that the search for best practices is often confined to the industry in which the business operates. Accordingly, it is a technique for catching up to competitors, not surpassing them. Moreover, the scope of potential changes is limited because there is less variation in the practices of businesses within industries than across industries.

In recent years, we have experimented with a modification of the technique—*benchmarking noncompetitors*—that creates new opportunities for production-capacity-focused businesses by opening the eyes of their managers to new possibilities. For example, we have taken people from Amoco to visit Champion International, and people from Intel to visit 3M and Dow Chemical. We have discovered that benchmarking noncompetitors has some definite advantages over benchmarking competitors. The most obvious advantage is that businesses are more eager to share information with noncompetitors than with direct competitors. Competitors may be able to study each other from a distance; learning between noncompetitors can be up-close-and-personal.

Observing how noncompetitors operate also encourages businesses to think outside the established practices of their industry. (This is especially true of noncompetitors that have chosen the same strategic option.) New opportunities are created by unfreezing thinking. Something that was previously viewed as either impossible or impractical is seen in a different or more attractive light.

Perhaps the most substantial benefit derived from benchmarking noncompetitors is that most of a noncompetitor's best practices do not translate perfectly across industry boundaries. They cannot be imitated verbatim. The ideas that businesses gain from noncompetitors, therefore, function like sparks that ignite further thinking. Businesses create new opportunities by adapting the ideas of noncompetitors to their particular circumstances. This, in turn, increases their ownership of the ideas and deepens their commitment to them.

DETECTING BACKGROUND NOISE

There is more to the outer game of strategic improvising than finding and creating business opportunities to align to current capabilities. In the long run, it is inevitable that fundamental shifts in industry structures will make existing capabilities obsolete and require the creation of new capabilities. For businesses to anticipate these fundamental shifts, individuals and teams must engage in detecting the background noises that foretell of major structural changes.

Detecting background noise is an important activity, but its importance is secondary to finding and creating business opportunities. The primary focus of the outer game of strategic improvising must be real-time developments. Accordingly, formal, labor-intensive, and time-consuming techniques are not recommended. Instead, we recommend two techniques that involve widespread sensing of the environment, forums for discussion of *relevant* information, and the use of a strategy filter in determining what information is relevant. We call these techniques: *listening for the winds of change* and *collecting weak signals*.

Listening for the Winds of Change

Before Fletcher Byrom left Koppers, a business he had led during the 1960s and 1970s, he proposed nine commandments in a message for his successor. The second commandment was: Listen for the winds of change. Byrom was a vocal critic of long-range planning, but he believed in doing it. Koppers used regression formulas, input–output matrices, and other tools as part of a sophisticated long-range planning process. However, planning at Koppers was a discipline more than it was a guide to future decision making. It was used as a thinking process to help Koppers people to understand the environment better and to recognize both Type I and Type II planning errors—unanticipated changes that did happen and anticipated changes that did not happen. According to Byrom:

> As a regimen, as a discipline for a group of people, planning is very valuable. My position is, go ahead and plan, but once you've done your planning, put it on the shelf. Don't be bound by it. Don't use it as a major input in the decision-making process. Use it mainly to recognize change as it takes place.[11]

Byrom believed long-range planning was one way of listening to the winds of change—it was a tool for anticipating fundamental shifts in the business environment.

During his years at Koppers, Byrom also championed a less formal method of listening for the winds of change. After spending one or two years at the company, young managers became eligible to participate in a Koppers seminar program: "A general survey of the nation and the world, past, present, and future, as seen from the fifteenth floor of the Koppers building." A wide variety of ideas were discussed in the Koppers seminar program, but they were always brought back and made relevant to Koppers's present and future business challenges.

There were 25 people scheduled for each seminar group, and Koppers would start about three groups each year. During the first year of the seminar, Byrom assumed the role of discussion leader for the seminar groups; in subsequent years, other senior executives took the lead. Sessions lasted about three hours and were held monthly. Participants were assigned to read one or two books in preparation for each session. During the sessions, discussions centered on world environments, world forces, and the struggle and tension of the world's economy. By thinking, reading, talking, and listening, seminar participants gained deep insights about the business environment in which Koppers operated.

Russell Ackoff, a well-known sage, strategist, and former professor at the Wharton School of Management, is another advocate of listening for the winds of change by thinking, reading, and talking. Ackoff tells a story about having dinner with the CEO of a major corporation. The CEO asked him the name of the last book he had read. Ackoff told him, and they discussed it for a while. Then the CEO asked about the book he had read before the last and they discussed it also. After the third request, Ackoff asked the CEO to explain his interest in books and ideas. The CEO told Ackoff that he did a great deal of reading "on his own time" but had no one to discuss it with at work. He observed that his colleagues read little that was not immediately relevant to their work and that discussion of his reading *at work* made him feel guilty because he assumed it would be perceived as unproductive.[12]

Ackoff later shared this discussion with several of the CEO's associates and discovered that they did a great deal of reading "on their own time," but also felt it inappropriate to discuss the books at work. They expressed interest in organizing periodic "brown-bag lunches" at which they could hold such discussions, but none of them was willing to take the initiative. Ackoff concluded: "What a pity that so many managers indulge in such self-deprivation and maintain a state of intellectual undernourishment."

During a recent trip to the Ground Systems Group of Hughes Aircraft, we observed an environment in which the need to think about, read, and discuss ideas is given genuine support, not just lip service. One of the reasons for this support is the Hughes culture, in which education is highly valued and managers with PhDs are addressed as "Doctor." In one division, the excitement for ideas is more directly traced to an assistant division manager who "always has a new book under his arm," and openly shares with colleagues the new ideas he reads and thinks about. In another division, the division manager is enrolled in a PhD program and is hungry to discuss with colleagues the new ideas he is reading and thinking about. These managers do not initiate random, aimless discussions; they always apply ideas to the challenges faced at Hughes. This is why it is appropriate, in both divisions, to make "company" time available for thinking about and discussing ideas. Discussions inevitably lead to a broadly shared, highly sophisticated understanding of the business environment in which the Ground Systems Group operates.

Collecting Weak Signals

Hillenbrand's people sense background noise by collecting weak signals in the business environment. Each person has a weak-signal "pot" in which is collected any piece of information that is believed to have some relevance to the company's business at some future time. Hillenbrand sponsors forums in which people share the weak signals they have collected. The forums help Hillenbrand's people translate diverse pieces of information into relevant and integrated insights about the business environment.

One advantage of collecting weak signals is the widespread employee involvement it fosters. Everyone needs to know Hillenbrand's strategic direction in order to collect relevant weak signals. Moreover, the thought process by which relevant signals are differentiated from irrelevant signals helps fine-tune strategic direction.

Another advantage of collecting weak signals is its anticipatory nature. It encourages people always to be forecasting fundamental shifts in the business environment and gives them time to develop new capabilities to align with changing opportunity structures. People resist changes that are thrust on them—even changes that they would normally embrace. Conversely, when people have time to think about the reasons for changing and to devise different means of accomplishing change, they move out in front of change and run interference for it.

CORPORATE SOCIAL RESPONSIBILITIES

Managers are responsible to many stakeholders, all of whom exert multiple pressures on them. The issue of corporate *social responsibilities* is not one that lends itself to easy, straightforward answers. Ultimately, however, every manager must ask herself or himself: "To whom am I responsible, and for what?"

Michael Jensen, a Harvard Business School professor, reminds managers that they are the agents of stockholders. At a basic level, Jensen is right. Public corporations are economic institutions owned by stockholders. Managers should be expected to operate a business as a business: the short-term and long-term profitability of the corporation should be their foremost concern. If companies fail to make adequate profits, they go out of business and nobody's interests are served.

Business corporations, however, are also important threads holding together the fabric of society. They are another form of human enterprise, which has prompted Anita Roddick, the managing director of The Body Shop, a chain of eco-conscious cosmetic stores headquartered in Little-hampton, England, to ask:

> Why should we expect and accept *less* from it [business] than we do from ourselves and our neighbors? . . . The idea of business . . . is not to lose money. But to focus all the time on profits, profits, profits—I have to say I think it's deeply boring.[13]

Once managers decide to whom they are responsible, it is important that they respond. In many cases, a key factor is how quickly they respond. There is no reason to believe that strategic improvisers operate at a higher level of social responsibility than strategic planners, but there is a distinct difference in their *social responsiveness*. Strategic plans create a one-track, goal-oriented mind-set that is not easily interrupted. Like the passersby in the parable of the Good Samaritan, strategic planners are so intent on getting to their destination that they ignore a calamity on the side of the road.

Strategic improvisers are less programmed. Like the Good Samaritan, they are able to interrupt ongoing activity in order to respond to critical needs. Strategic improvising facilitates greater social responsiveness because companies do not need to complete a planning cycle before responding to emerging social needs. This flexibility translates into fewer incidences of benign neglect.

There has been a lot of talk in recent years about the profession of management: managers want to be considered professionals on a par with doctors, dentists, and lawyers. One of the fundamental characteristics that distinguishes professionals from nonprofessionals is their allegiance to a code of conduct. For different groups of professionals, the codes of conduct differ, but all of them devote significant attention to public service and social welfare. If managers are to become professionals, in the traditional sense, their *social responses* need to involve more public service and promote more social welfare.

We categorize social responses along two dimensions:

1. *Behavior.* Does a person's or a business's behavior contribute to the welfare of society?

2. *Motive.* Is the purpose behind a social response directed at doing good or at looking good?

Social responses that are socially acceptable fit somewhere along a continuum. At one end are actions that persons are not ashamed to tell their families they are taking; at the other end are actions they want to stand up and shout about because they are so proud of what they are doing.

The minimum requirement of socially acceptable corporate behavior was introduced to us by Fletcher Byrom, the former chairman of Koppers. Byrom wrote in a letter to Koppers employees:

> The dictates of conscience for a person with a family might be to think whether you would be happy to tell your spouse and children or other family members the details of the actions you are contemplating. If you would not want to do so, Koppers would not want you to take the action.[14]

There are a lot of business actions that individuals may be willing to describe to their families, but would not want broadcast outside their homes.

The other end of the continuum is an extension of Byrom's statement to a higher level of social acceptability. When people provide products or services that are truly needed and furnish tremendous societal benefit, they want to tell everyone about them.

The second dimension, dealing with motive, differentiates social responses taken in order to look good from those intended to do good. A politician we know speaks of the lower road and the higher road to voter approval. Politicians who take the lower road anticipate what the voters want, and then run out ahead so that they appear to be leading public opinion. On the higher road are politicians who vote their conscience: they do what they believe is right whether or not it conforms to public opinion. Politicians on the lower road are only concerned about looking good to their constituency; the principal concern of politicians on the higher road is doing good.

Typically, when the purpose of companies' social responses is to look good, they respond only when pressures from external interest groups might make them look bad. For example, when a steel mill sends out press releases announcing installation of new antipollution equipment, it is usually in response to pressures from environmental groups and the EPA. The steel mill is attempting to neutralize the effect of negative press and avoid further regulation and penalties through its actions. If the pressure and potential embarrassment were lifted, the steel mill would likely behave in a less socially responsible manner.

The purpose behind many companies' social responses is to do good. The Body Shop, for example, built a soap factory in a poverty-stricken section of Glasgow, Scotland, with the explicit purpose of providing jobs for local people, some of whom had been unemployed for over 10 years. Days Inn hires homeless people to answer telephones at its corporate reservations center. Corning, Inc. acquires and rehabilitates commercial properties, then tries to make them available to minority tenants. All these companies are quite open about their social agendas, and, naturally, they come away looking good in the business press. They are perceived as examples to other companies, not publicity seekers, because their social responses begin with a firm commitment to improve the communities in which their business is located.

Figure 6–3 represents the two dimensions that define corporate social responses. It is important to realize that all four categories of social response represented in Figure 6–3 are socially responsible, but some are more responsible than others. When a company's social responses are concentrated in quadrant 1 of Figure 6–3, issues of social responsibility are exercising great influence on the outer game of strategic improvising. The

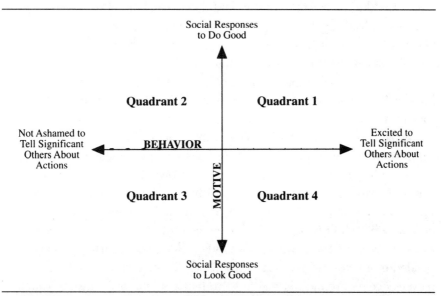

FIGURE 6–3.   Quadrants of corporate social responses.

motive is a desire to do good, not just look good, and people are behaving with excitement and energy—they want to talk about their socially responsible actions.

Social responses always have a *social impact;* in some instances, the social impact is significant. The Body Shop's social agenda is long and decidedly liberal. Its franchisees have contributed hundreds of thousands of dollars to defend the native inhabitants of the Amazon rain forest. It has worked to save the whales and to free political dissidents. The company has helped many communities in developing countries by setting them up as suppliers under a program it calls Trade Not Aid. The Body Shop has also contributed to countless community projects by expecting all its employees to contribute at least one hour a week—which is paid and on company time—to community service.

Another company whose social responses have carried significant social impact is Corning, Inc. The company has made significant progress toward its goal of making life in upstate New York more attractive to minorities. For example, it has increased minority employment in local stores and has persuaded the cable-TV operator in its area to offer the Black Entertainment Television channel. Corning also plays roles as benefactor, landlord, and social engineer in Corning, New York (population: 12,000). It is half-owner of a racetrack, sponsors a professional golf tournament, and has funded such amenities as a hotel, museum, and library. The company provides affordable housing and day care. Through its Corning Enterprises subsidiary, Corning spearheads community investments to bring 200 new jobs to the Chemung River valley each year, making the region less dependent on its headquarters and 15 factories.[15]

Positive social impact does not automatically improve a business's bottom line, but there are several examples of definite benefits to being socially responsible. Corning, by improving circumstances for minorities, has expanded its labor pool. Harley Davidson's efforts to raise money for the Muscular Dystrophy Association balance the company's "tough guy" image and attract new customers. Harley owners are more easily portrayed as patriotic Americans with soft hearts than as members of motorcycle gangs. Zion's First National Bank's Annual Employee Paintathon not only benefits Utah widows with a new coat of paint on their houses, but, as executives do the painting alongside tellers, the bank's employees are bonded more closely together. At the Body Shop, a similar bonding of employees occurs around helping to solve major social problems by using the company's resources to come up with *real* answers.

THE FINAL COMPONENT

Several of our colleagues are highly critical of microeconomics-based competitive strategies that concentrate on finding favorable positions for businesses to operate within industries, but underestimate the value of internal organizational capabilities and the challenges associated with their development. These colleagues make the point that analysis that leads to favorable positioning within an industry can prevent a business from being "dumb," but only by focusing on the development of internal capabilities do businesses become "smart." Accordingly, they recommend that businesses compete from the inside out.

An understanding of the outer game of strategic improvising depolarizes this thinking. By focusing on aligning opportunities and capabilities, both perspectives become important. What is really "dumb" is getting caught up in a debate over the comparative value of two strategic perspectives—inside-out and outside-in—when it is the tension between them that creates an effective strategy.

Recent events at WordPerfect Corporation illustrate this point. For several years, WordPerfect closed itself off to the software industry. Its neighbor, Novell, was very connected and very active in the affairs of the industry. WordPerfect kept its distance. The company was not necessarily resting on its laurels, but it had chosen to compete exclusively from the inside out. This led to the development of a very effective international product development strategy, the addition of PlanPerfect™ and DrawPerfect™ to its software line, and new versions of its popular word-processing software. The U.S. software market, however, was experiencing a fundamental shift toward platform-based, integrated software. Microsoft, the developer of WORD,™ WordPerfect's principal competitor, was leading the charge with its WINDOWS™ platform. Long before WordPerfect realized what was happening, the opportunity structure of the software industry had been dramatically altered, and WordPerfect began to lose significant market share to Microsoft WORD.

Recently, WordPerfect appeared to wake up to the importance of competing outside-in. It realized that it needed to open its borders and develop closer ties to other software producers. At highly visible gatherings in San Francisco and New York, it announced new cooperative agreements and a small acquisition. Unfortunately, there was no indication that WordPerfect had clarified its strategy enough to play the outer game of strategic improvising.

The concern with WordPerfect is that it will overreact to having been closed and will open its borders to every opportunity that comes along. By moving from competing inside-out to competing outside-in, the company will miss the significant benefits of competing both ways.

In a sense, information about opportunities and a way of thinking about social responsibilities complete the input requirements for strategic improvising. When they are combined with an understanding of organizational capabilities and human energy, businesses have everything they require to think and act strategically. Recent experiences at WordPerfect, however, suggest that businesses still need a way of guiding their strategic thoughts and actions. The final component needed to make strategic improvising fully operational is a guidance system that balances the inner game and the outer game of strategic improvising.

7

AIN'T MISBEHAVIN':
REAL-TIME MEASUREMENT
AND INFORMATION
SYSTEMS

Ain't Misbehavin' A composition by Fats Waller, with words by
Andy Razaf, that Louis Armstrong introduced in "Connie's Inn Hot
Chocolates," a 1929 revue; more recently, an immensely successful
Broadway musical.

Jack Welch, GE's CEO, tells a story about how the North American Division of GE Appliances invited managers from a Japanese competitor to visit for a few weeks. The Japanese contingent thoroughly analyzed the business; at the end of the visit, they presented their observations. The Japanese began by praising the North American Division for its world-class measurement and information system. They expressed awe at the amount of detailed information that was available, and the speed at which the information could be processed. In fact, they held the North American Division up as a model for others who might aspire to such a system. Their final comments, however, revealed their true feelings: notwithstanding their awe, the Japanese team could not figure out why anyone would want such a system.

We do not know why the Japanese questioned the North American Division's formal, centralized measurement and information system, but we have several questions of our own about such systems. What is the role of the system designers? Do they use technology in a disciplined or an undisciplined manner? Some designers use technology for technology's sake. They fail to consider a business's strategic direction when they are deciding whether one technology is better than another. Businesses store

149

much more information than they need, when they have no way of differentiating between useful and useless information. Ultimately, this lack of discipline leads to a need for greater capacity. As the capacity of the system expands, it becomes increasingly difficult to synthesize vast amounts of stored information.

A system that does something that no other system can do is certainly unique, but not necessarily valuable. The value of a system is based on the contributions it makes to a business's strategic objectives. The best measurement and information systems concentrate on what is strategically important.

There is also a cart-before-the-horse kind of problem when measurement and information systems function independent of strategy. At a mid-size, urban law firm, the principal measure of productivity (and the basis for compensation) is an attorney's billable hours. There are five ways in which this system of measuring productivity undermines attempts at the firm to promote the interdependent teamwork needed to support its customer-focused strategy:

1. Rainmakers (attorneys who develop their own clients) hoard legal work, especially when work is scarce, instead of going out and finding new clients.

2. Little cross-selling of work is done with current clients, because rainmakers refuse to share clients.

3. The growth and development of junior partners and associates is stifled, because they are denied direct contact with important clients.

4. The firm's strategic direction is fragmented, because senior partners see themselves as individual contributors who are only responsible for defining direction for their own practice areas.

5. Little attention is given to providing strategic direction for the firm, because members of the executive committee either bring work to do during their meetings or schedule their time so tightly that they need to leave meetings, to keep appointments with clients, before important issues are resolved.

The maxim—what you measure is what you get—certainly applies here. A measurement and information system that is aligned to strategy encourages individuals and teams to work in support of the strategy. They realize that what is noticed and ultimately rewarded is what contributes to the accomplishment of strategic objectives.

Another question can be raised about the role of the controller and staff. When a problem occurs, is it caused by the information being provided by the system or by the way the information is being collected and used? Often, the controller and staff forget their support role, make unrealistic demands on line managers, and, as a result, impede the accomplishment of core work. Measurement and information systems provide value-added support, but they do not involve core work. Accordingly, it is a mistake to give them the same attention and time as core work. By getting bogged down in detailed measurement and information systems, businesses can miss the bigger picture provided by their strategic direction.

At a large Texas-based chemical company, the Corporate Analytical Center, an arm of the corporate controller's office, serviced all the measurement and information needs of several plants. The Center appeared to be performing a value-added support role for the plants, and most of its work was done in response to requests from the plants. Employees at the Center, however, had chronic problems with absenteeism, low morale, racism, and sexism. There had even been a few instances of apparent sabotage.

The Center's manager decided to reorganize his people into self-directed teams and hired us to help with the redesign effort. First, we gathered some information about the service the Center provided to the plants. We were surprised to discover that the plants were using only about one-third of the information contained in reports issued by the Center. This was not necessarily the Center's fault. It was standard operating procedure for the plants to request a full report, even though their information needs were quite specific. It became increasingly clear that a lot of effort was being wasted because the plants did not know how to request specific information from the Center. A redefinition of the role of the Center's employees was recommended: they needed to spend less time preparing standardized reports and more time consulting with plants about ways to fill their specific information needs.

The study ultimately led to a decision to discontinue the Corporate Analytical Center and to transfer the analysts to individual plants. A few of the Center's analysts were retained in the corporate controller's office because their work required extremely expensive equipment, but over 70 percent of the costs associated with running the Center were either eliminated at the corporate level or allocated to the plants. Moreover, morale problems disappeared when analysts were transferred to the plants and were able to establish closer client relationships.

The most remarkable fact about the decision to discontinue the Corporate Analytical Center is that it was made by the Center's employees. Given access to information about problems with the current system, they made a tough, company-minded decision. In fact, their decision was much more radical than any of the suggestions that their managers had been willing to make. This example raises a third potential concern about formal, centralized measurement and information systems: in addition to providing the wrong information, do the systems put information into the wrong hands for the wrong use?

Most measurement and information systems are designed to support the top-down, "plan and control" model of management. In essence, measurement and information systems are tools used by top managers to track progress, promote accountability, and ensure that businesses operate according to plan. Nevertheless, there is a fundamental problem associated with using measurement and information systems to control behavior. Armen Alchian and Harold Demsetz, two institutional economists, call it the meterability problem.

Alchian and Demsetz argue that the purpose of organizations is to perform tasks that are technologically inseparable.[1] In other words, organizations are based on the premise that people work together because one individual cannot do everything—or even most of what needs to be done. When the work performed by people in organizations is highly interdependent, then individual productivity cannot be assessed by measuring output. Because resources and contributions are typically shared, it is also extremely difficult to assess individual productivity by measuring inputs.

In the case of nonroutine work where means cannot be specified, the meterability problem is compounded because there are no step-by-step actions that individuals and teams can be held accountable to perform. The control function is effectively disabled. Therefore, the meterability problem affects all phases of organizational work: inputs, throughputs, and outputs. Measurement and information systems fail to control behaviors because the requirements for precision are greater than the measurement system can provide.

A REVISED SYSTEM DESIGN[2]

One possibility we did not consider when we discussed Jack Welch's story was that the Japanese visitors were wrong to dismiss so quickly the North

American Division's measurement and information system. The Japanese may have underestimated the power of information, and may have allowed concerns about the creators and implementers, and the system itself, to blind them to its immense potential. Although this final interpretation runs counter to our natural inclination to believe the Japanese and doubt ourselves, it raises the intriguing possibility that well-designed measurement and information systems are a potential source of worldwide competitive advantage.

One of the major contributions of game theory to competitive strategy is the idea of *information asymmetries*. Game theorists who apply their knowledge to strategic management believe that the key to competing effectively is knowing more than one's competitors know; in their invented world of moves and countermoves, a real-time measurement and information system is always central to the creation of competitive advantage.[3]

A guidance system based on a real-time measurement and information system is also the core of the strategic improvising model (see Figure 7–1). Real-time measurement and information systems need to provide adequate guidance, to keep strategic thrusts aimed in the right direction. This requirement is very different from providing detailed measurement of inputs, throughputs, and outputs to be used for top-down control purposes. It is not necessary to measure who uses what resources, how work is accomplished, or who does what work. It is only necessary for individuals and teams to measure collective progress toward strategic objectives. In strategic improvising, measurements and rewards are also interrelated, but people are rewarded for how well they work together and improve as teams, rather than for their individual contributions.

What are the characteristics of a real-time measurement and information system designed to handle the faster pace of strategic improvising? Most current systems cannot accommodate the real-time demands of strategic improvising. Fortunately, a recent merging of new information technology and accounting practices has radically altered the way some organizations view measurement and information systems. Two leaders of this movement, Thomas Johnson and Robert Kaplan, have announced:

> Accounting systems can and should be designed to support the operations and the strategy of the organization. The technology exists to implement systems radically different from those being used today. What is lacking is knowledge. But this knowledge can emerge from experimentation and communication.[4]

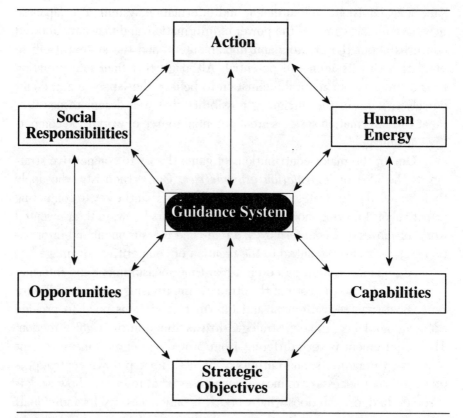

FIGURE 7–1. The role of a guidance system in the strategic improvising model.

A great deal of experimentation and communication has already occurred and has resulted in several advances in measurement and information systems design.

One of the more exciting advances has emerged from the idea of data integration and a single integrated store of information called the *enterprise information warehouse.* An enterprise information warehouse stores nonaggregated information about business events and processes. New technologies facilitate the collection and storage of real-time information in enterprise information warehouses, and then provide information customers with real-time access to information.

The idea of a single enterprise information warehouse is a dramatic departure from present practices. Most corporations and businesses create several poorly integrated measurement and information systems that have significant information gaps and overlaps. According to Eric Denna, Owen Cherrington, and David Andros, the key to data integration is a focus on essential business events and processes, which are quite stable, rather than on information artifacts, which change radically over time.

IBM is a company that has come a long way but still has a long way to go in the creation of an enterprise information warehouse. In 1979, IBM conducted a survey to determine the number of separate measurement and information systems used to support its accounting function worldwide. It discovered that there were 315 separate systems in operation. IBM actively pursued the common systems concept throughout the 1980s; by the end of 1991, it had trimmed down to 36 systems. More importantly, the work at IBM continues toward an ultimate goal of consolidating its measurement and information systems into a single enterprise information warehouse.

Advocates of the enterprise information warehouse are beginning to realize that efforts to consolidate information require strategic direction. Technology will not solve the massive storage and access problems associated with an enterprise information warehouse, at least in the near-term future. If companies are to consolidate many stores of information into a single warehouse, they need a way of determining what information is relevant. Strategic direction provides an important filter: ideally, information that is irrelevant to a corporation's or a business's strategic direction is filtered out, reducing the total amount of information that is finally stored. Moreover, when information passes through a strategy filter, it more naturally links up with other information. The linkage facilitates access to and synthesis of information.

Under the new approaches to measurement and information systems, the control function changes significantly. The controller, for example, assumes custodianship of the enterprise information warehouse, with responsibility for maintaining the warehouse. Information customers are thereby relieved of the burden of maintaining their own information systems.

The controller's function changes in other ways, as companies move from a "plan and control" to an "improvise and guide" model of management. In addition to maintaining the enterprise information warehouse, the controller and his or her staff become the chief information providers. In that role, they must develop close relationships with information customers and provide value-added support, especially to individuals and teams engaged in core work. When the system operates as it should, information customers are proactive, directing their inquiries to the office of the controller.

When value-added support is provided, the result is: support of real-time strategic decisions, and facilitation of the continuous refinement of business processes. When the controller's office provides the specific information needed by information customers, the quality of decisions improves significantly. When self-directed teams are informed by information providers and assume responsibility for making strategic decisions, their decisions are just as company-minded as those made by top management and are usually more easily implemented.

The continuous refinement of business processes is facilitated by access to real-time information. Provision of real-time information is dependent on two additional, closely related design features of the new measurement and information systems. The first design feature involves real-time measurement. Information technology is embedded in business events and processes so that information about them is recorded as they occur. The second design feature involves query tools. It is not enough to have real-time information stored in the enterprise information warehouse. Information customers must possess the necessary tools to retrieve pertinent, real-time information from the warehouse. The controller's office can furnish value-added support by providing information customers with the tools they need to access real-time information that is relevant to their strategic objectives. When information customers have special information needs, the controller's office may need to design special query tools for them.

In summary, this revised system design eliminates many of the problems associated with formal, centralized measurement and information systems. An enterprise information warehouse is centrally controlled, but the fact that it provides broader access to nonaggregated, real-time information encourages more team-based participation. When strategy filters are used to determine what information is relevant, a necessary discipline is provided.

The controller's function is also revised: instead of controlling, the controller concentrates on providing value-added support by maintaining the enterprise information warehouse, informing team-based strategic decisions, and equipping information customers with query tools to access real-time information. When individuals and teams have direct access to measurement and information systems and possess the tools needed to guide their real-time strategic decision making, the know-how exists to refine business processes continuously. Thus, real-time information empowers individuals and teams and moves them significantly closer to becoming self-managing.

A TYPOLOGY OF REAL-TIME MEASURES

Real-time information guides strategic improvising, but the necessary information would not exist without real-time measures, which are embedded in business events and processes, and fill the enterprise information warehouse. The principal challenge of real-time measurement is the need to keep up with rapid, unpredictable change. Real-time measures must be easily (or automatically) made, naturally recurring, and readily interpretable.

Two questions arise concerning real-time measures:

1. Are single measures or multiple measures being applied?
2. Are events or processes being measured?

These two questions are the basis of the typology presented in Figure 7–2.

The distinction between single measures and multiple measures is obvious. Single measures provide real-time information from one perspective; multiple measures provide real-time information from multiple perspectives.

The distinction between events and processes is less clear. In many ways, the distinction is artificial: when many events flow together, they

	Events	**Processes**
Single Measure	Cybernetic Models	Single-Element Focusers
Multiple Measures	Sensor Fusion	Distributed Expert Systems

FIGURE 7–2. A typology of real-time measures.

become processes. Business events are defined as both economic and noneconomic actions, transactions, and interactions. When events are measured, actions, transactions, and interactions are isolated, to facilitate repeated measurement.

Processes are more difficult to define than events. The capabilities within a business's unit of competitive advantage (UCA) need to be linked together by processes. Strategic thrusts are processes designed to accomplish strategic objectives. Ultimately, all organizational work is accomplished through processes.

A deeper understanding of organizational processes is emerging from a technology called *process mapping*. A process map is a flow chart showing every step, no matter how small, that goes into doing something. Many process maps use different shapes, such as diamonds and squares, to differentiate value-added from non-value-added work. Some of the process maps we have seen literally stretch around entire rooms and have taken weeks to draw.

There are important differences between measuring events and processes. Typically, events-based measures are not unique; they are widely known measures that develop around competitive necessities, like quality, speed, service, and low cost. Events are easily observed and imitated. They may be integrated into business processes, but they are like easily separated components. Events-based measures perform an important function by enabling businesses to keep up with their competitors; however, they do not help them create competitive advantage.

The advantage of measuring processes is that they already carry the same genetic code as a business's strategy, whether strategic direction is implicit or explicit. Therefore, when we measure processes, we are measuring the implementation of a strategy. Sometimes, process-based measurement results will surprise people and will lead them to clarify strategic direction, then redesign processes with *strategic* discipline. When businesses understand the order of strategic improvising, however, processes become a reflection of an explicit strategic direction. As measures develop around processes, they become firm-specific. In other words, measures actually conform to processes, which is why process-based measures are more precise than events-based measures.

Some real-time measures are more sophisticated than others, depending on their uniqueness and how precisely they guide strategic thrusts toward the accomplishment of strategic objectives. The typology in Figure 7–2 represents a continuum from less to more sophisticated uses of real-time measures: from *cybernetic models* (single measure/ events-based), to *sensor fusion* (multiple measures/events-based), to *single-element focusers* (single measure/processes-based), to *distributed expert systems* (multiple measures/processes-based).

All real-time measures must, by definition, remain easily made, naturally recurring, and readily interpretable, but they provide different levels of learning based on their level of sophistication. An added benefit of more sophisticated real-time measures is that, by offering more opportunities for deliberations among individuals and teams, they offer a wider assortment of perspectives.

The higher the level of sophistication of real-time measures, the less experience with them is available. This gap creates both a problem and a challenge. The problem is finding enough concrete examples of the more sophisticated real-time measures to demonstrate their greater potential; the challenge is to continue to develop new information technologies that will support more sophisticated measures, in order to gain more experience with them.

Cybernetic Guidance Systems

Two very different guidance systems are used to guide missiles. *Inertial guidance systems* originally made intercontinental ballistic missiles possible. These systems rely on gyros and servomechanisms and attempt to replicate the characteristics of the external environment internally. In other words, missiles with inertial guidance systems are programmed to follow a designated flight plan toward a prespecified target. When inertial guidance systems are front-loaded with accurate topographical information, they are clearly the most accurate systems for attacking stationary targets.

Missile developers also use *cybernetic guidance systems.* Missiles equipped with these systems use different sensors—including heat, metal, and motion sensors, as well as television cameras—to collect data about the external environment. Based on the information received through sensors, the guidance system locks onto a target until it is hit.

Inertial guidance systems are not externally self-adjusting. Once intercontinental ballistic missiles are launched, they must run their course. If the target does not move, it is likely that it will be hit; if the target moves even a little, it is almost always missed. Missiles with cybernetic guidance systems may not be as accurate at hitting stationary targets, but, because they are interactive and self-adjusting, they have a chance of hitting moving targets.

Cybernetic guidance systems are a class of real-time measures that involve single measures applied to business events. In many respects, they are similar to both the antecedent–behavior–consequence chains of learning theory and what Chris Argyris, a Harvard University professor, calls single-loop learning. Repeated measurements and adjustments are the key to continuous improvement. In learning theory, positive or negative *consequences* provide feedback in real time, and then become the *antecedents* for the next round of *behavior*. Over time, this learning process refines behaviors. Similarly, Argyris compares single-loop learning to a thermostat that reacts when it is too hot or too cold by turning the heat off or on. In single-loop learning, information is received and corrective actions are taken.[5]

Charting technologies provide a systematic way of using cybernetic real-time measures to track improvement. By charting a single measure of a business event over time, it becomes clear whether progress is being made. There are many kinds of charts—for example, pareto charts, trend charts, histograms, scatter diagrams, and control charts. Depending on the business events being measured, some charts have clear advantages over others. In most cases, however, the best chart is the one that is easiest to use and to interpret. It is also important, when charting measures of business events, to establish a baseline so that both the rate and amount of *real* progress can be determined.

Opportunities to learn about cybernetic guidance systems are widely available because events associated with competitive necessities are common across businesses. Moreover, the fact that cybernetic guidance systems involve single real-time measures makes it easier to share them across organizations. One of the great advantages of cybernetic guidance systems is how easy it is to place them in the hands of members of self-directed teams. Another advantage is how simple it is for individuals and teams to use cybernetic guidance systems to track continuous work improvement.

The key design requirement of cybernetic guidance systems is that they must be comprehensible to workers. One of the reasons the contributions of both W. Edwards Deming and Joseph Juran have been so significant is that they advocate cybernetic real-time measures that are easily comprehended. For this reason more than any other, their tools for measuring quality events are widely used by businesses.

Many cost-cutting measures are also easily effected and readily interpreted by production workers. Among these measures are: the time it takes to set up the manufacturing line to produce a particular batch of products; the amount of material that has to be scrapped because of worker error; or the percentage of purchased parts that are rejected because they do not meet specifications. Real-time measures of another competitive necessity, customer service, are also the focus of significant development efforts.

Cybernetic guidance systems offer a real-time alternative to questionnaires and surveys. These media are used widely to measure employee commitment, a fundamental source of human energy for driving strategic thrusts. However, questionnaires and surveys that measure employee commitment do not provide real-time information because they are not easily made, naturally recurring, and readily interpretable. At the Hughes Ground Systems Group, instead of using questionnaires and surveys, members of self-managing teams monitor the commitment of their co-workers with subtle, real-time measures, such as:

Do they arrive at meetings on time?

How often do they have to be called and reminded to attend regularly scheduled meetings?

How often do they volunteer to do something?

What percent of the time do they follow through on assignments?

How involved do they get in team discussions?

At Hughes, individuals and teams find it useful to keep track of the number of stories they hear that show either trusting or cynical accounts of people and events. When people at Hughes put all their real-time information together, they have a pretty good reading of employee commitment. Because much of their information is qualitative, they also gain significant insights about what they need to do to improve employee commitment.

Cybernetic guidance systems lend themselves to the outer game of strategic improvising. One of the best measures of a business's social responsiveness, for example, is how it is portrayed by media events. Real-time measures of these events provide answers to the following questions:

Does the business have a consistent image?

How much media coverage does the business get?

What percentage is"good" and what percentage is "bad" media coverage?

Is the business singled out for its positive contributions to the community, or is it tolerated because of the jobs it provides?

How often does the business find itself in the center of a storm of controversy?

We believe it is particularly important for businesses to focus on local media attention. The national media report on corporate social responsiveness, but their coverage tends to be more sporadic and less current; they do not provide as complete or contemporary a picture of a business's social image as the local media do. Moreover, the local media provide a much more accurate account of how a business is being perceived by its neighbors.

Because cybernetic guidance systems focus a single measure on a single business event, they focus people's attention on a single desired change. This improves the odds that the single desired change will be adopted throughout the organization. At Northwest Airlines, improving first-class customer service became a competitive necessity. In response to this competitive necessity, the airline distributed coupon books containing ten $20 coupons to all of its high-frequency, first-class passengers. They were instructed to give a coupon to their flight attendant each time they received exceptional service. When flight attendants were given coupons, they could redeem them for cash.

This was both a motivation and a measurement system. When flight attendants provided exceptional service, they received immediate, positive feedback. This reward improved their overall service to passengers. When they redeemed coupons frequently, the airline discovered who were its most service-minded flight attendants. Information about how to improve their service to first-class passengers was shared informally among flight attendants. The program also led to the formal sharing of ideas: the flight attendant who received the most coupons during the program's first year was appointed to be the head of flight attendant training.

Sensor Fusion

Cybernetic guidance systems provide a way for individuals and teams to make the real-time adjustments that are an integral part of strategic improvising, but they do not provide a way of stepping back to rethink business events in more fundamental ways. They enable many independent factors to be improved simultaneously, but they do not promote integrated improvements. For more fundamental and integrated improvements to occur, the viewpoints of different individuals and teams must be shared, compared, and brought together. This convergence of opinion is facilitated by multiple real-time measures of single business events.

Sensor fusion, or the use of multiple real-time measures, is rooted in more recent developments in the design of missile guidance systems. A long time ago, missile developers realized that cybernetic guidance systems that relied on single sensors were easily fooled. Using artificial intelligence and multiple sensor technologies, they significantly increased the success ratio of missiles equipped with cybernetic guidance systems. Because they can interpret and integrate the multidimensional information they receive, they are extremely difficult to fool, and they are even capable of selecting prime targets in areas where multiple targets exist.

The artificial intelligence supporting sensor fusion is based on a system of priorities. Depending on what is being targeted, the information provided by one type of sensor is registered as being more important than information provided by another type of sensor. The sensors operate differently when together than when separated.

A system of priorities is also necessary when multiple measures focus on a single business event. One measure is always primary and the other measures are secondary. Moreover, the information provided by secondary measures is always interpreted in terms of information provided by the primary measure. Even when measures come off-the-shelf, they are used in unique ways and, therefore, provide unique information.

Hot 'n Now stores employ sensor fusion technology to help improve team performance. Each store is equipped with an electronic scoreboard placed in full view of every team member. The scoreboard keeps track of three measures: points, fouls, and team productivity. When a customer places an order, an electronic clock is automatically set into motion. If the customer is served in 30 seconds or less, a point is scored. Fouls occur when a customer waits more than 35 seconds. The team productivity score is based on sales per team member for a defined period of time. Higher team productivity scores are recorded when fewer people serve the same number of customers or when the same number of people serve a greater number of customers.

The electronic scoreboard makes work at a Hot 'n Now store more like a game, and team members receive real-time information about how they are doing. It is important to score high on team productivity, but that measure is clearly secondary to the two speed-of-service measures (points and fouls) because this customer-focused business differentiates itself by providing a low-cost, acceptable quality product, *FAST.*

There are clear benefits from the interaction between the team productivity and speed-of-service measures. As team members try to maximize all three measures, they learn about relationships among them. They discover how small a team can get during a certain time of day before it starts committing an unacceptable number of fouls. When they consistently fill orders in 20 seconds or less, they realize that it is time to reduce team size.

Up to a point, the number of real-time measures used by individuals and teams increases the opportunities to learn. Hot 'n Now, for example, might benefit from adding a quality measure to its electronic scoreboard. Speed-of-service would still be king, but understanding its relationship to product quality would give team members another way to tweak the system. Sensor fusion offers significant advantages because the leverage of individual real-time measures increases each time they are fused with other real-time measures.

Single-Element Focusers

Tom Peters discussed *single-element focusers* as part of a typology of current change tools. He proposed that two criteria for inducing effective change were at or near the top of the list, in the minds of most senior managers: speed of effect and control over outcomes. Single-element focusers were high-speed, high-control tools of change. In other words, single-element focusing is a temporary and limited, but extremely fast and focused approach to organizational change.[6]

We use single-element focusers differently. Initially, they are single measures applied to business processes. Focus, however, is still the key operational term. At one company, a decision was made, by a team charged with boosting overall competitiveness, to focus attention on improving 15 different "global processes." The team even devised metrics for measuring improvements in each global process. When top managers heard about the team's extensive wish list, however, they panicked because they believed the company possessed neither the resources nor the will to drive improvement along two, much less 15, different processes. Their counterproposal was to focus on a single global process at a time. The change team was able to start a chain reaction of significant improvements in global processes because they accepted top management's counterproposal and began by picking the "lowest hanging fruit." In other words, they chose to focus first on the global processes that were the easiest to improve and offered the most leverage for increasing overall performance. With each round of success at single-element focusing, they gathered momentum and support for the next round.

A defining characteristic of single-element focusers is that they evolve over time as they are applied to processes: they acquire some of the characteristics of the processes they measure. Also, as single-element focusers are applied to processes, they retain a dominant focus but produce variations of the same measure. This occurs because different variations of a measure provide more precise information at different stages in a process.

Our colleagues, Chuck House and Ray Price, developed one of the first applications of single-element focusers while working at Hewlett-Packard (H-P). Initially, they assisted development teams interested in the relationship between time-to-market and revenue return from new products. They began by measuring the relationship between time and money over the course of the new-product development process. Over time, they developed several unique metrics, including:

Break-Even Time (BET). The time from the start of an investigation until product profits equal the investment in development (a measure of the total time until the break-even point on the original investment, and the best measure of the *whole* product development effort).

Time-to-Market (TM). The total development time from the start of the development phase to the manufacturing release (a measure of R&D efficiency and productivity, and obviously the most important R&D measure).

Break-Even-after-Release (BEAR). The time from manufacturing release until the product investment costs are recovered in product
profit (a measure that focuses on how efficiently the product was
transferred to marketing and manufacturing and how effectively it
was introduced to the marketplace; the most important measure for
marketing and manufacturing).

Return Factor (RF). A calculation of profit dollars divided by investment dollars at a specific point in time after a product has moved
into manufacturing and sales (an indication of the total return on the
investment without taking into account how long it took to achieve
that return).[7]

In what is called the investigation phase at H-P—the time when
decisions are made about whether to develop a new product—a return
map is used by product development teams to establish estimates of new-
product investment, sales, and profit. According to House and Price,
these initial estimates "are a 'stake in the ground' [a strategic objective]
for the team and will be used for comparison and learning" throughout
the duration of the product development process.[8] Over the course of the
product development process, the return map establishes a common language for the discussion and resolution of differing perspectives. As real-
time information is received, deviations from initial estimates are not
punished by management. Instead, they are used by product teams to examine whether the process is misguided or the estimates were unrealistic.
The original "stake in the ground" sets the stage for continuous investigation and learning.

We applaud these efforts, but the story of an H-P team's development of a new ultrasound machine suggests that the company's measurement system needs additional strategic focus. Two months into the
ultrasound machine team's development phase, H-P labs had a break-
through in ultrasound technology that offered significantly clearer images.
A decision needed to be made by the team about whether to incorporate
this new technology into their machine. To assist in making the decision,
the team revised the return map, incorporating the new technology. The
results surprised team members. What seemed like a golden opportunity
did not significantly increase the expected economic return.

The problem with the team's thinking, and the reason for the
team members' surprise, was that they were not thinking strategically.
H-P is a product-focused business. Its primary strategic concern involves

developing a successful line of products that gain significant market share. Its unique time-to-market metrics actually were misleading because they were related to profit return on investment, not to product/market impact. This is the danger of using a general measure of success instead of one that is strategically important.

Ultimately, the H-P ultrasound machine team's story ended happily. Team members, remembering that they were part of a product-focused business, decided to incorporate the new technology anyway. Their strategic objective was more consistent with their strategic direction—to capture greater market share, and, in turn, set up future generations of ultrasound machines. The metrics had misled the team but they promoted discussion that, in the end, proved to be an important saving grace. The final decision was not made based on the numbers alone, but resulted from a discussion of the differing perspectives offered by the numbers.

Distributed Expert Systems

Today's expert systems provide artificial intelligence by replicating the judgment of a single expert. The next step in artificial intelligence research is the development of expert systems that rely on a group of experts with differing perspectives. Distributed expert systems, as they are called, will be applied to poorly structured problems where the relevant issues and the nature of expertise are less clear-cut. When a common understanding can be reached, multiple perspectives guide better than a single perspective.[9]

A pioneer application of distributed expert systems, developed by Composition Systems, Inc., employs the perspectives of the editor, edition manager, production manager, and space manager to guide the publication of a newspaper. Multiple real-time measures operate much like the perspectives of different actors in guiding business processes. Ideally, multiple real-time measures bring to the discussion table all team-based perspectives. Although some perspectives are more or less important and, therefore, need to be weighted differently, they all affect in some way the total process flow.

When multiple perspectives are involved, reaching a common understanding is never automatic. Contentions will require constant cajoling, up, down, and across the ranks. Andrew Grove, Intel's CEO, comments that, at his company, such deliberations are necessary but they are not a pretty sight.

To reduce contentions by providing a common point of reference, a few companies—for example, General Electric and Hughes Aircraft—have experimented with process mapping. Most process maps set up multiple real-time measures by bringing together the perspectives of many teams around a common, visual understanding of business processes.

Fortune has reported the successes of GE's Evendale, Ohio, plant with process mapping and multiple real-time measures. The plant mapped the process of making turbine shafts for jet engines. The map and measures helped shaft teams pinpoint sources of flawed parts as well as ways to rearrange equipment in order to achieve a more continuous flow through the factory. A specific instance will illustrate the potential of distributed expert systems. A process map showed that all rotating parts went to a central steam-cleaning facility between operations, to ensure 100 percent utilization. After studying the process and making multiple efficiency and effectiveness measures, teams decided to give each of the shaftmakers an individual cleaning booth because it was obvious to everyone that the time saved more than compensated for the cost of the additional equipment.[10]

The process map provided teams at GE's Evendale plant with a view of how their work fit together. It showed how the shaft-cleaning operation interrupted the flow of the work and had become a significant process bottleneck. Nevertheless, other problems with the process, viewed from the perspective of a single measure, were either more or less important. The overall perspective provided by multiple real-time measures helped the teams to decide that the cleaning operation was one of their highest priorities. The perspective of multiple measures also helped them to anticipate the effects of proposed solutions. Ultimately, they decided to provide the individual cleaning booths for two reasons:

1. It was the best solution for a major process problem, among all the proposed solutions.

2. In the context of other priorities, the solution was acceptable to all partners in the process.

The applications of distributed expert systems in organizations, like applications of artificial intelligence, are very much in the pioneer stage. Only a few organizations are taking even preliminary steps to test distributed expert systems. The great expectations surrounding distributed expert systems are linked to their potential for promoting deeper inquiry and broader advocacy, but their actual contribution to the real-time measurement of business processes is yet to be determined.

PERCEPTION, POLITICS, PRESENTATION, AND FACTORS OF SAFETY

At Corning Asahi Video Products Company, the biggest supplier of color television glass in the United States, changes were underway. Corning's CEO, Jamie Houghton, and the senior vice president of specialty materials, Norm Garrity, mandated that the State College, Pennsylvania, plant was to become a partnership plant. At partnership plants, there is increased employee involvement and team-based management, and the levels of hierarchy are reduced. All of these practices are founded on the premise of a joint union–management partnership. The mandate was prompted by Corning Asahi's changing competitive environment. The business needed to become more focused strategically, reduce costs, and improve quality, in order to survive in the mature and crowded television glass business.[11]

One of the barriers to change at Corning Asahi was its history. Corning had invented television glass and had monopolized the market for decades. The State College plant paid premium wages. Layoffs had not been considered since the time, several years ago, when another Corning television glass plant had been closed.

Another barrier to change was Corning Asahi's culture. The business was a sleeping giant. In the eyes of local employees, their company was the biggest, best, and only major supplier of color television glass in the United States. Pervasive cultural assumptions of invincibility destroyed the felt need for change at the plant, seriously wounding the "partnership plant" effort.

The plant's management reasoned that, by sharing more information, they could challenge current cultural assumptions, and, in turn, secure greater commitment from the unionized employees. The plant manager assembled the plant's employees and explained the plant's quarterly budget and performance. His report showed that the plant's performance had never been worse. However, after playing to a silent, seemingly disinterested audience for almost an hour, the frustrated plant manager threw up his arms and asked: "How many of you think I just made these numbers up?" To the plant manager, it was a rhetorical question asked to generate discussion. However, the hands of several employees shot up.

This experience holds several implications for measurement and information systems:

1. The "eye of the beholder" is critical because people's beliefs affect their perceptions. Employees at Corning Asahi had held a set of basic assumptions about the business. When information challenged those basic assumptions, they tended to doubt the information before they questioned their assumptions.

2. Information is political fodder. It represents the point of view of the information provider as much as it communicates objective fact. Accordingly, when information is presented as the absolute truth, as Corning Asahi's plant manager had presented it, information customers will often question the motives of the information provider. On the other hand, when information is presented in a more tentative, qualified manner, it breeds trust and promotes discussion. Information customers do not get the impression that they are being "snowed."

3. There is a huge difference between "sounding the alarm" and being perceived as an "alarmist." People need to be prepared to receive information, especially when that information challenges their assumptions about themselves or their circumstances. Corning Asahi's plant manager simply "dropped a bomb"; with the plant's employees, he "bombed out." His information failed to generate an irresistible force, and Corning Asahi's people knew how to be immovable objects.

4. Culture *matters,* and it needs to be managed. Corning Asahi's assumptions of invincibility developed under a culture of complacency and arrogance. People had perceived the best of times for so long that they did not see the worst of times coming. They assumed that once they had the lead, they would always keep it.

One way to manage cultures that tend to develop assumptions of invincibility is by building in *factors of safety.* Structural engineers, significant players in the design of buildings, dams, and bridges, always build a factor of safety into the structures they design. The reason is simple: they can make relatively straightforward predictions regarding the common stresses on structures, but there are uncommon stresses that cannot be predicted. Hurricanes can start suspension bridges resonating; the structural integrity of buildings and dams may be tested by earthquakes. One of our friends, a civil engineer, likes to refer to factors of safety as *factors of ignorance*.

A parallel to engineered systems exists with measurement and information systems: there is no virtue in imprecision, but there is virtue in recognizing the limits of precision. Businesses that overestimate the precision of their measurement and information systems leave themselves highly vulnerable because they do not believe it is necessary to build in factors of safety.

An example of a factor of safety is the idea of "exceeding customer expectations." When it is difficult to measure what customer expectations are, the safest approach is to provide customers with services they do not expect. In a competitive business environment, this also reduces the risk that competitors will lure away customers by offering them new and improved standards of service.

Businesses do not build factors of safety into everything they do. Exceeding customer expectations would be more important for a customer-focused business than for a business that is production-capacity-focused. Again, the logic of strategy suggests the focusing of effort. It is especially important to build factors of safety into processes that are strategically important. However, building them into processes with limited strategic importance is usually unnecessary and often will spread organizational resources too thin.

SOLID SENDER: A LAUNCHING PLATFORM FOR STRATEGIC IMPROVISING

8

Solid Sender A term used to describe jazz that has everything right about its sound and delivery.

Recently, the first Wal-Mart store opened in the community in which we live. Several years of reading about Wal-Mart in the business press should have prepared us for this event, but it still held many surprises. The spectacle had nothing to do with what Wal-Mart was doing to mark its arrival, which seemed quite ordinary. It was the reaction by other merchants, most noticeably K mart, that really caught our attention. At the local K mart store, senior citizen greeters suddenly appeared at store entrances. As part of a national effort, the K mart store was remodeled to look a lot like a Wal-Mart store. In many other, subtler ways, it was clear that a threatened K mart was trying to copy everything it could from Wal-Mart in an effort to cut its losses.

The K mart store might have looked a lot like a Wal-Mart store, but it never quite felt like one. Sometimes the senior citizen greeters were stationed at the entrances, but many times they were not. Even when they were present, they seemed a bit uncomfortable and unclear about their role. K mart's layout resembled Wal-Mart's, but many of the shelves were understocked. The K mart people seemed less responsive and less willing than the Wal-Mart people to volunteer to assist customers. K mart and Wal-Mart had similar strategies, but the strategy seemed to be more in sync at Wal-Mart than at K mart.

We might conclude from this story that it is a mistake to imitate the strategy of a competitor. The problem with that conclusion is that Sam Walton, Wal-Mart's founder, claimed in his recent autobiography that almost everything he did was copied from somebody else.[1] How then can we attribute Wal-Mart's success to the uniqueness of its strategy, or K mart's failure to the fact that it copied its strategy from Wal-Mart? We must look elsewhere for an explanation.

The different results at Wal-Mart and K mart can be explained by the different levels of compatibility between their competitive strategies and their strategic assumptions. Wal-Mart's strategy was compatible with its strategic assumptions; the same strategy was less compatible with K mart's strategic assumptions. As indicated in Figure 8–1, strategic

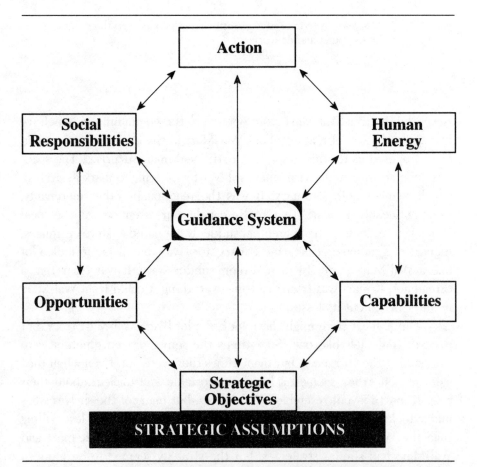

FIGURE 8–1. Strategic assumptions and the strategic improvising model.

assumptions provide a platform for launching strategic thrusts. Strategic assumptions are like a computer operating system, and strategic thrusts are like pieces of computer software. When a business launches strategic thrusts from a compatible platform of strategic assumptions, the thrusts work as intended; they are like software that is compatible with a specific operating system. Strategic thrusts launched from one platform of strategic assumptions, however, do not have the same trajectory when launched from another platform of assumptions. Accordingly, it is important to ask about the compatibility of strategic assumptions before strategic thrusts are launched.

Strategic assumptions tie a business's strategy to its culture. Most people agree that a connection exists between the two, but they mistakenly assume that cultural assumptions are the bedrock of organizations and competitive strategies are merely one of many artifacts of cultural assumptions. They do not explore the connection enough to understand how strategic assumptions are created out of cultural assumptions.

A Swedish school of strategic thinking, developed around the Scandinavian Institutes for Administrative Research (SIAR), links culture and strategy at a basic level. The problem with the thinking of the SIAR theorists is their assumption that cultures are unified and relatively stable. Given this point of view, cultural assumptions become the anchor in the organizational alignment process—it is taken for granted that strategic assumptions need to be aligned to cultural assumptions. Because organizational culture is complex and difficult to change, it imposes a repressive form that restricts strategic freedom. It promotes strategic continuity, not strategic change.[2]

Organizational cultures may be difficult to change, but they are not necessarily unified. Our colleague, Alan Wilkins, believes that most large organizations have many subcultures. It is the essential nature of organizations to assign pieces of an overall task to various subunits and to hold these subunits responsible for their piece of the task. Groups of people who associate with each other and share common backgrounds and objectives tend to develop and share common orientations that may differ from the orientations of other groups. Over time, they develop separate and distinct subcultures.[3]

When organizations are conceived as collections of subcultures, each with its own set of assumptions, it is no longer helpful to think of cultural assumptions as the anchor in the organizational alignment process. Diverse subcultural assumptions need to be anchored to something else; if they are not, organizational subcultures are likely to drift further apart instead of pulling together. This problem is compounded by the difficulty of changing these subcultural assumptions. It becomes almost impossible to align them to each other once they have come apart. Therefore, using cultural assumptions as an anchor in the organizational alignment process not only limits strategic change; it hardly ever works. Consequently, we need to rethink what should happen when strategic assumptions are created out of cultural assumptions.

Ideally, the process begins when a strategic direction is specified. Because strategic direction is unified and relatively stable, it provides a good anchor for aligning culture and strategy. Strategic assumptions are created when different subcultural assumptions are aligned to a business's strategic direction. Accordingly, strategic assumptions pick up the elements of subcultural assumptions that blend with a business's overall strategic direction.

Businesses can imitate some of the strategic thrusts of other businesses if they are willing to do some preliminary groundwork. K mart, for example, should have begun with a business-level strategy clarification process. The outcome of that process, a specific strategic direction, would have provided an anchor for a new round of organizational alignment. K mart then would have been able to create a platform of strategic assumptions by aligning its subcultural assumptions to its strategic direction. Broad-based learning about strategic assumptions, which is an important by-product of such actions, would enable individuals and teams in each K mart store to decide which of Wal-Mart's strategic thrusts were compatible.

Taken a step further, it is possible to think of strategy in terms of a portfolio logic. There are a lot of strategies that will work, but individual businesses need a way of being certain that the strategies they choose will work for them. The best way for businesses to have that certainty is to be clear about their strategic assumptions and make sure they choose only compatible strategies. Another way is to adapt or "affinitize" strategies to their own platform of strategic assumptions.

A VARIATION ON THE SAME THEME

During our consulting with a large manufacturing company, we ran into a different kind of problem that required a similar response. We were first contacted by people from the human resources department, who wanted to have an immediate impact on organizational performance. They asked us to help them in building high-performance work teams. As we later learned, their sense of urgency was fed by feelings of insecurity that were prevalent in the human resources subculture. A very different request came from the company's president and CEO. He had heard some of our ideas about strategy and wanted us to help create leaders throughout the company by putting strategic tools in their hands. He was a highly participative senior executive who was anxious to share strategic responsibilities. We also met with the company's management executive committee. They did not believe that the people at the company were ready to learn about strategy. They asked us to offer a basic management training program to all the company's managers.

We interpreted the situation as one in which only one strategic thrust would be launched; however, separate subcultures were asking for our help in launching three different strategic thrusts. We needed one meeting attended by representatives from the three subcultures, to decide what strategic thrust to launch. Because the representatives would approach the decision from their respective subcultural perspectives, we realized that, left untended, the decision-making process would be politically driven, and the representative of the dominant subculture would win out. We had learned that the management executive committee carried the most political clout, so we could predict what the politically driven decision would be.

At the meeting, we invited the human resources representatives, the CEO, and members of the management executive committee to make their respective cases. We did not allow comments on the proposed strategic thrusts. Then we explained that we did not yet have a process for choosing the best course of action, and proposed that we conduct an abbreviated strategy clarification exercise to begin that process. The strategy clarification exercise helped the attendees agree that the company was product-focused (quality-anchored). Discussion progressed about what the unit of competitive advantage (UCA) might look like for a product-focused (quality-anchored) business.

We began the process of aligning subcultural assumptions to the company's product-focused (quality-anchored) strategy by asking the representatives of the three subcultures to consider how their proposed strategic thrusts might affect the company's core capabilities. After a lengthy discussion, we were able to ask all the representatives to participate in the development of a platform of strategic assumptions. The group debated the appropriateness of each proposed strategic assumption and arrived at the following final platform:

1. Maximum leverage is gained by focusing efforts in the new-product development and design areas.
2. Team-based structures concentrate human energy.
3. Self-managing teams must be given the strategic tools they need to set and accomplish strategic objectives.
4. When training is guided by strategy, it becomes a powerful strategic tool.
5. Broad-based employee involvement and participation must be encouraged, to maximize the impact of strategy.
6. Consultants can help to launch strategies, but the company should drive the strategy.
7. If the company makes mistakes, it will learn from them; the most important thing is to keep moving in the same overall direction.
8. It will take a lot of different strategic thrusts to accomplish all of the strategic objectives.

Acting as scribes, we significantly influenced the language of this company's platform of strategic assumptions, but we played only a minor role in its development. We facilitated discussion, but made every effort not to direct it.

Once the platform of strategic assumptions was created, decisions on what strategic thrust to launch were relatively easy. Sharing common strategic assumptions, the group decided to organize people in the new-product development and design areas into high-performance work teams, and to train them in team-based management skills. The group wanted us to weave some basic strategy tools into this initial training, but it was decided to save the complete set of strategic improvising tools for future strategic thrusts.

Three important lessons were gained from our experience with this company:

1. By using strategic direction to align the subcultures, we were able to remove decision making from the political arena. A strategic anchor

reframed the decision-making process by providing new, legitimate criteria for making an informed decision, and it helped redraw battle lines. By the time we completed the process, the representatives of the three subcultures had become a group empowered by a strong spirit of cooperation.

2. The flexibility of strategic improvising tools was demonstrated. The tools can be used in varying applications, depending on the situation. We need to understand the difference between an abbreviated strategy clarification exercise and the complete strategy clarification process, and to recognize the times when it is better to use the short form rather than the long one.

3. It is not necessary to change cultural assumptions directly, when aligning strategy and culture.

The concept of cultural assumptions was first introduced to the organizational literature by Edgar Schein, a professor at MIT's Sloan School of Management. He proposed that organizational cultures can be analyzed at multiple levels ranging from *artifacts* to *basic assumptions*. Visible artifacts are the constructed environment of the organization—everything from architecture to manner of dress and decisions. At the other end of the cultural continuum, basic assumptions are typically unconscious but actually determine how organization members perceive, think, and feel. Artifacts are the concrete outcroppings of culture; basic assumptions are its abstract roots.[4]

Some respected culture theorists have cited Schein's work to argue that the only way to change an organization's culture is by understanding its basic assumptions and changing them. They criticize most efforts to change organizational cultures as being superficial and ineffective because they change only visible artifacts.[5]

We agree with these respected culture theorists that organizational cultures do not change until the basic assumptions underlying culture change, but we also believe that they make cultural change harder than it needs to be because they concentrate exclusively on changing basic assumptions. An important point they have missed is Schein's belief in *mutual* influence between basic assumptions and visible artifacts.

Our view is also based on research about cognitive dissonance/consonance. When there is a difference between visible cultural artifacts and basic assumptions, cognitive dissonance is created. Because

basic assumptions are difficult to change, dissonance is more easily de-
creased by changing visible artifacts. When visible artifacts are anchored to a strategic direction, however, the balance shifts. Again,
dissonance is created (differences exist between visible artifacts and basic assumptions), but the visible artifacts are less likely to change. Over
time, if strategic direction remains consistent, basic assumptions become
more consonant with visible artifacts.

When we aligned subcultural assumptions and strategic direction at
the large manufacturing company discussed above, we used surrogates for
both—the subcultures' proposed strategic thrusts, and the core capabilities inside a product-focused (quality-anchored) UCA. This more workable and less time-consuming approach was possible because visible
cultural artifacts can influence basic cultural assumptions.

The narration of our experiences at the manufacturing company,
combined with our ruminations about K mart and Wal-Mart, are intended
to put the relationship between strategy and culture into perspective.
People debate endlessly over which is more important—strategy or culture. Both are important. The role of strategy is to define purpose and
direction. People organize together for a reason, and strategy should play a
central role in making that reason explicit. When strategy does its part, it
can infuse organizational cultures with increased meaning and provide an
anchor that pulls together different organizational subcultures. The influence of culture shows up when organizations act to accomplish their
strategic objectives. In the creation of strategic means, which are the
building blocks of strategic thrusts, culture plays a defining role.

It is important to acknowledge that our bias is clearly away from culture for culture's sake and toward more instrumental and disciplined organizational cultures. We believe that either replacement or corrective
surgery needs to be performed when cultural or subcultural assumptions
conflict with a business's strategic direction.

POURING A NEW FOUNDATION FOR
STRATEGIC IMPROVISING

A more general way to view strategic assumptions is as a platform for
strategic processes, such as strategic improvising. Where strategic processes begin largely determines where and how they develop; this same
lesson is learned in fields as diverse as the study of human development, or

chaos theory. Although developmental psychologists have recently come to appreciate changes in adult life structures, more has been written about the first five years of life than about all the other periods of life combined. The developmental work of these early formative years is fundamental to all subsequent development.

Chaos theorists discuss how, in modeling systems, tiny differences in input can quickly result in overwhelming differences in output. They have named this phenomenon *sensitive dependence on initial conditions.*[6]

The analog in competitive strategy is a sensitive dependence on *initial strategic assumptions.* All businesses engaged in strategic improvising start with a platform of implicit or explicit strategic assumptions. Strategic improvising is sensitively dependent on these assumptions. If the assumptions are compatible with strategic improvising, strategic improvising will thrive; if they are not, it will fail. This is the basis of our belief that, for strategic improvising to be successful in today's complex, dynamic, and unpredictable business environment, it needs to be plugged into a platform of unique strategic assumptions about *leadership and people,* the *purpose of strategy,* and *organizational change.*

Strategic Assumptions about Leadership and People

The strategic assumptions of top-down strategic planning are incompatible with strategic improvising. Chester Barnard, for example, in his book, *The Functions of the Executive,* concluded that one of the three functions of a high-level executive is "to formulate and define the purposes, objectives, ends, of the organization." Barnard likened this function to "that of the nervous system, including the brain, in relation to the rest of the body. . . . It exists to maintain the bodily system by directing those actions which are necessary more effectively to adjust to the environment."[7]

Barnard's strategic assumptions about leadership and people are clear. Leaders, functioning as the nervous system, should command people, who are expected to respond as commanded. Leaders think and people do.

Strategic improvising assumes that people both think *and* do. What then is the role of a leader? In a metaphor from a more traditional era, the role of the man was to be the *head* of a household, and that of the woman was to be the *neck* that turned the head. When leaders function as the necks that allow the organizational minds to turn in various directions, they lead in a powerful, yet uncontrolling way. Leaders provide direction, but they do not overdirect.

Four strategic assumptions support leadership that provides direction without overdirecting:

1. *It should never be assumed that legitimate power, based on a person's position in an organization, overrides expert power, based on what a person knows.* In strategic improvising, the experts lead. As Kenan Sahin, the president of a software consulting firm, observes: "Before, when markets were slower, leaders had time to absorb information from experts. Now markets and technologies are becoming so complex, the experts will have to do the leading."[8]

Most businesses are filled with experts who, for many reasons, have been denied strategic responsibilities. A General Electric employee hit the nail on the head when he said to Jack Welch: "For 20 years you paid for my body, and for the same price you could have had my mind." Ralph Stayer, the CEO of Johnsonville Foods, has said: "The strategic decision is who makes the decision."[9] Stayer believes that he should provide strategic direction for his company, but that his people are the real strategy experts. In his view, people are more motivated, committed, and empowered when they see themselves as strategic thinkers.

2. *Most people can lead themselves.* Becton Dickinson, a maker of high-tech diagnostic systems such as blood analyzers, has started exploring ways to let its informal organization come alive. The company is encouraging its people to take the initiative, form teams to innovate, and go after business in new ways—within specified directional parameters. Instead of directing strategy from the top, Raymond Gilmartin, Becton's CEO, lays out a very broad vision—develop proprietary ideas and beat the competition to market with them—and then lets his 15 divisions improvise their own business strategies. Gilmartin wants Becton's people to understand that there is no rigid master plan.[10]

What Raymond Gilmartin does at Becton Dickinson is similar to what our partners, Gene Dalton and Paul Thompson, call *mapping the environment.* The leader's role is that of a mapmaker, but the maps resemble the crude drawings of the New World that were circulated in the 16th century. The maps organize what is known, project relationships, encourage exploration, and gradually become more accurate. It is not the role of leaders to provide detailed maps of the business environment. Instead, they fly at 30,000 feet and provide a general overview.[11] As General Norman Schwarzkopf explained to a reporter in the concluding hours of the Persian Gulf War, "Generals always speak generally."

Provided with general directions, but left unbridled, the people of Becton Dickinson structure their businesses to meet their needs. Chuck Baer, the head of the company's consumer products division, says: "We reorganized ourselves by the way we work. We organized cross-functional teams that include not only our own people but also vendors, suppliers, and people from other divisions. We set the strategy and the team carries it out."

3. *Once strategic freedoms are granted to individuals, teams, and businesses, they should not be withdrawn.* During much of its history, Hewlett-Packard (H-P) has been a company in which top management does not overdirect. In its early years, H-P's business units were granted enormous autonomy and encouraged to be entrepreneurial in pursuing two broad categories of opportunities—scientific instruments and computer technology. The company was extremely successful following this model and became a world leader in the development of new, innovative products.

Then, in the mid-1980s, H-P's computer businesses came under attack because of several incompatible products. John Young, H-P's CEO, decided the company's computer businesses needed to become more tightly integrated so that, like its major competitor, Digital Equipment Corporation, H-P could offer highly integrated systems. This decision necessitated changes in H-P's strategic assumptions. Top management began to direct operations, not simply provide strategic direction.

H-P lost more than it gained by attempting to change its strategic assumptions. The company's computer business has never adjusted to more centralized control; in fact, the only recent major success in H-P's computer business resulted when a maverick plant manager in Boise, Idaho, decided to go his own way by launching the LaserJet printer. Presently, H-P's line of LaserJet printers accounts for nearly all of the profits in the computer division. This state of affairs recently prompted Bill Hewlett and Dave Packard, now in their early 80s, to voice their displeasure. In a speech at H-P's Colorado Springs facility, Packard threatened to come out of retirement to return the company to its entrepreneurial roots.

4. *Leadership is not just a matter of tightening the focus; it also must provide leverage.* Business leaders are pioneers who go where no one has gone before. They are disciplined by strategy, but they choose to test the limits of strategic parameters instead of playing it safe.

We are intrigued by one company that defines its strategy as product-focused (quality-anchored). The product at the core of the company's product-focused strategy is *image*. We have not yet decided whether a product-focused strategy of selling an image is focused enough, but it does provide significant leverage. The company has leveraged its image across a broad range of products from clothing to low-calorie entrées, sports equipment, and cologne.

Decisions about strategic direction are not always clear-cut. Strategy is a discipline: its intent is to focus organizational effort. Nevertheless, because too much focus imposes too much form and can be damaging, issues of leverage also need to be considered. They give life to the ongoing strategic debate by stoking the fires of creative tension between freedom and form. Leaders who practice strategic improvising sometimes appear to be teetering back and forth on a high wire, but, over the long run, strategic improvising ensures that they will maintain their balance.

Strategic Assumptions about the Purpose of Strategy

Microeconomics-based approaches to competitive strategy assume that the purpose of strategy is to aid businesses in finding industry positions where they can best defend themselves against the forces of competition.[12] For strategic improvising, the underlying assumption is that competition is good for businesses because they get better when they compete against world-class competitors. In business, as in isometric exercise, resistance builds strength, and, up to a point, increasing the resistance builds more strength. Because it assumes that the purpose of competitive strategy is to compete, strategic improvising is an offensive strategy.

Carl von Clausewitz, a 19th-century Prussian military strategist, observed that the purpose of strategy is to seize, retain, and exploit the initiative. There may be periods during which a defensive posture must sustain offensive gains, but only offensive actions accomplish strategic objectives.[13] There is a desired balance between the defensive and offensive components of strategy. Strategic operations can be thought of in terms of "vertical" and "horizontal" dimensions (see Figure 8–2). The vertical dimension represents a strategic thrust, and the horizontal dimension

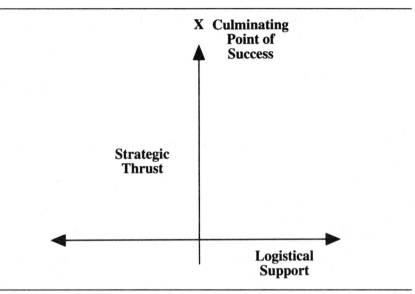

FIGURE 8–2.   The vertical and horizontal dimensions of strategy.

represents the logistical support necessary to sustain the strategic thrust. To prevent the strategic thrust from extending beyond its culminating point of success, it is important to stop intermittently and rebuild the supporting resources and capabilities. Companies, however, move forward and accomplish their strategic objectives only through offensive actions.

In the Middle Ages, kings and knights built walled castles to protect themselves from attack. The art of fortification and the strategies of military defense were cultivated during this period. With the introduction of artillery, however, the rules of war changed dramatically, and walled castles were suddenly vulnerable to attack. A new era began as the military balance shifted markedly in favor of the offensive. Francesco di Giorgio Martini, one of the great Italian architects of the 15th century, complained that "the man who would be able to balance defense against attack, would be more a god than a human being."[14]

Like the strategies of kings and knights during the Middle Ages, the strategies of companies in the U.S. automobile, consumer electronics, machine tool, microelectronics, steel, and textile industries during the 1970s and 1980s focused on the construction of entry barriers and the defense of domestic markets from outside attack. When Asian competitors invented a new, more aggressive form of capitalism and went on the attack, the walls protecting American businesses came tumbling down.

Kenichi Ohmae, the managing partner of McKinsey's Tokyo office, argues that companies should avoid competition whenever and wherever possible. He quotes the Chinese philosopher and military strategist, Sun-tzu, to reinforce his point. According to Sun-tzu, the smartest strategy in war is the one that allows a combatant to achieve its objectives without having to fight.[15] Sun-tzu, however, did not recognize that, in both military and economic warfare, there are objectives that cannot be realized without a fight. These objectives are related to the growth, development, discipline, and order of organizations and people. Military strategists, for example, describe the difficulties of keeping a peacetime army battle-ready when there is no rallying sense of purpose to foster discipline and order. Moreover, leaders and their people cannot really prove themselves until they have been tested in battle.

At the time when Marshall Hahn was named chief executive at Georgia-Pacific (G-P), housing starts had plunged in response to high interest rates, and the company was mired in debt after a capital spending binge (including $150 million for its new Atlanta headquarters). In masterminding a differentiation strategy for G-P's recovery, Hahn focused on deepening the strength of the company's distribution network. G-P had huge covered warehouses spread across the country, and no competitor in the building materials business had anything like them. Hahn added more warehouses and he changed the mix of products from basic materials to items for remodeling and do-it-yourself projects, to move the company away from dependence on interest-sensitive new-home construction.[16]

In addition to deciding what to do, Hahn reviewed the basic assumptions underlying G-P's competitive strategy. Long-standing agreements not to attack one another were honored among members of the building supplies and paper industries, and G-P was reluctant to engage in direct competition. Hahn reasoned that, if G-P's basic assumptions about competition were not challenged, the company would never regain its competitive edge. Specifically, Hahn was concerned that G-P's strategy of creating an unrivaled distribution system could make the company's mills less competitive because, by creating huge captive markets, it buffered them from the discipline of direct competition.

To avoid this potential outcome and intensify direct competition, Hahn decided to stock supplies from other manufacturers in G-P's warehouses. G-P's mills had to compete against some of their toughest competitors for space in their own warehouses, and the warehouses had to compete with other wholesalers for products from G-P's mills.

A company's decision to be offensive, although it does not guarantee success and will not remove all the barriers to success, can offer significant leverage. NCR's Self-Service Systems Division, headquartered in Dundee, Scotland, is a case in point. In 1980, James Adamson was hired away from a subsidiary of ITT and given the assignment of saving the Dundee Plant, which, at the time, was a second-source supplier of cash registers for the U.K. and Commonwealth markets. Adamson was told by NCR that if he could not turn the plant around in six months, it would be closed.[17]

In conjunction with NCR's U.S. operations, the Dundee Plant had developed an automatic teller machine (ATM). This was a significant first for the plant, because it offered a new source of potential business. When the first of Dundee's ATMs were installed in two major British banks, however, the overall quality was so poor that the banks sent them back. What did Adamson do? He challenged his engineers to develop an ATM that was twice as reliable as the competition's. The engineers laughed, but Adamson persisted. Eventually, Dundee's engineers tripled the reliability of NCR's ATMs.

By 1984, the Dundee Plant was producing all of NCR's ATMs, and NCR was third behind IBM and Diebold, with over 4,000 installations per year. In 1987, NCR became the worldwide leader, with the largest installed base spanning about 90 countries. In September 1990, however, Diebold and IBM decided to gang up on the leader. They formed a joint venture, InterBold, to grab the lead position in installed ATMs away from NCR.

How did NCR respond to the new challenge presented by InterBold? It went on the offensive. "This is a survival issue for us," James Adamson told the Dundee plant's employees. "If we don't step up to the challenge now, the game will be lost forever. If we don't react in a positive way, we'll probably be involved in redundancies and layoffs. At worst, we could go into plant closures and lose the business." Adamson forgot to mention that, if NCR were to just keep installing units at the previous year's rate, and if InterBold did the same, NCR would be first again in three years.

W. Edwards Deming understood the value of direct competition against the world's best competitors. He once said: "If you're going to have a competitor, be thankful you have a good one. . . . Nothing can do you so much harm as a lousy competitor." Deming was trying to drive home the idea that one company can force its competitors to raise their performance by launching an aggressive strategic thrust.

In Foster City, California, a battle recently broke out over which of three competing grocery stores would attract the most walk-in customers. Before the battle began, the Safeway store was the unquestioned leader in attracting walk-in traffic because it was located near most of Foster City's office complexes; equally important, the Safeway store was the best-run store in Foster City. The Alpha-Beta store in Foster City had recently been converted to a Lucky's store. The management of the Lucky's store decided that the current equilibrium was disadvantageous. They wanted to puncture it. Although their store location was clearly inferior to Safeway's, they believed they could draw new walk-in customers by offering special promotions.

The battle was officially launched when the Foster City Lucky's store decided to offer freshly baked French bread four times each day. Lucky's had been selling only between 15 and 20 loaves of French bread per day. It sold 100 loaves on the first day of the promotion. On the second day, it sold 200 loaves, and sales then held steady. More importantly, the store's overall sales volume increased 20 percent. New walk-in customers were buying more than freshly baked French bread.

The Lucky's store was drawing its new customers away from its competitors. The Foster City Petrini's store was the hardest hit by Lucky's more aggressive strategy. It soon responded with its own hot French bread promotion, to neutralize the advantage gained by Lucky's.

Although Petrini's response lacked inventiveness, it attracted back some of the store's lost customers and reestablished equilibrium for Foster City's three competing grocery stores. If Lucky's, Safeway, or Petrini's wants to continue to improve its position in the Foster City market, it cannot be content with this return to business as usual. It must launch new, rapid-fire strategic thrusts in an attempt to stay at least one step ahead of its competitors.

Strategic Assumptions about Organizational Change

Most businesses accept change as inevitable, but they avoid change when they can. Strategic improvising requires a different attitude toward change because it involves continuous change. A strategic assumption compatible with strategic improvising is that change should be embraced, not avoided. Businesses that practice strategic improvising are perpetually adapting organizations. They always want to be managing in the middle of change.

PepsiCo's people love managing in the middle of change. This attitude has been fine-tuned over the past century as the company has played the part of scrappy second-place competitor behind the industry leader, Coca-Cola. According to Wayne Calloway, PepsiCo's CEO: "Nothing focuses the mind better than the constant sight of a competitor who wants to wipe you off the map." PepsiCo is always trying to stir up the pot. The company has quickened its response time over the years, but it also specializes in revamping its operations, marketing, or management when everything is running smoothly, simply to gain a step on the competition. Calloway observes: "The worst rule of management is 'If it ain't broke, don't fix it.' In today's economy, if it ain't broke, you might as well break it yourself, because it soon will be."[18]

A love for managing in the middle of change is evident in PepsiCo's fast-food businesses, especially Taco Bell and Pizza Hut. At Taco Bell, change follows the course of offering better value: the chain aggressively advertises a menu with 25 items under a dollar as well as 39-cent tacos, burritos, and tostadas. To maintain desired margins, Taco Bell has simplified operations. The key to lowering costs in the fast-food business is to increase volume while employing fewer people in less space. The business has reduced labor costs and kitchen space by switching to ground beef that is cooked outside the store, tortillas that are already fried, and prepared cheese and vegetables. In the process, volume has increased significantly; customer traffic recently rose 60 percent.

At Pizza Hut, continuous change is moving in two directions simultaneously. First, the company entered the fast-food business by introducing five-minute service at lunch, and it is creating a rash of new opportunities by redefining where it sells its pizzas. Through a joint venture with Marriott Corporation, it is selling pizzas at football stadiums and basketball arenas, in grade-school cafeterias, and at airport kiosks, and it is negotiating to sell them on airline flights.

The second road of change on which Pizza Hut is moving will take it right to Domino's and a challenge for a bigger piece of the pizza-delivery business. Steven Reinemund, Pizza Hut president, views his business as a pizza distribution company. The company is building most new units exclusively for delivery and carryout, and these new units are delivering returns on investment of more than 25 percent a year.

What is most impressive about the changes at PepsiCo is the momentum that appears to be building. Its people's initial reluctance to change has been transformed into an addiction or insatiable appetite for change. They have discovered that it is incredibly exciting to know roughly where you are going, but to be inventing how you get there all along the way.

Individuals and teams learn the most when they are in the middle of change. Under stable conditions, opportunities to learn something new do not arise very often. People adopt routine behaviors and close themselves off to new learning. A major reason why organizations and people avoid change may be that they have forgotten how to learn and they are afraid that change will make them obsolete. People who continuously stay in the middle of change never forget how to learn; they avoid the self-doubt and emotional upheaval associated with discontinuous change.

Continuous change is not always comfortable. At one company, we were observers at a meeting of a high-level strategy team. One of the consultants to the team—a company employee—shifted the discussion to process issues. He suggested that the team's meetings were not as effective as they should be and proposed using a survey to identify the characteristics of high-quality meetings. This idea was met with some resistance by several team members, for some very good reasons:

1. In recent months the division had been "surveyed to death";

2. A hand-out about how to hold effective meetings had been distributed recently;

3. The problem had more to do with execution than lack of knowledge (it was noted that conducting an effective meeting is not "rocket science");

4. Focusing on meetings seemed trivial, given the many deeper and more urgent problems facing the company.

The consultant accepted these concerns and then explained that he viewed the survey as an instrument to engage people in thinking about ways to improve their meetings. A team member suggested that a better approach might be to model desired behavior at their team meetings and then get information in real time about whether the meeting had hit or missed its mark. His suggestion appeared to capture the team's interest and resulted in several ideas about improving team meetings. Among them were: establishing a norm to empower people ("If anyone thinks a meeting is not being well-run, he or she can walk out"); developing the next meeting's agenda at the end of each meeting; starting and ending meetings on time; and conducting a brief evaluation at the end of each meeting.

The interesting features of this snapshot of one team's efforts to manage in the middle of change were the blunt honesty of team members and the fact that nobody's ego left the meeting badly bruised. The consultant had intervened with the intent of stimulating further change. His proposed intervention—a survey—was shot down by members of the team. Still believing that the team's meetings needed to be improved, the consultant had persisted by explaining why he had thought a survey would be helpful. This led to a counterproposal from a team member that received support. Once team members were engaged by the counterproposal, they generated a list of procedural changes intended to improve team meetings. In the end, the consultant got what he wanted, but not the way he wanted it. He was satisfied that he had stimulated positive change, and team members were satisfied because they had hammered his initial proposal into a change they could live with.

Change is continuous when strategic improvising tools and responsibilities are given to individuals and teams, high-frequency strategic thrusts are encouraged, and strategies are being formulated and implemented together in real time. Strategic improvising, by definition, writes a never-ending story of change, which is why assumptions that promote resistance or avoidance of change can be so damaging to the process. A commitment to engage in strategic improvising, therefore, requires a commitment to be changing continuously.

FROM A THREE-LEGGED TO A FOUR-LEGGED PLATFORM

Returning to Sam Walton's statement that he copied everything he did from somebody else, there is one possible interpretation we did not consider. Was the crafty retailer pulling our leg, or deliberately trying to mislead us? If his approach to retailing was unique, one of the ways he could keep it that way would be to deny its uniqueness.

Whether plausible or remote, this possibility introduces a new set of variables to the strategy equation—deception and surprise. Most approaches to strategy are based on a linear logic that is highly predictable. In strategic improvising, we assume the superiority of a paradoxical logic.

Paradoxical logic promotes unconventional solutions to problems. By thinking about perplexing problems from another perspective or at another level, paradoxical thinkers are able to break free of existing paradigms and pierce through stifling complexity.

Three metaphors are especially useful for identifying different ways to think paradoxically. When businesses are like *pitchers with a change-up*, the purpose of paradoxical logic is to fool competitors. We learn from *jet fighter pilots* how businesses can think paradoxically by moving outside established ways of thinking. Finally, businesses that think paradoxically are like *stock market contrarians:* they turn common, everyday market signals upside-down and convert them into unique business opportunities.

A Pitcher with a Change-Up

In baseball, when a batter is expecting a fastball, a properly disguised change-up will either leave him flat-footed or throw him completely off balance. Once a change-up is thrown, it makes a pitcher's fastball appear faster because it creates a moment of indecision for the batter.

A classic example of slowing down a competitor's ability to respond occurred when Canon invented distributive copying and left Xerox flat-footed, unable to respond. Eventually, Xerox recovered, but it took the giant several years to undo the damage Canon had done when it threw a change-up.

Another company that undermined a much stronger competitor is Novell. Novell's NetWare software made it possible to link microcomputers in a way that made their combined processing capacity and speed rival those of IBM's mainframe computers. The company made available, to everyone with a networked microcomputer, a computer processing capacity equivalent to that of a mainframe computer.

People at Novell claim that, early in their history, one of their real advantages over IBM and the rest of the computer industry was their Utah location. They were not taken seriously until they had established a strong beachhead. IBM was never certain it wanted to respond; Novell ultimately became its biggest customer for microcomputers. IBM probably would have counterattacked if it could have, but it did not know how, without cannibalizing its mainframe computer business. Recently, IBM threw in the towel and entered into a joint agreement with Novell. Now its giant sales force sells Novell's NetWare.

Another lesson taught by a pitcher with a change-up is that a mix of pitches can effectively create competitive advantage. Paradoxical logic, instead of always capitalizing on strengths, will sometimes recommend strengthening weaknesses. Businesses that strengthen weaknesses are more likely to surprise competitors that are using traditional competitor analysis as the basis for their strategy formulation. Mixing strategies—capitalizing on strengths and strengthening weaknesses—makes the actions taken by a business significantly less predictable.

Jet Fighter Pilots

Businesses think paradoxically like jet fighter pilots. In the training of a fighter pilot, a critical transition must occur from thinking in two-dimensional space to thinking in three-dimensional space. When fighter pilots think only in two-dimensional space, their options are limited and their maneuvers are highly predictable. They can always be outmaneuvered by an enemy pilot who is thinking in three-dimensional space. When fighter pilots think in three-dimensional space, however, enemy pilots can only guess what they will do next, because their options are practically limitless.

Like jet fighter pilots, businesses can think paradoxically by introducing new dimensions to their strategic thinking. At PepsiCo, for example, managers use the term "out-of-the-box thinking" to describe strategic thinking along a new dimension. The company initially improvised the strategy for its restaurant businesses along three dimensions: providing *high-quality* food *faster* and at a *lower price.* But it really leapfrogged its competitors and expanded its business by introducing a new dimension to its strategic thinking: nontraditional locations for selling fast food.

In this vein, Martin Starr of Columbia University says: "For years we've been talking about inching up, closing the gap, getting almost as good as the Japanese. That's not enough. We've got to leapfrog ahead."

Stock Market Contrarians

Because stock market contrarians believe in acting counter to the conventional wisdom, they become more bullish when everyone else is predicting a bear market. There are several reasons for businesses to be like contrarians. When everybody is moving in one direction, they are likely to *find many unexplored or abandoned opportunities* in the other direction. Because most high-tech companies focus on early adopters, significant opportunities are often available to companies that focus on serving late adopters. One Utah-based company, for example, experienced meteoric growth by purchasing, at sell-out prices, excess inventories of Apple IIs, then selling them to parents of children who used Apple IIs in school and wanted to buy an inexpensive first computer that their children already knew how to use.

In industries where businesses are competing against time, competitive advantage may go to a business that puts on the brakes and focuses on improving the quality of its products, innovates radically new products, or improves customer service. Xerox, for example, prided itself on its ability to ship a copier from its factory faster than the competition. When Xerox put on the brakes, however, it realized that what its customers really wanted was to know when the copier would arrive, to have it installed on schedule and in working order, and to be presented with an accurate bill. By responding to what its customers really wanted, Xerox was able to boost customer satisfaction, as measured by a company survey, from 70 percent to 90 percent.

Because business is usually cyclical, companies that do what everyone else does are never the first to *take advantage of a new business cycle.* They do not set the rules and are typically left picking up the crumbs of someone else's success. Contrarians, although they sometimes have to wait for success to catch up with them, are the first to arrive and stake out their claims in new or reemerging markets. When cycles reverse themselves, contrarians are uniquely positioned to clean up on late arriving competitors.

Basic Manufacturing and Technologies (BM&T) of Utah bought the aging Geneva Steel plant when nobody else wanted it because of depressed world steel prices. Soon afterward, the worldwide demand for steel turned around, and BM&T made phenomenal returns on its original investment in the plant. BM&T applied a large percentage of its profits to modernizing the Geneva facility and transformed it into one of the lowest-cost steel producers in the world.

Because contrarians take the road less traveled, they are *forced to improvise.* General Electric, consistent with the contrarian philosophy, launched Work-Out in 1989, after the best year in its corporate history. What is especially interesting about GE's Work-Out successes is that the divisions in which the process has been pushed the fastest are divisions that had initial disasters. Apparently, the initial disasters reinforced the idea that new ways of working could not be extrapolated from previous experience, and unique Work-Out solutions needed to be improvised.

A contrarian's viewpoint *keeps successful businesses from becoming overconfident.* At Novell, Ray Noorda, the CEO, describes the development of organizations in five stages. The fourth stage is *euphoria* and the fifth stage is *extinction.* Noorda views his principal responsibility as keeping Novell out of the euphoria stage. This is sometimes a difficult task in a company that owns roughly 60 percent of the networking market. Nevertheless, Noorda continually reminds his people that there are never any guarantees in business, and that the only competitive advantage that means anything is the ability to stay ahead of competitors. Novell's people, he says, are not just building a company; they are creating an industry. He is always pushing them to introduce new products, even at the risk of cannibalizing existing product lines.

THE HOT SEVEN: PREPARING INDIVIDUALS FOR MOVING FROM STRATEGIC PLANNING TO STRATEGIC IMPROVISING

9

Hot Seven A jazz group led by Louis Armstrong. Its members were Armstrong (cornet), Kid Ory (trombone), Johnny Dodds (clarinet), Johnny St. Cyr (banjo), Lil Armstrong (piano), Pete Briggs (tuba), and Baby Dodds (drums).

Ray Smith, a talented jazz musician and close friend, likes to tell a story about how he was first introduced to musical improvisation. As a music student at Brigham Young University, he was studying classical music and preparing for his senior concert. Woodwind instruments are Ray's specialty, and he decided to play Handel's oboe sonata as one of his concert selections. Generally, he loved the sonata, but he had a problem with its third movement—it had fewer notes per page than any piece of music he had ever played. It was boring to practice, and he feared it would be even more boring to his audience.

Two weeks before Ray's senior concert, a world-famous oboist performed at the university, and one of his selections was Handel's oboe sonata. When he played the third movement, Ray could not believe his ears. The oboist filled in the spaces in the composition with a flood of improvised notes. It was beautiful and immensely interesting to listen to.

After the concert, Ray approached one of his professors and asked about the liberties that had been taken with Handel's third movement. The professor explained that Handel composed his oboe sonata *expecting* musicians to improvise during the third movement.

197

This revelation put Ray in a quandary. After the performance he had heard, he could not go back to playing the third movement as it was written. As he practiced improvisations, however, he realized that he did not have the skill necessary to play it adequately. When the day of Ray's senior concert came, he performed the first and second movements of the sonata flawlessly, then signaled his accompanist to skip the third movement.

Ray Smith's first experience with improvisation illustrates that it is not an easy thing to do. Most people will see the benefits of improvisation but they may be reluctant to try it. Practiced strategic improvisers, like the world-renowned oboist, get results in complex, dynamic, and unpredictable business environments that strategic planners both admire and desire. Still, planners feel unprepared to improvise. When moments of truth come, they lose their nerve and fail to take the leap of faith required by strategic improvising. Because they are used to planning what they do before they take action, it is difficult for them to formulate and implement strategies together in real time.

As we discuss strategic improvising with executives throughout the world, we hear one message over and over: it is easy for them to agree that their companies need to do more strategic improvising, but they personally are uncomfortable with the idea. When we spoke to one executive recently, he suggested that strategic improvising would be a lot more palatable if we could help prepare individuals for the profound changes associated with moving from strategic planning to strategic improvising. This began our thinking about the *hot seven,* our name for the individual orientations required of strategic improvisers. They must:

Learn to go toward anxiety;

Continuously aspire higher;

Keep their eyes on the ball;

Leverage themselves through others;

Accept dynamic imbalances;

Learn to laugh at themselves and with others;

Keep the faith.

Each of these orientations is described in the sections that follow.

GOING TOWARD ANXIETY

Clayton Alderfer, a professor of organizational behavior at Rutgers University, counsels his students to go toward anxiety. He believes that individuals both learn more and develop more quickly when they force themselves to go in directions that initially feel uncomfortable to them. Alderfer believes that what people need to learn most is behind the walls created by their own anxieties.

John Keats described a characteristic of persons of achievement that he called "negative capability." In a letter to his brothers, George and Thomas, on December 22, 1817, Keats wrote:

> . . . it struck me what quality went to form [a person] of Achievement, especially in Literature, and which Shakespeare possessed so enormously—I mean Negative Capability, that is, when a man is capable of being in uncertainties, mysteries, doubts, without any irritable reaching after fact and reason.

The world is a complex place, and individuals often struggle to navigate their way through life. Persons of achievement are somehow able to face the unknown and the unresolved, in their pursuit of answers to questions and solutions to problems. They are comfortable with uncertainty and do not force a premature resolution of a problem in order to avoid feeling anxious.

Most individuals, however, have comfort zones in which they prefer to operate—safe havens from stress and anxiety. A reluctance to leave a comfort zone eventually transforms it into a trap. When people go toward anxiety, they test out what life is like outside their comfort zones. Some people are cautious—they dip their toes into new waters, lift them out, then dip them in again. Others dive deep into new waters and never look back. Either way, people are likely to find that living outside their comfort zones is an exciting and enriching experience; there is nothing more exhilarating than accomplishing something that fear had always prevented them from trying. By moving beyond their preconceived limitations, they are able to redefine who they are and what they are capable of doing.

Scott Peck, a psychotherapist and the author of *The Road Less Traveled,* makes an interesting observation about individuals, families, and leaving home that has some important implications for going toward anxiety. He notes that those individuals who grew up in warm, nurturing homes usually have the easiest time leaving home. Individuals from homes filled with backbiting, hostility, coldness, and viciousness have a much more difficult time leaving. The reason, according to Peck, is that individuals tend to project onto the world what their early-childhood home was like. Individuals from loving homes have an easy time leaving the nest because they see the world as a loving place; individuals from difficult home environments see the world as cold, dangerous, and uncaring.

Similar projections can color the perceptions of corporate employees. When their companies are caring and humane, employees will be much more likely to leave their comfort zones. Conversely, when companies are cold and impersonal, employees will be reluctant to venture outside their comfort zones because they fear the unknown.

The objective of programs like Outward Bound and Japanese "Hell" Camps is to force individuals out of their comfort zones. People are uprooted from their familiar surroundings, in some cases exposed to derision and contempt, and challenged in ways they have never been challenged before. These are not pleasant experiences, but they can be extremely fulfilling when fears are faced head-on and conquered.

Do individuals have to submit themselves to such programs, in order to learn how to go toward anxiety? The advantage of such programs is that they break people out of their normal routines, but this can also be their downfall. Individuals may establish a new self-identity in a new place, but will they keep their new identity when they return to the workplace? This transfer-of-learning problem is associated with most off-site training. People need the help of others to validate the new patterns of behavior they learn when they are away. In the absence of external validation, people tend to revert to previous patterns of behavior. If they were unwilling to go toward anxiety before they left, they are unlikely to be any different when they return.

For this reason, we recommend naturally occurring opportunities to go toward anxiety. In most organizations, everything anyone needs to know about going toward anxiety can be learned by urging more openness in interpersonal relationships. Individuals confront some of their worst anxieties when they tell their boss something he or she doesn't want to hear, or ask a question that nobody dares ask, or vote their conscience irrespective of how they will be perceived by others. Going toward interpersonal anxiety tests the level of trust people can have for each other in an organization; more often than not, when honest opinions are openly expressed, the rumored causes of distrust disappear and people realize they can trust each other more than they had ever thought possible.

In a major metropolitan law firm, there was a real reluctance on the part of many of the junior partners to speak their minds publicly. They feared retribution, particularly from the senior named partner, who controlled about 70 percent of the firm's business and had a reputation for being quite arbitrary about whom he gave "his" work to. The consequence was that concerns about the firm were being expressed by junior partners behind closed doors, but never shared with the key decision makers of the firm. Ultimately, a group of the junior partners became so frustrated with the status quo that they decided to confront the senior named partner. Predictably, he disagreed with some of their views, but he surprised the junior partners with the number of times he agreed with them. By going toward the anxiety surrounding their relationship with the senior named partner and risking alienating someone with significant control over their livelihoods, this group of junior partners was a catalyst for significant, positive change at the firm. They were harbingers of a new era of openness and trust.

Chris Argyris, the James Bryant Conant Professor at the Harvard Graduate School of Business, has developed an exercise to help people see how they manipulate situations to avoid interpersonal anxiety. He calls it "exposing the left-hand column." Argyris instructs participants to select a specific situation in which they are interacting with one or several people in a way that is clearly not working. They write out a sample of the exchange on the right-hand side of the page, in the form of a script. Then, on the left-hand side, they write anything they would think or feel but probably would not communicate during the discussion. By analyzing the left-hand column, participants discover the assumptions about others that strongly influence their interactions, although they are reluctant to share them. They learn how to share those assumptions and move discussions forward more productively, if they are willing to go toward interpersonal anxiety.[1]

Strategic improvising is extremely dependent on an open flow of information. Only when people are quickly and fully informed can they make the ongoing adjustments to strategic thrusts that characterize strategic improvising. Therefore, going toward interpersonal anxieties greatly increases the probability that the immense information needs associated with strategic improvising will be met.

ASPIRING HIGHER

When we counsel people to aspire higher, we assume that something to aspire to really exists for them. We call their response the Apollo Creed effect. If Rocky Balboa, the central character in the movie *Rocky,* had not gotten the chance to fight Apollo Creed, the heavyweight champion, he would probably have continued living the life of a no-good neighborhood bum. He would have fought mediocre fighters, beating some and losing to some, and supplemented his income by supplying loan sharks with a little muscle.

Being given the chance of a lifetime, a fight with Apollo Creed, inspired Rocky to get out of his rut. He worked at getting better and reached out to others to help him get better. Before the fight, all Rocky wanted to do was go the distance with the champ; during the fight, he gained new confidence. He realized the champ was not invincible: he had weaknesses like everybody else, and, although he threw lightning-quick combinations, he did not have the devastating power that Rocky had feared. In the end, Rocky's transformation was more psychological than physical. He became a world-class contender by believing he belonged in the same ring with Apollo Creed.

Recognition of the Apollo Creed effect suggests that one of the best ways to aspire higher is to step up to a higher level of competition. Many people simply stop at a level of competition that feels comfortable, then coast along; like Rocky, they win some and lose some. The only way one can coast for a long time is to go downhill. Going uphill requires a continuous push, and standing toe-to-toe against stronger competitors is one way to get pushed.

Another way to aspire higher is to compete against a standard, preferably a rising standard. Career development literature discusses the "success spiral syndrome," a psychological process in which success at one level creates a desire for success at a higher level. Several warning labels are attached to the success spiral syndrome. If spiraling success is the only incentive guiding their lives, people will be easily ruled by obsessions. Sometimes, when individuals become consumed by spiraling, unidimensional successes, the things that matter most receive the least attention. There is also a positive side to the success spiral syndrome. As people aspire higher and succeed, they learn that they can aspire still higher.

We visited Tektronix's Forest Grove, Oregon, plant a few years ago, and observed there a culture in which every individual technician was encouraged to aspire higher. Technicians were expected to assume greater responsibility, participate in decisions, develop personal skills, and, of course, do the work. They were taught to think developmentally about themselves and the work they performed. The philosophy at the plant was that individuals could work at 50 percent of their capacity and remain employed, but real growth came from being fully engaged both physically and intellectually. The natural outgrowth of being fully engaged was a limitless capacity for developing new capabilities.

Forest Grove's plant manager, Gene Hendricksen, talked about the stages of development of the plant's technicians, from the embryonic stage, where a high-performance work system is simply a concept, all the way to full maturity, where wisdom and commitment have been acquired after years of extensive experience. Along this developmental path, technicians take greater initiative, become more achievement-motivated, develop a tolerance for ambiguity, become more interdependent with others, develop increased versatility, gain perspective and awareness, and acquire sophisticated process skills.

Hendricksen, who assumes the roles of teacher, inspirer, facilitator, and coach, ensures that the decisions the technicians are required to make coincide with their stage of development. For example, decisions about the layout of the cafeteria and the plant interior preceded decisions about the compensation system, a plant performance plan, and plant strategy. Hendricksen's ultimate goal is for every plant technician to think strategically all the time, but he realizes that the first steps in that direction need to be modest. Nevertheless, by continuing to inspire technicians to aspire higher, his goal is becoming a reality. Even before Hendricksen's goal is realized, the technicians are reaching beyond it with their own goals for the plant.

Aspiring higher is not a romantic concept; rather, it is mundane because it involves self-discipline, persistence, and hard work. "You don't need talent to succeed," insists Irwin C. Hansen, chief executive of Porter Memorial Hospital in Denver. "All you need is a big pot of glue. You smear some on your chair and some on the seat of your pants, you sit down, and you stick with every project until you've done the best you can."[2] Many people are content with the immediate successes that come to them because of their natural abilities. They become self-satisfied and complacent, and they stop reaching higher. Only people who set their sights high continue to aspire higher. Intermediate successes bring feelings of satisfaction; more importantly, they instill the needed confidence to continue upward toward a distant, ultimate goal.

Before Super Bowl XXV, we read a column about Matt Bahr, the placekicker for the New York Giants. Bahr had been the hero in the National Football Conference championship game against San Francisco. He kicked the winning field goal with four seconds left in the game. According to the columnist, Bahr was not proclaiming himself the Greatest, nor was he having his right leg bronzed. He was not even walking with a swagger.[3]

"I have one motto in this business," said Bahr, referring to the kicking business and explaining his demeanor. "You're only as good as your next kick." The purpose of aspiring higher is always to make your next kick better than your last.

KEEPING THE EYES ON THE BALL

Whenever we get a little off-balance in life, we like to imagine ourselves on a baseball diamond, dug into the batter's box, swinging at a pitch. Our image is of a batter keeping his head down and not taking his eyes off the ball. He is swinging level. Too often, as batters in life, we get caught up in swinging for the fences when all we really need to do is make contact. When a batter swings too hard, he almost always loses sight of the ball because his shifting torso forces him to step away from the pitch and his head lifts up prematurely to see where the ball is going. Our imagined swing is smooth and level. Our weight shifts at exactly the right moment, and we are *not* looking at where the ball is going before we hit it.

In too many organizations, people run too hard and too fast with new ideas, and then burn out. The individual efforts that accomplish the most in organizations are sustained efforts. Almost always, slow-and-steady wins the race.

According to Jim Gott, the Los Angeles Dodgers' relief pitcher, there is a time late in the season when players on teams that are still contenders in a division championship race try to run faster, throw harder, or field cleaner. They try to exceed their capabilities. Gott wants his teammates to play hard, but he does not believe they should play beyond their limits. They are more likely to be injured if they play in an uncontrolled way, and their performance tends to go up and down, making it less predictable. Potential damage to team unity threatens, when individual players either think they can do everything themselves or criticize other players because they are not playing with the same level of intensity. Gott's remedy is simple: "[Y]ou have to still go out there with a boyish enthusiasm and just play like you're thankful to be there."[4]

In successful companies, it is important for people to find a pace that pushes them but is sustainable. When people are constantly turning their afterburners on and off, they waste energy. Besides being exhausting, flat-out performance is unsustainable because it operates under the assumption that there is an end in sight and things will be qualitatively different once the end is reached. There are fiscal years and quarterly reports in business, but there is never an end to the business season.

Spectacular success stories do happen, but they are few and far between. An image of explosive growth and success is at best a harmless fantasy and at worst a distraction from the business basics that are the bedrock of consistency. The best way to keep a business growing is to keep the eyes focused on strategic objectives and take controlled, level-headed actions. If people and organizations keep their weight evenly distributed and resist the urge to overreact, they are less likely to be thrown off-balance when competitors or unpredictable changes in the business environment throw them a change-up or a curve.

Our discussion has focused on individuals, but it is important to understand that there are parallel organizational dynamics. David Birch, director of MIT's Program on Neighborhood and Regional Change, observes that "the best predictor of a big company's decline is previous rapid growth, the best predictor of rapid growth is a previous big decline, and stability is tied to a big decline as the best predictor of [company] death." Birch believes that the key to corporate success is hanging on through the natural ups and downs of the organizational life-cycle. When explosive growth does happen, it is more likely to occur in mature companies that have accumulated the cash flow, wisdom, and experience to recognize and take advantage of opportunity when it presents itself. According to Birch, the potential for explosive growth is like a planted seed "waiting for the right combination of water and light to bring it alive."[5]

National Applied Computer Technologies (NACT), a small company based in Orem, Utah, makes telephone switching equipment. NACT's early history was quite successful: its switches became popular with both small, rural telephone companies and large corporations. NACT sat on its technical advantage and was soon overtaken by larger, more aggressive competitors. In response to the sudden downturn, the founders signed personal lines of credit to keep the company afloat. After months of continuous bleeding, there were layoffs of two-thirds of both the professional and nonprofessional staffs. Costs were taken down to the point where the company could be profitable selling just one switch a month. In the meantime, the small group of hardware and software engineers who remained with the company went to work building a new switch and writing new software. The result was a very competitive new product that the company is currently selling at a rate of almost 20 switches per month.

Because of its recent slump, NACT is not taking its current success for granted. The company continues to operate in a highly disciplined manner, solicits comprehensive feedback from its customers, and attempts to be as responsive as possible. NACT was able to keep its head down and swing level when it was getting nothing to hit; now, when pitches are being delivered with NACT's name on them, the company is cleaning up.

Keeping the eyes on the ball means that most of the attention of individuals and companies is riveted on the here-and-now. No one looks back at what happened the last time at bat or thinks about what the plans are for after the game. It is important to know the score, the inning, the count, and whether runners are on base, but that information is secondary to one's primary task of making contact with the ball. The best hitters seem to be able to tune-out everything that is going on around them and to have peak concentration at the only instant that really matters: when the ball crosses the plate. This kind of real-time, everything-is-on-the-line concentration makes individuals successful at strategic improvising—and most other business activities.

LEVERAGING THROUGH OTHERS

Jacqueline Wexler, the current president of the National Council of Christians and Jews, has a sister who has spent her life teaching children with reading disabilities. To Wexler's sister, every child is a unique detective mystery, and her job is to find clues to unlock the child's potential.

We strongly believe that all organizations would be better, more productive, and more humane places to work if all of us looked on everyone below us, above us, and working at our same level as having a unique detective story. We need to focus more on unlocking the vast reservoir of potential in others.

Franklin Murphy, one-time chancellor of UCLA and later chief executive of the Times-Mirror Company, believes he succeeded on the talents of others. He has said: "I always sought out people who were talented, who had self-discipline. Then I developed their affection and loyalty. I recruited them, motivated them, and when we achieved something, I shared the credit with them."[6]

Recently, we have spent a great deal of time in professional service organizations because we believe increasingly complex, nonroutine work will require businesses to operate more like professional service firms. One of the primary ways professional service organizations increase their profitability is by leveraging senior partners through junior partners, associates, and staff. This is especially true when professional service firms contract to provide prespecified services for a fixed fee. The best way to improve margins is to reduce the overall costs by involving lower-salaried associates and support staff in the delivery of services.

In most professional service organizations, however, there is a problem with underdelegation: senior partners do not push work down to more junior members of the firm. Senior partners are especially reluctant to invest time in coaching and supervisory activities that result in more effective delegation. According to David Maister, of Maister Associates, Inc., a consulting firm that specializes in working with professional service organizations, on any single engagement it is always more costly to get a junior person involved because the task will take longer and will require supervisory time. Although supervised delegation and coaching will increase leverage and decrease costs in the long term, senior people usually make short-term decisions not to involve junior people in specific projects. Accordingly, most professional service organizations underinvest in good supervision and coaching, even when they preach it fervently.[7]

When delegation occurs, there is some question about *how* it occurs. When organizations are engaged in nonroutine work, the most valuable people are not clones of stronger personalities—they are individuals who know how to think and act for themselves. Nonroutine work is comprised of a series of original episodes, not reruns. The longer junior people work alongside senior people, the more they learn, but to succeed at nonroutine work they must be able to improvise novel solutions to unique problems on their own.

Thomas Plummer, a professor of Germanic and Slavic languages at Brigham Young University, discusses the "Ophelia syndrome," based on the relationship between Polonius and his daughter, Ophelia, in Shakespeare's *Hamlet*. In a brief exchange during Act I, Scene 3, Polonius asks his daughter whether she thinks Hamlet's intentions are genuine. She answers: "I do not know, my lord, what I should think." Ophelia wants to be controlled, and Polonius wants to control her. He says: "I'll teach you. Think yourself a baby . . . ." Leveraging oneself through others is the antithesis of the Ophelia syndrome. At times, leveraging may promote interdependence, and at other times, independence; but it never promotes dependency. As long as dependencies remain, senior people do not let go and junior people do not take charge.[8]

If leveraging oneself through others does not mean answering their questions for them, what does it mean? How do senior persons help junior persons learn to think for themselves? One answer was suggested during a nationally televised interview with Itzhak Perlman, the virtuoso violinist. As a child, Perlman was sent to New York, far from his friends and family, to attend the Juilliard School of Music. His teacher was Dorothy Delay, a gentle but demanding woman who never told young Perlman what to do. This both frustrated and liberated him. He reported: "She would stop me in the middle of a scale and say, 'Now, Itzhak, what is your concept of a C-sharp?' It made me furious. She refused to tell me what to do. But I began to think as I played. My playing became an engaging intellectual exercise in which I understood every note and why I played it the way I did, because I had thought about it myself."

Perhaps the way to develop others' ability to think is the Socratic method. The key could be as simple as responding more often with questions and less often with answers, when individuals are unclear about what they should think. Real leveraging through others is accomplished when appropriately timed questions are asked, such as: What is your concept of a strategy? What strategic objective were you trying to accomplish here?

Another way to think about leveraging oneself through others is by using the career stages model developed by our two partners, Gene Dalton and Paul Thompson. According to the model, professionals move through four distinct career stages:

I. Apprentice stage, a period of maximum dependency; the key activities are helping, learning, and following directions.

II. Independent contributor stage, which requires increased independence; individuals are entrusted with their own projects or parts of projects.

III. Mentor stage, a period in which individuals train and assume responsibility for others.

IV. Director stage, the career stage of individuals who provide strategic direction and exercise power to get things done in organizations.[9]

In many ways, the movement of individuals between stages I and II depends on how successful stage III professionals are at leveraging through them. Stage IV represents ultimate leverage: the stage IV professionals leverage the leverage of stage III professionals.

One of the key ideas presented by Dalton and Thompson is that professional work is accomplished best by teams. Moving through the stages of career development involves changes in roles, relationships, and psychological orientation of team members. When these changes occur, both individuals and teams operate more effectively because the entire spectrum of teamwork is being covered: people are learning how to do the work, doing the work, and managing the work—all while other people are finding the work.

ACCEPTING DYNAMIC IMBALANCES

Some of our research has been in the area of career and adult development. Among other projects, we did a major study of businessmen in their 30s and concluded that theirs was a time of imbalance. We have also learned, from observing friends, colleagues, and clients, that every decade of life has its own potential for imbalance. There is more to do than there is time to do it in, and most people are forced to make ongoing choices about what they do and do not do. Because the choice never seems to be between having a balanced life or an imbalanced life, we prefer to concede to the inevitability of imbalances and think in terms of managing dynamic imbalances.

The same changes in the business environment that have rendered strategic planning ineffectual are increasing the pace at which life must be lived. In a slower, planned life-style, events are anticipated and responses are chosen in a deliberate, planful way. There is a time for everything, and everything can be given time. As events accelerate and become less predictable, people are forced to improvise a hectic, unplanned life-style. Decisions about what to do next are often made on the run. The world turns so fast that planning and thinking never quite catch up to action.

The answer to this modern-day condition is planning, thinking, and acting together in real time. What enables individuals to do this? Clear, long-term choices about life—a kind of personal strategic direction—that sets parameters within which they can improvise short-term choices. Early, long-term choices are expressions of fundamental values. When they are solid and immovable, they provide an anchor to life, a standard to which emerging patterns of short-term decisions can be compared. When short-term decisions seem to be veering too far from goals, adjustments can be made in real time to steer them on a more direct path.

Robert Wood, currently a Distinguished Professor of Finance at the Fogelman College of Business and Economics, Memphis State University, enjoys discussing his students and the characteristics that make some students better than others. He believes that the worst students are the ones who always try to maintain a perfect balance in their lives. From his perspective, these are students he can never trust to keep their promises when the pressure is on, because they refuse to upset the delicate balance in their lives.

Bob Wood realizes that there are more important things in life than writing another article for *The Journal of Finance*, but at the same time he understands that the relationship between effort and output is nonlinear. A threshold effect is associated with nonroutine work: unless one's efforts exceed a certain threshold, outputs will be negligible. Moreover, when one goes beyond that threshold of effort and stays there for a substantial period of time, the accomplishments are likely to stack up quickly. In many ways, nonroutine work is an all-or-nothing proposition.

If this sounds like a well-designed trap, it can be, unless one thinks in terms of dynamic imbalances. With dynamic imbalances, individuals must be unwilling to rationalize away their long-term choices, while still realizing the benefits of short-term imbalances.

Peter Vaill makes a distinction between micro-time (hours worked each day) and macro-time (length of commitment, in terms of months and years, to a project). He then argues that high-performing systems require people who are committed to putting in both micro-time and macro-time.[10] If companies are going to reach their potential, their people must be willing to make periodic sacrifices. However, when the pressure is off, people should be able to expect the company to have a memory because their long-term happiness is involved. Companies should actively encourage their people to reexamine their priorities at the conclusion of periods of intense effort. It is important for companies to realize that, from time to time, they need to provide their most valuable players with opportunities to readjust their commitments.

LAUGHING AT ONESELF AND WITH OTHERS

It is important to keep perspective in the games of business and of life. Although people sometimes construe situations in all-or-nothing terms in order to increase their commitment to a course of action, most successes do not change life much for the better and most failures do not change life much for the worse. Life goes on pretty much the same, whether individuals succeed or fail.

When organizations and people engage in strategic improvising, success and failure should be considered forms of feedback, not measures of relative worth. Fewer instances of grand successes or resounding failures occur with strategic improvising than with strategic planning, because minor adjustments are being made all the time.

When failures occur, as they inevitably do, it is important to be able to laugh at oneself and with others. Laughter ensures that nothing is taken too seriously. It is a pressure-release valve for individuals and organizations. When failure is caused by adverse circumstances, laughter helps people accept and make the best of them. Seve Ballesteros, the professional golfer, has said: "I'll play anywhere. If there are bad greens, then I am going to be the greatest bad-greens golfer. You just accept it . . . the great players don't get irritated." When failure is attributed to personal mistakes, laughter enables people to shrug them off, learn from them, and then apply that learning to a new and improved course of action.

John Cleese, an actor and comedian, suggests: "If you can get people to laugh at counterproductive behavior, they will be more likely to behave productively." He contends that people operate in two contrasting modes, open or closed. The open mode is more relaxed, more receptive, more playful and humorous; the closed mode is tighter and more rigid. Only in the open mode are people able to receive feedback from their actions. Accordingly, the ability to learn is greatly enhanced when people are in the open mode. Cleese suggests that humor and laughter perform a helpful role in organizations because they switch people into the open mode, in which they are "most intelligent, most efficient . . . and most competitive."[11]

Generally, we like and respect successful people who relish telling about their failures—perhaps even more than telling about their successes. Because experience tells us that failure is a part of most successes, such people seem more real to us. In spite of their obvious successes, they acknowledge their fallibility. These people appear to approach life as an adventure. Both the ups and downs of life bring them joy. They exhibit a playfulness that is both disarming and refreshing.

W. Edwards Deming makes another point that relates to the ability to laugh at oneself. He argues that organizations need to reduce the fear of failure before people will be able to discuss their failures openly and learn from them. When high-level or highly respected individuals are able to laugh at their failures, it loosens up people in organizations. They don't just tell their bosses the good news because they think that's all they want to hear. In fact, the focus shifts to reporting the bad news because it offers the most opportunities to learn from experience.

It is also important to laugh *with* people, because laughter together fosters interpersonal bonds and bolsters unity around strategic direction and purpose. One of the more significant events in the history of the informal system at Hughes Ground Systems Group was a talk given by Warren Mathews, on November 20, 1986. Mathews, a company old-timer and insider, recounted the history of Hughes Aircraft and, in a very humorous and often irreverent way, supported his hypothesis that the firm's culture was formed between 1951 and 1956, and then remained fundamentally unchanged. His talk was videotaped, retaped, and disseminated throughout the Hughes Ground Systems Group. It became a bona-fide, word-of-mouth hit throughout the company, largely because Mathews was able to make sense of Hughes Aircraft's distinctive culture while also making fun of it. In the process, Hughes's people were able to see both the functionality and dysfunctionality of their unique way of doing business. This summoned great pride and esprit de corps, while opening up the company to thinking about areas where changes were sorely needed. By using humor to describe the Hughes culture, Mathews was able to honor the past and then to galvanize commitment around a strategy for the future.

KEEPING THE FAITH

Karl Weick recounts an intriguing story that happened during military maneuvers in the Alps. The story illustrates the power of keeping the faith:

> The young lieutenant of a small Hungarian detachment in the Alps sent a reconnaissance unit into the icy wilderness. It began to snow immediately, snowed for two days, and the unit did not return. The lieutenant suffered, fearing that he had dispatched his own people to death. But the third day the unit came back. Where had they been? How had they made their way? Yes, they said, we considered ourselves lost and waited for the end. And then one of us found a map in his pocket. That calmed us down. We pitched camp, lasted out the snowstorm, and then with the map we discovered our bearings. And here we are. The lieutenant borrowed this remarkable map and had a good look at it. He discovered to his astonishment that it was not a map of the Alps, but a map of the Pyrenees.[12]

This story is open to several possible interpretations, but the most likely interpretation is that the map provided the soldiers in the reconnaissance unit with the faith they needed to find their way home. Because they kept the faith, they acted; in the course of acting, they were able to determine at every juncture what they should do next. In many ways, their faith in the map turned their confusion into meaning and became a self-fulfilling prophecy.

William James once observed that the faith that life is worth living generates the action that makes life worth living.[13] People make sense of the world by taking positive actions, but they must first believe that their actions will have positive results. In their mind's eye, individuals see something they want to accomplish, but they will simply throw up their arms in frustration unless they perceive some level of probability that their efforts will result in desired outcomes. This is the essence of faith as a motivator of action.

Another side to faith is important to consider, as part of our concern about individual behavior in organizational settings. Our colleague,

Alan Wilkins, discusses institutional faith: the faith individuals have in the fairness and adaptability of their organizations. He argues that the wrenching change introduced by corporate restructuring destroys the character of organizations and damages employee faith. Without faith, employees either develop self-protection skills or they become overly cautious because they are reluctant to take necessary and appropriate risks to improve operations.[14]

We agree with Wilkins, but we believe there is another side to the story: the onus of responsibility for maintaining faith is not only the institution's. Our experience tells us that individuals often overgeneralize and then overreact to isolated organizational events. Moreover, as they passively wait for the organization to act, they criticize instead of lending support to the actions that are taken. These observations lead us to conclude that the institutional faith of employees is often too fragile, too easily destroyed. Generally, individuals should cut their organizations some slack by being less suspicious of organizational actions. Faith is reciprocal: the more faith individuals have in organizations, the more faith organizations will have in them and the tighter will be ties that bind them.

If strategic improvising is to be successful, individuals must have faith in themselves, their organizations, and their strategic direction, and then keep their faith through thick and thin. This is the message of a sign Ross Perot keeps on his door: "Every Good and Excellent Thing Stands Moment by Moment on the Razor's Edge of Danger and Must Be Fought for."

Strategy is more of a motivational problem than a cognitive, forecasting problem. Most people can do what they think they can do, as long as they see it clearly, are willing to invest whatever effort is necessary, and remain focused to the end. One of the fundamental lessons of life is that successful people create the future by imposing their view on the world. They are the ones who never give up. Their unwavering faith and persistent behavior are the keys to accomplishing strategic objectives because they consistently make things happen.

Tom Sawyer, the president of NACT, likes to remind us that the difference between success and failure is trying something 18 times versus trying it 17 times. The Wright brothers were unsuccessful on their first 147 attempts to fly. They are recognized as the inventors of the first airplane because they refused to give up. They succeeded with attempt number 148.

GET OUT OF THE WAY

When individuals have internalized the "hot seven" individual orientations, it is important for their managers to get out of the way. In Tracy Kidder's *The Soul of a New Machine,* the secretary of the Eclipse project, Rosemarie Seale, described what it was like working for the project leader, Tom West:

> The bottom line . . . is that effort was done; it was done well, with very little help from the corporation, if any; a lot of people were allowed to grow; a lot of people were allowed to feel good about themselves—not a pat on the back—but deep-down good about themselves. . . . He [Tom West] set up the opportunity and he didn't stand in anyone's way. . . . He never put one restriction on me. Tom allowed me to take a role where I could make things happen. . . . He let me go out and see what I could get done. You see, he allowed me to be more than a secretary there.[15]

A Japanese word, *nemawashi,* refers to a process by which gardeners bind the roots of a tree for replanting. In Japan, where space is limited and great value is attached to a single tree, nemawashi is an intricate art form. One of the critical steps in nemawashi occurs after the tree is transplanted. The gardener has given the tree a new opportunity to grow by transplanting it, but once it is in the new soil he must stand back and allow the tree to grow. The worst thing a gardener can do during this pivotal stage in a tree's development is disturb it.

When Sparky Anderson, the manager of the Detroit Tigers, was asked about the secret to his success as a big-league manager, he responded: "I don't trip the players when they run out of the dugout." Susan Mooney, the president and CEO of Daw Technologies, a company that builds ultraclean manufacturing environments, explains her philosophy of management in similar terms: "Harness the brain power in people and then get out of their way." According to Mooney, the capability and energy of a company's people drive its strategy.

As managers step back to give people room to grow, they can still support personal development by removing bureaucratic barriers that obstruct change. Individuals feel more empowered and they preserve a lot more energy for change when their managers are leading interference for them against hierarchical structures and the policies and procedures that reinforce the status quo.

RIDE-OUT: FINAL COMMENTS ABOUT A CONTINUING PROCESS

10

We spent some time during the summer of 1991 at Division X of the Giant Radar Technology Group.[1] We were trying to understand the changes that had been occurring there since Giant Aircraft's acquisition by UniTrans Corporation. Division X makes radar displays for the Army and is one of the more progressive and profitable divisions in the Radar Technology Group.

As we helped Division X clarify its strategy, the debate focused on whether it should be customer-focused or product-focused. The argument for a customer-focused strategy was that, because of the division's many years of experience with the Army, it knew the defense contractor business. The customer-focused strategy would provide the clearest focus, through its concentration on providing excellent service to military customers. It was decided, however, that the customer-focused strategy failed to provide adequate leverage, especially in an era of shrinking defense spending. The product-focused strategy also fit the division, which was in the business of making radar displays. The strategy was more attractive to Division X's people because it offered greater leverage, through the development of products for commercial markets.

The clarification of Division X's strategic direction made it possible to decide that the division should be organized around three process guidance teams: the design-the-parts team (Design Team), the build-the-parts team (Build Team), and the support-the-business team (Support Team). Because Division X was product-focused, the Design Team and Build Team constituted its unit of competitive advantage (UCA). Other types of value-added work were considered support work and were relegated to the Support Team. It was also decided that, before it could move into commercial ventures, Division X needed to organize a service-the-product team (Service Team). Currently, a Service Team was unnecessary because of the Army's policy to provide its own service.

The Design, Build, and Support Teams provided Division X with a basic structure, and strategic improvising operated within that structure. The influence of Division X's team-based structure was especially evident in the way strategic alignment processes conserved energy to drive strategic improvising. Each of the three teams appeared to be focusing on a specific alignment problem.

Division X's Design Team concentrated on aligning culture to strategy. Historically, the product engineering subcultures had been dominant at Giant. Giant's product-focused strategy, however, challenged previous cultural assumptions. Product engineers became members of cross-functional teams that included representatives from the procurement, marketing, manufacturing, testing, and quality departments, as well as from suppliers and customers. Instead of serving the engineers, the other members of the team worked with them to create the best possible product designs.

The alignment of Division X's culture to its product-focused strategy met initial resistance. For example, it was difficult for engineers to allow manufacturing people to influence the design of products. It was even more difficult, given their history as second-class citizens, for manufacturing people to stand up to engineers. Caught in the confusion of cultural change, team members had to be reminded constantly that they had to speak up if they had reservations about a design: they were only going to see it once.

The cross-functionality of the Design Team enabled it to improvise a product-focused strategy. Technical considerations, marketing considerations, procurement concerns, and customer preferences all influenced product strategies. Team members worked to build consensus around strategic objectives so they all could get behind a strategic thrust and make it successful.

The key issue for the Build Team was reducing temporal misalignments in order to get the product out the door more quickly. To improve productivity, the division replaced its production-line system with manufacturing cells. The manufacturing cells solved many problems, but they created others. For example, on the production line, people could see how the manufacturing process worked. When bottlenecks occurred, it was obvious what needed to be done to get the line moving again. Many wonderful things happened in manufacturing cells, but they had difficulty reacting quickly to unanticipated events, especially in the early stages of their development. They were not yet programmed to deal with nonroutine work. They needed engineering and design expertise, and access to materials. Without them, the work stopped.

The Build Team responded to this problem by assigning a cross-functional focal team (a search-and-rescue team) to each manufacturing cell. When a buzzer went off, a focal team sprang into action to provide the necessary engineering and design capability or the required materials, to get the manufacturing cell back on track. Focal teams also had developmental responsibilities. While they assisted, they taught members of the manufacturing cell how to solve their own problems. The key skills that the Build Team wanted transferred from the focal teams to the manufacturing cells were: problem identification, problem validation, and solution strategies that combine formulation and implementation in real time.

The Support Team had a different kind of alignment problem. Information was once synonymous with power at Division X. Individuals bragged about being one of only four or five people who "knew what was going on" at the division. This perception was especially strong in the finance department, which exercised power through the control of information. For example, a common practice at Division X was for the finance people to hold managers accountable for financial targets that were never shared with them, then humiliate the managers, during sessions with the division manager, for not meeting the uncommunicated goals.

Given the history and orientation of members of Division X's Support Team, critical efforts focused on moving it into horizontal alignment—first internally, and then externally—with the Design and Build Teams. Representatives from the finance department were especially resistant to changes, which they viewed as a direct challenge to their power and authority. Their instinctive response was to try to hold on to power and not empower others. For example, the finance people would not attend meetings of the Support Team which, in their minds, exempted them from sharing their information. In response, the Support Team decided to hold meetings in a conference room next door to the office of the finance manager. They even considered walking into his office together and holding a meeting there.

Events at Division X furnish insights into the relationship between strategy and structure. Because strategy provided the overall direction for the division, structure followed strategic direction. Strategic improvising, however, was influenced by and occurred within existing organizational structures. Therefore, strategy also followed structure.

A DIVISIVE DEBATE

"Structure follows strategy," said Alfred Chandler in 1962. Nobody could have foreseen the consequences of this simple assertion made by a business historian. The point Chandler was trying to make seemed innocuous enough—strategy defines an organization's purpose, and structure is the means of realizing that purpose. Therefore, structures are designed to implement strategies.

Competitive strategists used Chandler's statement to confirm the primacy of their field which, in turn, irritated organizational designers. Designers countered Chandler and the strategists who embraced his maxim by proposing that strategy follows structure. Existing organizational designs, they insisted, impose constraints on what organizations can do. Structures confine strategies to specific courses of action.

To many people, this debate was silly; however, the consequences were tragic. Battle lines were drawn, and the fields of competitive strategy and organizational design developed along separate paths. Many good ideas about organizational design bogged down because they lacked strategic focus, and a lot of good ideas about strategy met a similar fate because limited knowledge of organizational design confounded implementation.

One of the most disturbing consequences of this divisive debate has been strategists' ignoring important ideas from the sociotechnical systems (STS) literature. One STS concept, *equifinality*, means that a variety of "good" ways can be used to accomplish something. An organizational designer explores a variety of ways to design a job, a process, or a set of tasks in order to realize a desired set of outcomes. Because the concept of equifinality increases flexibility, it should be as important to strategic thinking as it is to organizational design. There is more than one way to accomplish strategic objectives within an established strategic direction. The STS concept of *minimum critical specifications* also enlightens strategic thinking. Strategies cannot be overdetailed at the top of an organization, if everyone is expected to become a strategic thinker. A jazz group's lead sheets provide minimum critical specifications; improvising is expected. Strategies, like lead sheets, should be stated simply, to allow embellishment by strategic improvisers throughout each organization.

What used to be called the field of "policy formulation and administration" preceded the rift between strategists and organizational designers. This field of study had blind spots traceable to its preoccupation with the top-management perspective, but it also offered several advantages. A primary advantage was that it treated the activities of a general manager as a seamless garment: there was no artificial separation of functions, roles, and skills. All general managers were expected to manage current operations, formulate strategies for the future, and forge organizational structures to fit the needs and characteristics of businesses. Management, competitive strategy, and organizational design were bundled together as one problem—to be solved by the general manager.[2]

The old policy formulation and administration perspective is injected with new life when the functions, roles, and skills of general managers are distributed throughout organizations. One of the early influences on our ideas about strategic improvising came from a visit to a plant that was run by a committee comprised of representatives from each of the plant's business-element units. The level of sophistication demonstrated by the members of this committee caught our attention. They were individuals with high school diplomas who were able to think like general managers.

Experiences at Giant's Division X told us that getting people to think like general managers is easier said than done. Division X had both top-down and bottom-up resistance. At the top, managers were concerned about the impact of participation on their ability to control processes and outcomes. In the trenches, some employees were reluctant to assume additional responsibilities. These attitudes prevented both groups from engaging in strategic improvising. Top managers wanted to provide more than a strategic direction; employees colluded with the managers' plan-and-control orientation by spurning their own expanded functions, roles, and skills.

It remains a challenge to change the functions, roles, and skills of people in organizations, but if businesses are to gain or regain competitive leadership in the 1990s, their people must begin to think like general managers and combine competitive strategy and organizational design into one problem. Strategic planners and organizational designers both try to respond to complex, dynamic, and unpredictable conditions in the business environment, but they are never quite responsive enough because they work separately. Either organizational designs are fine-tuned independent of events in the business environment, or businesses reposition themselves in their industries without making appropriate internal adjustments.

WANTED: NEW WAYS TO EDUCATE STRATEGISTS

One of the major barriers to expanding the use of strategic improvising is a pedagogical problem: How can it be taught? Business organizations are ideal laboratories for learning-by-doing. In the daily affairs of businesses operating in a complex, dynamic, and unpredictable business environment, there are many opportunities for individuals and teams to practice real-time strategic thinking. Opportunities to practice strategic improvising exist; the problem is whether people are prepared to take advantage of them. Many opportunities to practice strategic improvising are missed because businesspeople are still wedded to strategic planning.

Henry Mintzberg goes right to the source of the problem. He believes that the way strategy is taught in business schools explains why strategic plans continue to be formulated long after their many shortcomings have been exposed. According to Mintzberg, the case-study method is probably more responsible for strategic planning's longevity than anything else. Because strategic planning models match perfectly the pedagogical requirements of the case-study method, students walk away from their case-study-driven strategy classes believing they can plan their way out of any management situation. They carry with them a mistaken impression that, by setting its strategy, their firm's future is in their hands.

Mintzberg attributes many of the current problems in American industry to the case-study method. He writes:

> If the case method . . . has encouraged leaders to oversimplify strategy, if it has given them the impression that "you can give me a synopsis and I'll give you a strategy," if it has denied strategy formation as a long, subtle, and difficult process of learning, if it has encouraged managers to detach thinking from acting, remaining in their offices instead of getting into factories and meeting customers where the real information may have to

be dug out, then it may be a major cause of the problems faced by contemporary organizations.[3]

The case-study method reinforces the top-down, low-frequency (high-impact), and front-loaded foundations of strategic planning. It is a pedagogy perfectly designed for strategic planning; it does not fit in with strategic improvising.

Business school professors may question the usefulness of strategic planning, but they are reluctant to teach anything else because it would force them to give up the case-study method. They might more readily accept the strategic improvising approach to strategy if a related pedagogical alternative were available.

On the surface, simulations appear to be a viable alternative to the case-study method because it is possible to simulate an enormously complex competitive environment. However, it would be difficult to use simulations to teach strategic improvising because the assumptions of most simulations about complex organizations are quite simple. For example, most simulations assume that a competing firm can make any move it wants—an assumption that completely ignores the many social, cultural, and political problems associated with implementing a strategy. Simulations leave students of strategy with a misperception that the perfect execution of their strategic decisions is automatic.

Projects are a better alternative for teaching strategic improvising, but only when they provide hands-on experience. Too often, projects are viewed in the same way as cases. The project team contracts with a business to provide it with a strategy. Team members collect information about the business's strengths, weaknesses, opportunities, and threats; they analyze it, propose a list of strategic recommendations, and then leave. They never stay long enough to help implement their recommendations.

Projects are limited by the fact that students do not have the credibility to significantly influence a business's strategic thinking. If a business is immersed in strategic planning methods, a student group is not going to convert it to strategic improvising. The best learning opportunities for students might be with businesses already engaged in strategic improvising: a group of students might join intact work teams in formulating and implementing strategies in real time. Ideally, they would become valued members of their teams. The product of their project would be real-time suggestions that they would take some role in implementing.

Most students would also need to write papers that report on their experiences and the lessons learned, to satisfy class requirements.

Another option is "live" cases. Representatives of a firm could visit a class once or a few times, to discuss their strategies. One of the great advantages of "live" cases is that they require students to acquire, filter, and digest information in real time. Students learn to probe deeply into the circumstances surrounding a "live" case. What they learn about the business is secondhand, but the experience fine-tunes their observation skills.

When we arrange for representatives of companies to visit a class and they can come only one time, we get the best results from the "live" case discussions when we have had previous consulting or research experience with the companies. The representatives tell the class their company's story. Our previous experiences with their company enable us to rehearse the narrative for best effect. We encourage the representatives to stop at key decision points and ask students what they would do, before they describe what the company did. It is also important to ensure that formulation and implementation issues receive equal time and attention.

When someone comes to us with an interesting strategic problem but does not have the resources to pay us to consult with their business, we sometimes invite them to participate in another kind of "live" case experience involving several visits to classes during a semester. The visitors present a real-time strategic problem, and the class participates in helping them solve it. Most of the time we begin with strategy clarification, but occasionally we meet with representatives of businesses that already have a defined strategic direction. During subsequent visits, the class receives real-time information from the visitors and participates with them in making real-time decisions. This approach does not provide hands-on experience with strategic improvising, but students receive feedback about decisions they helped make in real time.

Another alternative that shows great promise, but with which we have only limited experience, is what we call *expanded case discussions*. Instead of confining a case to a single session of class, we spend multiple sessions on an expanded case discussion. We choose undisguised cases that provide the information needed for strategy clarification. During the first session of the expanded case discussion, we focus on the identification of strategic options. We work at understanding what three or four strategic options might mean to the company described in the case. Then, three or four student groups are formed and each group is assigned to explore one of the strategic options. We violate one of the golden rules of case teaching by considering cases as being incomplete. Student groups are encouraged to find out more information about the company to support the validity of their strategic option.

During the second session, the student groups present arguments for their assigned strategic options. After hearing the presentations and debating the positives and negatives of each strategic option, the class chooses to pursue one strategic option. Next, we work at specifying a strategic direction and defining a business concept for the company. The final discussion activity involves defining the company's unit of competitive advantage (UCA). We assign student groups to represent teams inside the UCA, and a value-added support team. For example, in an expanded case discussion about the Giant Radar Technology Group's Division X, we would assign three student groups to function as a design-the-parts team, build-the-parts team, and support-the-business team respectively. With a more typical product-focused business, we might also assign a student group to function as a service-the-product team.

Typically, we devote one more session of class to the expanded case discussion. Student groups representing different teams present their strategic objectives. The instructor provides an external business environment by describing a variety of actions taken by competitors, suppliers, and customers. The teams are invited to recommend actions. Class members who are not assigned to one of the teams play the role of a high-level strategy group. They deal with vertical misalignments (defined as actions that are inconsistent with the company's business concept) as they arise. Team members learn about reducing horizontal and temporal misalignments as they adjust to actions taken by other teams. Because teams of students engage in making high-frequency, real-time strategic decisions in a complex, dynamic, unpredictable business environment, they inevitably develop their strategic improvising skills.

DRIVING OFFENSIVE STRATEGIES

In *Offensive Strategy: Forging a New Competitiveness in the Fires of Head-to-Head Competition,*[4] we proposed a new way of thinking about competitive strategy. We argued for a change in attitude about competition: instead of positioning businesses to avoid and defend themselves against competition, managers should engage in direct competition. We reasoned that, to become global industry leaders, businesses need to compete directly against the best businesses in the world.

Offensive Strategy was about how to *think about* strategy. This book has been about how to *do* strategy. Strategic improvising is a technology for driving offensive strategies, and our purpose here has been to equip businesses with the tools they need to formulate and implement offensive strategies together in real time.

There is a great need for tools to drive offensive strategies. Across the landscape of American and international business, we see examples of companies that have missed significant windows of opportunity in their industries because they did not attack aggressively enough. These companies realized the need for change and wanted to change, but when the time came to change, they did not know how. It is not enough to espouse the philosophy behind direct competition and offensive strategies: companies need to do something about it—they need to know *what to do*. A case from the bottled water industry illustrates this point.[5]

The Perrier Group controlled 24 percent of the U.S. bottled water business when catastrophe struck. In February 1990, traces of benzene, a known carcinogen, were discovered in Perrier's bottled water. The contamination was attributed to a faulty filter. The problem for Perrier was that its customers now knew that benzene occurs naturally at the source of the company's spring at Vergeze, France. The advertising slogan, "It's perfect, it's Perrier," became a source of embarrassment for the bottler.

Derek Quibell, vice president of Quibell Corporation, another bottler, described Perrier's demise this way: "It's as if, in one day, the world's biggest army has waved the white flag." Surprisingly, however, Perrier's competitors were reluctant to step forward and assert themselves. Even big competitors like PepsiCo and Adolph Coors held back from attacking the inviting target. The litany of excuses—lack of marketing money, limited bottling capacity, fears that a weak Perrier would weaken the overall market—all made sense, and probably justified restraint on the part of some of Perrier's competitors. Given the lack of response, it appeared as if Perrier had psyched-out an entire industry.

The fact that none of Perrier's competitors wanted to step forward and take advantage of this once-in-a-lifetime opportunity was in part a tribute to Perrier's reputation and the relationships it had been able to build, especially with food retailers. Ronald Davis, Perrier's CEO, said at the time: "I've learned how important a reputation is. If we had faced this problem with a bad reputation, we'd be dead." Davis helped Perrier's reputation by writing letters to 550 retail CEOs and pledging that the company's marketing budget would rise from $6 million to $25 million in 1990. This compared quite favorably to the $14 million spent by *all* of Perrier's rivals in 1989. Moreover, the Perrier Group had other brands of sparkling water—Arrowhead, Poland Spring, Great Bear, and Calistoga—to pick up the shelf space vacated by its flagship brand.

Still, it made no sense for David Daniel, CEO of Evian's U.S. bottled-water business, which markets Saratoga, a major competitor, to say that Perrier's problems "haven't affected our strategies one iota." A lot of talk about long-term considerations and gentlemanly behavior among Perrier's competitors supports the conclusion that they did not go after the leader because they did not want to change their strategies. The Perrier tragedy actually upset their plans because they had settled into the role of industry followers. In essence, Perrier had no competitors because the other industry players were neither inclined to engage in combat nor combat-ready.

Another plausible explanation is that Perrier's competitors did not change their strategies because they did not know how. In the stable industry structure they colluded to create, strategic planning worked like a charm. They could anticipate sales and profits by projecting industry trends. They had little incentive to develop real-time tools to respond to unanticipated industry events. They were stunned when the unthinkable happened and Perrier went down. It was as if they had lost their leader and they did not know what to do next.

Perrier's competitors might have prevented Perrier from jumping back into the game with its lead intact. Instead, they encouraged it back, because none of them was equipped to enter the brave new world of direct competition that Perrier's loss of market leadership would have ignited.

How important is it to *think* about competitive strategy? Our current advice to companies is: DO IT. While discussing paradigm changes, John Trani, head of GE Medical Systems, said: "They do not shift by thinking about them. Actions need to be taken, something must be done."

In the crisis within the bottled-water industry, nobody seemed willing or able to make the first move. Thinking about offensive strategy might have convinced Perrier's competitors that they should make a first move, but they did not know how to do it. Strategic improvising is a technology for making the first move, and, in turn, provides access to the kinds of information needed to determine subsequent moves. For these reasons, it is the right technology for driving offensive strategies.

SEMPRE AVANTI: FOREVER FORWARD

The motto of a proud Italian-American family is Sempre Avanti, meaning Forever Forward. This is also a fitting motto for strategic improvising.

The core idea behind strategic improvising is: from small beginnings, great things can come, if a strategy is directed and purposeful and people are willing to improvise. Gateway 2000 Inc., which sold 230,000 IBM-style personal computers in 1991, has a simple strategy: charge the fewest bucks for the bang. Ted Waitt, Gateway's CEO and founder, started down the road to building a billion-dollar, product-focused (low-cost) company when he dropped out of college in 1984 and went to work for a computer retailer. After a year, he and partner-to-be Mike Hammond started a users' club for owners of the Texas Instruments (TI) 99 computer. Once membership rolls were large enough, they negotiated with manufacturers to build products to order, creating a lucrative mail-order market. Using the TI-users market as a beachhead, they earned enough money to branch out into the mail-order business for complete personal computer systems.[6]

Gateway's next direction is gradually becoming clear to Gateway's people as the company moves forever forward on several fronts. Internally, they are moving toward self-managing teams and more formal meetings to share information and make collective decisions. They are also moving aggressively into the computer notebook market, in response to new offerings by competitors (Zeos, Dell, and Compaq). Externally, Gateway is shifting direction more toward the corporate market by offering machines that are NetWare-certified for corporate computer networks and by beefing up its corporate sales force. Gateway's people realize that they need to cut their two-week delivery time at least in half, to become attractive to corporate customers. The company also wants to go international; with the lowest price-tags in the industry, their reliable machines should be very popular in the global marketplace.[7]

Businesses need to move forever forward because the only way they learn is by taking action and then thinking about the consequences of their action. Chaos theorists tell us that the only way to know how complex systems will behave after they are modified is to modify them and see how they behave.[8] The only way to know how a strategy will affect a complex organization is to take action on multiple fronts, monitor the effects, and then make appropriate adjustments.

Miles Davis, the great jazz trumpeter who recently died, epitomized the spirit of Sempre Avanti. He was the innovator of more distinctive styles than any other jazz musician, including cool jazz, hard bop, modal playing, and free-form explorations. According to Max Roach, a drummer and long-time friend: "He was musically one of the restless ones, constantly seeking."

In business, the restless ones invent new strategic objectives and launch new strategic thrusts within existing forms. They also modify current forms and create new forms. This book has offered one form, but strategic improvising, like jazz improvisation, is not limited to a single form. Our message would be inconsistent with the spirit of Sempre Avanti if we did not encourage the invention of other forms.

In *Miles,* his 1989 autobiography, Miles Davis wrote:

> To be and stay a great musician you've got to always be open to what's new, what's happening at the moment. You have to be able to absorb it if you're going to continue to grow and communicate your music. . . . I want to keep creating, changing. *Music isn't about standing still and becoming safe.*

Neither is business.

Notes

Chapter 1
Pickup: An Introduction to Strategic Improvising

1. We use the term "strategic planning" because it is the term that is most commonly used in industry. Among our academic colleagues, the more common term used to represent our intended meaning is "strategic management." Under the umbrella of strategic management are several schools of strategic thought, including the Harvard Policy School, Michael Porter's Competitive Forces School, and the Strategic Planning School. Common to these three schools of strategy is their recommendation of a top-down, low-frequency (high-impact), and front-loaded approach to strategic thinking. When we use the term "strategic planning," we are referring to any strategic approach with these three characteristics.

2. J. B. Quinn, *Strategies for Change: Logical Incrementalism* (Homewood, IL: Dow Jones-Irwin, 1980), 9.

3. A. D. Chandler, *Strategy and Structure* (Cambridge, MA: MIT Press, 1962), 11.

4. Cited from R. Henkoff, "How to Plan for 1995," *Fortune* (December 31, 1990), 76.

5. G. Stalk, Jr., "Time: The Next Source of Competitive Advantage," *Harvard Business Review* (July/August 1988), 41–51.

6. H. Mintzberg, "The Manager's Job: Folklore and Fact," *Harvard Business Review* (July/August 1975), 50–51.

7. Quinn, *Strategies for Change,* 15.

Chapter 2
A Cuttin' Contest: Strategic Planning versus
Strategic Improvising

1. R. L. Ackoff, *A Concept of Corporate Planning* (New York: John Wiley & Sons, 1970), 129–130.

2. Taken from R. H. Hayes, "Strategic Planning—Forward in Reverse?" *Harvard Business Review* (November/December 1985), 114.

3. J. B. Quinn, *Strategies for Change: Logical Incrementalism* (Homewood, IL: Dow Jones-Irwin, 1980), 38–39.

4. Hayes, "Strategic Planning," 111.

5. R. Henkoff, "How to Plan for 1995," *Fortune* (December 31, 1990), 70.

6. Robert McNamara actually served as president of the Ford Motor Company for only a few weeks before he was asked to serve as President John F. Kennedy's Secretary of Defense.

7. D. Halberstam, *The Reckoning* (New York: Morrow, 1986), 208.

8. Hayes, "Strategic Planning," 114.

9. H. I. Ansoff, *Corporate Strategy* (New York: McGraw-Hill, 1965).

10. K. E. Weick, "Substitutes for Strategy." In D. J. Teece (Ed.), *The Competitive Challenge: Strategies for Industrial Innovation and Renewal* (Cambridge, MA: Ballinger, 1987), 222.

11. *Ibid.,* 225–226.

12. Hayes, "Strategic Planning," 114.

13. The name of the law firm has been changed to protect its confidentiality.

14. See R. D. Lamm, "Crisis: The Uncompetitive Society." In M. Starr (Ed.), *Global Competitiveness: Getting the U.S. Back on Track* (New York: W. W. Norton, 1988), 12–42.

15. G. Stalk, Jr. and T. M. Hout, *Competing Against Time: How Time-Based Competition is Reshaping Global Markets* (New York: Free Press, 1989).

16. S. J. Gould, *Ever Since Darwin: Reflections in Natural History* (New York: W. W. Norton, 1979).

17. J. A. Schumpeter, *The Theory of Economic Development* (Cambridge, MA: Harvard University Press, 1934).

18. B. Dumaine, "Sega: When Delay Courts Disaster," *Fortune* (December 16, 1991), 104.

19. K. Vonnegut, *Player Piano* (New York: Delta Books, 1952).

20. F. W. Taylor, *Principles of Scientific Management* (New York: Harper & Row, 1907).

21. Taken from S. P. Sherman, "The Mind of Jack Welch," *Fortune* (March 27, 1989), 46.

22. Our initial interest in W.L. Gore & Associates was stimulated by Michael Pacanowsky's article, "Communication in the Empowering Organization," which appeared in John A. Anderson (Ed.), *Communication Yearbook/11* (Beverly Hills, CA: Sage, 1987). We have also had a discussion with Mr. Pacanowsky and spoken with several associates from W.L. Gore.

23. J. R. Hackman and G. R. Oldham, *Work Redesign* (Reading, MA: Addison-Wesley, 1980).

24. C. Pava, "Redesigning Sociotechnical Systems Design: Concepts and Methods for the 1990s," *Journal of Applied Behavioral Science, 22* (1986), 215.

25. Weick, "Substitutes for Strategy," 229.

Chapter 3
Gettin' into a Bag: How to Clarify Strategic Direction and Strategic Objectives

1. The name of the company and facts about it are altered to protect its confidentiality.

2. G. W. Dalton, "Influence and Organizational Change." In D. A. Kolb, I. M. Rubin, and J. M. McIntyre (Eds.), *Organizational Psychology: Readings on Human Behavior in Organizations* (4th ed.) (Englewood Cliffs, NJ: Prentice-Hall, 1984), 622–624.

3. N. R. F. Maier, "Assets and Liabilities in Group Problem Solving: The Need for an Integrative Function," *Psychological Review, 74* (1967), 241.

4. See G. Hamel and C. K. Prahalad, "Strategic Intent," *Harvard Business Review* (May/June 1989), 70–71.

5. Our early thinking about business focuses was influenced by the idea of driving forces presented in B. B. Tregoe, P. M. Tobia, J. W. Zimmerman, and R. A. Smith, *Vision in Action* (New York: Simon & Schuster, 1989).

6. E. Calonius, "America's Toughest Papermaker," *Fortune* (February 26, 1990), 83.

7. R. Henkoff, "How to Plan for 1995," *Fortune* (December 31, 1990), 70–79.

8. J. Barney, "Organizational Culture: Can It Be a Source of Sustained Competitive Advantage?" *Academy of Management Review, 11* (1986), 656–665.

9. J. Carlzon, "The Art of Loving," *Inc.* (May 1989), 41.

Chapter 4
The Front Line: Core Capabilities, Support Capabilities, and the Unit of Competitive Advantage

1. We have chosen not to divulge the name of the business and have modified facts about its technology, to protect client confidences.

2. P. C. Reid, *Well-Made in America* (New York: McGraw-Hill, 1989).

3. D. J. Teece, G. Pisano, and A. Shuen, "Firm Capabilities, Resources, and the Concept of Strategy: Four Paradigms of Strategic Management," unpublished paper (December 1990), 33.

4. C. K. Prahalad and G. Hamel, "The Core Competence of the Corporation," *Harvard Business Review* (May/June 1990), 79–91.

5. *Ibid.,* 82–83.

Chapter 5
In the Groove: Aligning Organizations to Conserve Human Energy

1. G. W. Dalton, "Influence and Organizational Change." In D. A. Kolb, I. M. Rubin, and J. M. McIntyre (Eds.), *Organizational Psychology: Readings on Human Behavior in Organizations* (4th ed.) (Englewood Cliffs, NJ: Prentice-Hall, 1984), 636.

2. R. H. Guest, *Organizational Change: The Effect of Successful Leadership* (Homewood, IL: Richard D. Irwin, 1962).

3. E. Luttwak, *Strategy: The Logic of War and Peace* (Cambridge, MA: Belknap Press, 1987), 11–12.

4. *Ibid.,* 13.

5. *Ibid.,* 12.

Chapter 6
Hep to the Jive: The Outer Game of Strategic Improvising

1. Both the name of the founder and the company he founded have been changed to protect confidentiality.

2. G. Hamel and C. K. Prahalad, "Corporate Imagination and Expeditionary Marketing," *Harvard Business Review* (July/August 1991), 87–88.

3. S. Caminiti, "The Payoff from a Good Reputation," *Fortune* (February 10, 1992), 76.

4. Entering new markets, a technique for finding business opportunities, also works for businesses with other business focuses, especially product-focused and technology-focused businesses.

5. Information about Vanport Manufacturing was taken from Joel Kotkin, "The New Northwest Passage," *Inc.* (February 1977), 92–96.

6. D. M. Maister, *Professional Service Firm Management* (Boston: Maister Associates, 1990), 2.

7. All of our information about Pitney Bowes, Inc. was taken from J. L. Roberts, "Common Interest: Pitney Bowes Thrives from Close Relations with Postal Service," *The Wall Street Journal* (April 4, 1991), A1, A6.

8. Information about the NBA under David Stern was obtained from E. M. Swift, "From Corned Beef to Caviar," *Sports Illustrated* (June 3, 1991), 74–90.

9. Most of the information for the Kodak case was taken from S. Moffat, "Picking Japan's Research Brains," *Fortune* (March 25, 1991), 84–96.

10. M. L. Dertouzos, R. K. Lester, and R. M. Solow, *Made in America: Regaining the Productive Edge* (Cambridge, MA: MIT Press, 1989), 52.

11. Information about Fletcher Byrom and Koppers comes from an interview of Byrom conducted by William F. Dowling. See "Conversation with Fletcher Byrom," *Organizational Dynamics* (Summer 1978), 37–60.

12. See R. L. Ackoff, *Management in Small Doses* (New York: John Wiley & Sons, 1986), 163–164.

13. Information about The Body Shop comes from Bo Burlingham, "This Woman Has Changed Business Forever," *Inc.* (June 1990), 38–42.

14. "Conversation with Fletcher Byrom," 38.

15. The information about Corning, Inc. is taken from K. H. Hampton, "Corning's Class Act," *Business Week* (May 13, 1991), 70–71.

Chapter 7
Ain't Misbehavin': Real-Time Measurement and Information Systems

1. A. Alchian and H. Demsetz, "Production Information Costs, and Economic Organization," *American Economic Review, 62* (1972), 777–795.

2. We attribute most of the information contained in this section to discussions with Eric Denna and Owen Cherrington. We have also had access to some of their writing about events-based accounting and information systems, including: D. P. Andros, J. O. Cherrington, and E. L. Denna, "Reengineering Your Accounting System: The IBM Way," *Financial Executive* (July/August, 1992); E. L. Denna, J. O. Cherrington, D. P. Andros, and A. S. Hollander, *Event-Driven Financial and Enterprise Systems* (Homewood, IL: Dow Jones-Irwin, 1993).

3. C. Shapiro, "The Theory of Business Strategy," *Rand Journal of Economics, 20* (Spring 1989), 129.

4. H. T. Johnson and R. S. Kaplan, *Relevance Lost: The Rise and Fall of Management Accounting* (Boston: Harvard Business School Press, 1987).

5. C. Argyris, "Double Loop Learning in Organizations," *Harvard Business Review* (September/October 1977), 115-125.

6. T. J. Peters, "Symbols, Patterns, and Settings: An Optimistic Case for Getting Things Done," *Organizational Dynamics* (Autumn 1978), 3–23.

7. Our understanding of these metrics and the Return Map came initially from personal discussions with both Chuck House and Ray Price and was later supported by their article, "The Return Map: Tracking Product Teams," *Harvard Business Review* (January/February 1991), 92–100.

8. *Ibid.,* 96.

9. C. Pava, "Redesigning Sociotechnical Systems Design: Concepts and Methods for the 1990s," *Journal of Applied Behavioral Science, 22* (1986), 217.

10. T. A. Stewart, "GE Keeps Those Ideas Coming," *Fortune* (August 12, 1991), 41–49.

11. This story was told to us by Brent Heslop, who worked at the Corning Asahi Plant in State College, Pennsylvania.

Chapter 8
Solid Sender: A Launching Platform
for Strategic Improvising

1. S. Walton with J. Huey, *Sam Walton: Made in America* (New York: Doubleday, 1992).

2. H. Mintzberg, "Strategy Formation: Schools of Thought." In J. W. Fredrickson (Ed.), *Perspectives on Strategic Management* (New York: Harper Business, 1990), 166–172.

3. A. L. Wilkins, "The Culture Audit: A Tool for Understanding Organizations," *Organizational Dynamics* (Autumn 1983), 29.

4. E. H. Schein, "Coming to a New Awareness of Organizational Culture," *Sloan Management Review* (Winter 1984), 3–16.

5. This argument has been made many times to us by our colleagues, Alan Wilkins and Gibb Dyer, both noted culture theorists.

6. J. Gleick, *Chaos: Making a New Science* (New York: Penguin Books, 1987), 9–33.

7. C. I. Barnard, *The Functions of the Executive* (Cambridge, MA: Harvard University Press, 1958), 231.

8. Mr. Sahin was quoted in B. Dumaine, "The Bureaucracy Busters," *Fortune* (June 17, 1991), 50.

9. B. Dumaine, "Who Needs a Boss?" *Fortune* (May 7, 1990), 52–60.

10. Dumaine, "The Bureaucracy Busters," 42.

11. G. W. Dalton and P. H. Thompson, *Novations: Strategies for Career Management* (Glenview, IL: Scott, Foresman, 1986), 133–158.

12. M. E. Porter, *Competitive Strategy: Techniques for Analyzing Industries and Competitors* (New York: Free Press, 1980), 4.

13. P. Paret, "Clausewitz." In P. Paret (Ed.), *Makers of Modern Strategy: From Machiavelli to the Nuclear Age* (Princeton, NJ: Princeton University Press, 1986), 186–213.

14. F. Gilbert, "Machiavelli: The Renaissance of the Art of War." In Paret, *Makers of Modern Strategy*, 15.

15. K. Ohmae, "Getting Back to Strategy," *Harvard Business Review* (November/December 1988), 149–150.

16. Information for the Georgia-Pacific case was taken from Erik Calonius, "America's Toughest Papermaker," *Fortune* (February 26, 1990), 80–83.

17. Information about NCR's ATM business was drawn from Geoffrey Colvin, "The Wee Outfit that Decked IBM," *Fortune* (November 19, 1990), 165–168.

18. Information for this case comes from our consulting work with PepsiCo and from Patricia Sellers, "Pepsi Keeps On Going After No. 1," *Fortune* (March 11, 1991), 62–70.

Chapter 9
The Hot Seven: Preparing Individuals for Moving from Strategic Planning to Strategic Improvising

1. C. Argyris, *Reasoning, Learning and Action: Individual and Organizational* (San Francisco: Jossey-Bass, 1982).

2. Mr. Hansen's statement was taken from Alan Loy McGinnis, "How 'Average' People Excel," *Reader's Digest* (August 1992), 73.

3. L. Benson, "Bahr's Philosophy Is to Only Care About the Kick Coming Up Next," *Deseret News* (January 25, 1991), D1.

4. L. Benson, "Gott Says Dodgers Must Focus on What They Don't Need to Do," *Deseret News* (September, 1, 1991), D1–D2.

5. D. L. Birch, "What Goes Up," *Inc.* (July 1988), 25; and "Late Bloomers," *Inc.* (September 1988), 30.

6. McGinnis, "How Average People Excel," 74.

7. D. H. Maister, *Professional Service Firm Management* (Boston: Maister Associates, Inc., 1990), 15–16.

8. T. G. Plummer, "Diagnosing and Treating the Ophelia Syndrome," *BYU Today* (September 1989), 25–39.

9. G. W. Dalton and P. H. Thompson, *Novations: Strategies for Career Management* (Glenview, IL: Scott, Foresman, 1986), 1–17.

10. P. Vaill, "The Purposing of High-Performing Systems," *Organizational Dynamics* (Autumn 1982), 32.

11. J. Cleese, "Serious Talk About Humor," *Executive Excellence* (September 1989), 15–16.

12. K. E. Weick, "Substitutes for Strategy." In D. J. Teece (Ed.), *The Competitive Challenge: Strategies for Industrial Innovation and Renewal* (Cambridge, MA: Ballinger, 1987), 222.

13. W. James, "Is Life Worth Living?" In W. James (Ed.), *The Will to Believe* (New York: Dover Press, 1956), 32–62.

14. A. L. Wilkins, *Developing Corporate Character* (San Francisco, CA: Jossey-Bass, 1989), 181–182.

15. T. Kidder, *The Soul of a New Machine* (New York: Avon Books, 1981), 274.

Chapter 10
Ride-Out: Final Comments about a Continuing Process

1. We are not using the company's real name, to protect its confidentiality.

2. C. R. Christensen, N. A. Berg, M. S. Salter, and H. H. Stevenson, *Policy Formulation and Administration* (9th ed.) (Homewood, IL: Dow Jones-Irwin, 1985).

3. H. Mintzberg, "The Design School: Reconsidering the Basic Premises of Strategic Management," *Strategic Management Journal, 11* (1990), 189–190.

4. L. T. Perry, *Offensive Strategy: Forging a New Competitiveness in the Fires of Head-to-Head Competition* (New York: Harper Business, 1990).

5. Information for the Perrier case that follows is taken from Patricia Sellers, "Perrier Plots Its Comeback," *Fortune* (April 23, 1990), 277–278.

6. A. Kupfer, "The Champ of Cheap Clones," *Fortune* (September 23, 1991), 116.

7. *Ibid.,* 120.

8. J. Gleick, *Chaos: Making a New Science* (New York: Penguin Books, 1987), 1–10.

Index

For more information about ideas contained in this book, contact Lee Tom Perry at Brigham Young University at (801) 378-4618 or Novations Group, Inc. at (801) 375-7525.

Special Offer
available to
Portable MBA readers

...Turn page for details ☞